The Task of Utopia

The Task of Utopia

A Pragmatist and Feminist Perspective

Erin McKenna

ROWMAN & LITTLEFIELD PUBLISHERS, INC.
Lanham • Boulder • New York • Oxford

ROWMAN & LITTLEFIELD PUBLISHERS, INC.

Published in the United States of America
by Rowman & Littlefield Publishers, Inc.
4720 Boston Way, Lanham, Maryland 20706
www.rowmanlittlefield.com

12 Hid's Copse Road
Cumnor Hill, Oxford OX2 9JJ, England

British Library Cataloguing-in-Publication Information Available

Library of Congress Cataloging-in-Publication Data
McKenna, Erin, 1965–
    The task of Utopia : a pragmatist and feminist perspective / Erin McKenna.
      p. cm.
    Includes bibliographical references (p.) and index.
    ISBN 0-7425-1318-1 (alk. paper)—ISBN 0-7425-1319-X (pbk. : alk. paper)
      1. Dewey, John, 1859–1952 2. Utopias in Literature. 3. Feminism. 4. Anarchism I.
    Title.

B945.D44 M35 2002
335'.02—dc21

                                                                                    2001049205

Printed in the United States of America

⊗™ The paper used in this publication meets the minimum requirements of American
National Standard for Information Sciences—Permanence of Paper for Printed Library
Materials, ANSI/NISO Z.39.48-1992.

Faith in the power of intelligence to imagine a future which is the projection of the desirable in the present, and to invent the instrumentalities of its realization, is our salvation. And it is a faith which must be nurtured and made articulate: surely a sufficiently large task for our philosophy.

John Dewey, *The Need for a Recovery of Philosophy*

Contents

Acknowledgments   ix

1   Introduction: The Problem of the Future   **1**
     The Need for Utopia   1
     Why Pragmatism, Feminism, and Utopia?   3
     An Overview   9

2   The End-State Model of Utopia   **17**
     Static Imagination   18
     The Desirability of Perfection   21
     The Possibility of Perfection   26
     Rousseau: Utopian Education   29
     Perfection as Process   34
     The End-State Vision of Women's Country   36
     Women's Country   37
     Problems of the Vision   40
     Women's Country: A Useful Utopian Vision?   44

3   The Anarchist Model of Utopia   **49**
     Anarchist Imagination   50
     The Cost of Freedom   53
     The Possibility of Freedom and Its Maintenance   58
     Anarchist Education   63
     Freedom as the Precondition of Progress   65
     The Anarchist Vision of Mattapoisett   68
     Mattapoisett   70
     Problems of the Vision   74
     Mattapoisett: A Useful Utopian Vision?   79

4   Dewey's Democracy: A Process Model of Utopia   **83**
  Intelligent Imagination   84
  The Possibilities of Imagined Ends   88
  Realizing the Possible   90
  Dewey Rejects End-State and Anarchist Visions   92
  Judging Future Possibilities   97
  Education and Experimentation   101
  The Need to Dream the Possible   105
  Dewey's Community   107
  A Picture of Community   113
  The Possibility of Community   118

5   Feminism, Pragmatism, Community, and Utopia   **129**
  A Feminist Critique of Dewey's Call for Community   131
  Feminst Utopias   135
  The Kesh   141
  The Hill Women   147
  The Valley and the Wanderground—Good Ends-in-View   153

6   The Future of Utopia   **161**

Bibliography   169

Index   175

About the Author   179

Acknowledgments

This work has been percolating for some time now. I have moved in different directions through the years, but I have always come back to the ideas expressed here and continued to find them important. While it is possible to single out some people and express my gratitude for their help with this project, there are many I am sure to pass over due to the passing of time.

First I would like to thank all those who sustain my interest in philosophy—students and colleagues. I would like to thank all the students at Pacific Lutheran University who have taken my freshman writing seminar "Making the Future." Their willingness to engage in thoughtful conversations about texts and ideas central to this project has been very valuable. Similarly, the students who have taken my "Women and Philosophy" class have given me much to think about and inspired me to continue my work. My colleagues at Pacific Lutheran University have also been much appreciated. Specifically I would like to thank Jim Albrecht, Susan Brown Carlton, Greg Johnson, and Kevin Olson for helping me think through my ideas on Dewey, feminism, and utopia. I would also like to thank Tracy Williamson, administrative assistant to the humanities and Susan Young, administrative associate to the humanities for retrieving information from my office while I was on leave; and most especially Gail Egbers, reference and instructional librarian, for tirelessly and patiently helping me track down sources.

I would like to thank John K. Roth (Claremont McKenna College) for putting me on the path of philosophy, and for his continued support and encouragement. Most recently, being asked to teach the philosophy seminar for the philosophy, politics, and economics major at CMC, while Roth was on sabbatical, gave me the opportunity to get a great deal of work done in the quiet of his office. It also gave me the opportunity to work with twelve very bright and engaging students whose conversations about political theory convinced me once again of the importance of this work.

The Society for the Advancement of American Philosophy has given me opportunities to present some of the ideas developed here and members of this society have provided me with valuable feedback and support. Specifically I would like to thank Jim Campbell, Ann Clark, Vincent Colapietro, Judith M. Green, Leonard Harris, Lisa Heldke, John McDermott, Scott Pratt, Charlene Haddock Seigfried and John E. Smith for their encouragement and help. Being part of SAAP is to be part of something very special—a real community. It is fun and inspiring. Thank you to all of you who have made this community possible and continue to sustain it.

I would also like to thank all the writers of utopias and science fiction who have inspired me. In the same vein, I would like to thank my family for encouraging my imagination and supporting my choice of an academic career. I would also like to thank my family, friends, and animals for their understanding and patience regarding my need to work.

I would like to thank everyone at the Hangar Inn in Puyallup, Washington, for letting me hang out, drink tea, read, think, and write. I would especially like to thank Sue Duff, Tom Ford, and Cindy Sleighter. And finally, I would like to thank everyone at Rowman & Littlefield for making this all come together so quickly.

Chapter One

Introduction: The Problem of the Future

THE NEED FOR UTOPIA

The twenty-first century has long held the promise of the future. Now that future is here and many people advise us not to dream anymore. Many of our classic visions of the future are now visions of the past. Nineteen eighty-four has come and gone, we look back on Edward Bellamy's *Looking Backward*, set in the year 2000, and we near the end of 2001 (*A Space Odyssey*). Visions of the future have been used both to inspire and warn. A specific version of such future-oriented literature is utopian literature. Utopian thought, by providing visions to which we might aspire, helps us to understand ourselves both as we are and as we might be. Such visions can help us decide what to do now to improve the social order; they also can provide a description of an ideal which serves to structure what goes on in our present actions. Utopian visions are visions of hope that can challenge us to explore a range of possible human conditions.

Utopian literature has fallen out of favor, though, because it tends to propose final perfect end-states. The twentieth century is, of course, littered with cautionary examples of why this model of utopia is unacceptable. Visions that seek specific ends, and encourage people to maintain a passive faith that the future will be better, run the risk of unleashing on the world, in an organized and devastating manner, genocide, nuclear destruction, sophisticated genetic engineering, and intentionally directed psychological manipulation.

Some people argue that in our complex world utopia is dead, or too dangerous to pursue. There is, however, a recent resurgence of interest in the idea. This interest comes in many forms: members of intentional communities and sociologists who study intentional communities; feminist science

1

fiction writers and literature professors who study feminist science fiction;
and political and social theorists.[1] This renewed interest is not naïve. These
writers recognize that we need such hopeful future-oriented thinking, but also
see the need to critique traditional utopian thinking. We need more than a critique, however. We need a new model of utopia—a process model of utopia
based on pragmatist and feminist political theory.

Those who call for (or lament) the end of utopia have a limited vision of
what utopia can entail. They tend to fall back on an end-state model of utopia.
If one can get beyond trying to achieve final perfect end-states and accept that
there are instead multiple possible futures-in-process, one has taken the first
step to understanding the responsibility each of us has to the future in deciding how to live our lives in the present. In *The End of Utopia*, Russell Jacoby
argues that we need utopian visions if we hope to make the future better, but
he worries that "a utopian spirit—a sense that the future could transcend the
present—has vanished."[2] Jacoby believes that the lack of such vision accounts for our current apathy and cynicism, and he provides an interesting
discussion of how and why utopianism fell out of favor. He believes that multiculturalism supports a notion of pluralism as an antidote to totalitarianism,
but that in this move utopianism became equated with totalitarianism. "Yet
the liberal consensus successfully established a rough equivalence of utopianism and totalitarianism, setting both against liberal pluralism. Damning totalitarianism meant damning utopianism."[3]

He also argues that those who embrace pluralism and multiculturalism
close down the utopian option by closing the door on universal concepts.
"Without an emphatic idea of freedom and happiness, a better society can
scarcely be envisioned; utopia withers. Those who celebrate differences and
discredit universals cannot think beyond the limited possibilities tossed up by
history . . ."[4] Totalitarianism, universal concepts, and utopia become equated
and rejected. Jacoby wants to revive utopia without totalitarianism, but he believes it inherently requires universal concepts and commitments. I believe
this analysis suffers from a lack of imagination and understanding. Jacoby
falls into the dualistic thinking of pluralism or absolutism, diversity or universality. As William James would have it, this appears to be the problem of
whether the universe is pluralistic or monistic—many or one. Jacoby acknowledges James' account of this dilemma, but he does not seem to understand the implications of embracing a pragmatist resolution. Jacoby falls back
on the either–or option and opts for the monistic, universalistic notion of existence, while James says, "it is clear that pragmatism must turn its back on
absolute monism, and follow pluralism's more empirical path."[5] Jacoby
thinks this monistic, universalistic view is necessary to revive utopia because
he believes such a view is necessary for people to make judgments about bet-

ter and worse possible futures and so be enabled to transcend the present. However, this is the end-state model of utopia and with it comes the dangers of stasis and totalitarianism which Jacoby wants to avoid. Pragmatism embraces a pluralism and dynamism, but does not reject the making of judgments. Pragmatism can keep utopia alive without falling back on the end-state model of utopia.[6] Utopia can become an ongoing task rather than a resting place.

Envisioning the future from a pragmatist and feminist perspective results in what I call the process model of utopia. In the process model it becomes important for us to critically examine the goals we choose to pursue because what we choose to pursue now defines what we will be able to pursue in the future. In this model we must accept responsibility for creating the future and develop a critical method of directing it, and not wait for it to simply unfold. We need to see life, and our visions of what could be possible, as an experimental process—an experimental coping with conflict and difficulties. Rather than seek perfection, the process model of utopia seeks to create and sustain people willing to take on responsibility and participate in directing their present toward a better, more desirable future. We need to continue to try; we must have hope and remain active agents in forming the future. The process of seeking meaning, not any final aim, is where our hope lies. The process model of utopia, manifested in the philosophy of John Dewey's pragmatism and in the feminist utopian fiction of writers such as Ursula K. Le Guin (*Always Coming Home*) and Sally Miller Gearhart (*The Wanderground*), represents an important new political vision. "As soon as we abandon the conventional concept of utopia, we find that the utopian is not dead at all, but very much alive in people's longing for a more just and human world, their belief that such change is possible, and their willingness to act on the basis of the belief."[7]

WHY PRAGMATISM, FEMINISM, AND UTOPIA?

Before I can present the process (pragmatist and feminist) model of utopia, it is important to examine what I mean by utopia and how I will use both pragmatism and feminism to develop the new model of utopia. Further, it is important to understand the need to connect pragmatism with utopian thought at all when so many people see them as incompatible.

The definition and scope of utopia are much debated. The full scope of this debate is not the focus of this work, though.[8] I use Lyman Tower Sargent's definition of "a non-existent society described in considerable detail" to support my selection of the feminist novels discussed in this book. I am, however, also concerned with the social and political theory that informs, and is represented by, such fictional societies. These theoretical perspectives are utopian in the sense that they present dreams of an alternate, and hopefully in some respects better, way of founding and organizing society.[9] "Utopia is about how we would live and what kind of a world we would live in if we could do just that. . . . Sometimes utopia embodies more than an image of what the good life would be and becomes a claim about what it could and should be."[10] I will discuss three models of utopia—end-state, anarchist, and process—from both the theoretical perspective of what could and should be and the fictional perspective of a non-existent society. In other words, I will try to merge theory and (potential) practice.[11] Both pragmatist and feminist theory reject the notion of theory and practice as separate. They understand theory as arising out of and guided by practice and practice as arising out of and guided by theory. This dialectical interchange energizes and enlivens both how we think and how we live. While the societies discussed here are imaginary potential societies, they do show people living out complex theoretical perspectives.

This merging of theory and practice is one of the ways in which this study is feminist. Further, to provide the reader with a common focus and to assist with the clarity of the comparison of the three models of utopia, I have chosen to discuss only feminist utopian novels which seek to address the problems male violence (in various forms) pose for women and the world. These novels bring to life, while simultaneously critiquing, a variety of feminist perspectives. This leads to the difficulty of defining feminism. As with utopia, there is no single definition of what is feminist and a full discussion of this debate is not the focus of this work.[12] I use a basic definition: the belief that the subordination of women is wrong, that the absence of women's perspectives distorts and limits traditional social and political theory, and that addressing male bias in both theory and practice will result in a society more inclusive of diversity.[13] The pragmatist and feminist perspective will, specifically, reject the traditional dualisms of academic philosophy which include male/female, mind/body, reason/emotion, objective/subjective, and theory/practice. For both pragmatists and feminists, experience is essential to forming theory and knowledge is influenced by one's situatedness. I refer to the process model of utopia as a pragmatist and feminist model in order to highlight these commonalities and to demonstrate the ways in which pragmatism is inherently feminist and the ways feminism, in all of its diversity, can be informed and modified by pragmatism.[14]

Now, why do I link pragmatist and feminist perspectives to utopia? While there is a clear tradition of feminist utopian novels, there is no clear connection of pragmatism to either utopian theory or utopian fiction. The history of feminist utopian fiction is well documented in Darby Lewes' *Dream Revisionaries: Gender and Genre in Women's Utopian Fiction 1870–1920* (1995), Carol F. Kessler's *Daring to Dream: Utopian Stories by United States Women, 1836–1919* (1984) and "Bibliography of Utopian Fiction by United States Women, 1836–1988" (1990). Women's utopian fiction began to gain strength in the nineteenth century and experienced a revival in an overtly feminist form in the 1970s and 1980s. It is interesting to note that these two periods closely correspond to the emergence of American pragmatism (1870s) and a marked revival of interest in pragmatism (1980s and 1990s). I am not arguing for any kind of causal link, but I do suggest that both are born of similar social and scientific climates. They both assume change is possible and provide an outlook that is hopeful and melioristic. Why then does the idea of linking pragmatism and utopia strike many people as a contradiction?[15]

Most people do not associate pragmatism with utopian thought. John Stuhr writes:

> Pragmatism, a faith in intelligence, carries no overarching or advance guarantees. It provides no specific assurances about the future existence or expansion of democratic life. Indeed, it provides no general warrant for any complacent expectation of progress. It finds nothing in human history, human nature, or the world situation today to support a rosy or comfortable vision of the future. Such mistaken visions merely treat present hopes as future realities. This faith in community, then, supports neither utopian thinking nor even optimism in the abstract.[16]

Further, pragmatism is often seen as being about what works while utopianism is seen as idle or dangerous dreaming about perfection. Richard J. Bernstein says, "Although Dewey was not utopian, he was, as Alan Ryan says in the concluding remarks of *John Dewey and the High Tide of American Liberalism,* a visionary—'a curious visionary, because he did not speak of a distant goal of a city not built with hands.'"[17] At their best, however, both pragmatism and utopianism are about hope. Both pragmatism and utopianism encourage people to think about the future as a guide to understanding the past and forming the present. Just as pragmatism has often been misunderstood as valueless instrumentalism, utopianism has often been unnecessarily limited to dreams of a static perfect world. I argue that a utopian vision, informed by pragmatism, results in a process model of utopia which can help us form the future based on critical intelligence. I piece together a variety of John Dewey's works to develop this process model of utopia.[18]

Dewey himself had some negative things to say about utopian thinking. In an essay on the logic of judgment he criticizes utopianism and discusses his view of the proper meaning of idealism. He says of idealism, "It is not blind instinct of hopefulness or that miscellaneous obscurantist emotionalism often called optimism, any more than it is utopianism. It is recognition of the increased liberation and redirection of the course of events achieved through accurate discovery. Or, more specifically, it is this recognition operating as a ruling motive in extending the work of discovery and utilizing its results."[19] Dewey implies that utopianism is a blind hopefulness. This critique may be well grounded, but I believe we can develop a model of utopia that embraces Dewey's notion of idealism as "the increased liberation and redirection of the course of events achieved through accurate discovery."

A second critique of utopian thought is offered by Dewey in *The Public and Its Problems*:

> There is no a priori rule, which can be laid down and by which when it is followed a good state will be brought into existence. In no two ages or places is there the same public. Conditions make the consequences of associated action and the knowledge of them different. In addition the means by which a public can determine the government to serve its interests vary. Only formally can we say what the best state would be. In concrete fact, in actual and concrete organization and structure, there is no form of state which can be said to be the best: not at least till history is ended, and one can survey all its varied forms. The formation of states must be an experimental process.[20]

This is a critique of a specific type of utopian theory—the end-state model of utopia. Utopian visions can avoid these problems when they no longer seek a final goal, but realize that it is the process of transformation itself that needs to be addressed. What is needed is to keep the possibility of change alive; what is needed is to introduce the notion of evolution into utopian visions.

Dewey makes it clear that he does not, and he does not believe anyone should, seek perfection but only betterment. There is always a possibility of improvement if people are willing to take on responsibility and participate in directing their present toward a more desirable future. This is an ongoing task.

> We have to be always learning and relearning the meaning of our active tendencies. Does not this reduce moral life to the futile toil of a Sisyphus who is forever rolling a stone uphill only to have it roll back so that he has to repeat his old task? Yes, judged from progress made in a control of conditions which shall stay put and which exclude the necessity of future deliberations and reconsiderations. No, because continual search and experimentation to discover the meaning of changing activity, keeps activity alive, growing in significance.[21]

Progress, for Dewey, is not getting further down the road to a perfect end-state. Rather, progress is to be found in the ongoing activity of people seeking meaning in a changing world. This sense of process is relatively new to utopian theory and some still argue that such visions are not utopian visions.[22]

In her book *The Concept of Utopia*, Ruth Levitas brings together the variety of definitions the word utopia has had and discusses the variety of purposes toward which utopian theory has been applied.[23] Utopian literature is defined by some in terms of content and by others in terms of form. There are also those who define it in terms of function, though Levitas argues that this is less common and a more recent development. What appears common to most definitions of content are the ideas of perfectibility and unattainability, and what is common in form is the description of particular states and political structures. "Utopia is fictional, it 'describes a particular state or community' and its 'theme is the political structure of that fictional state or community.'"[24] Some define utopia as the ideal commonwealth; utopian literature must draw a complete picture of the new society. "What is entailed is 'a new set of habits, a fresh scale of values, a different set of relationships and institutions, and possibly . . . an alteration of the physical and mental characteristics of the people chosen, through education, biological selection and so forth.'"[25] Others see utopias as unattainable goals that help push us forward. "Utopia is identified with an impossible perfection, contrasted with the virtue of evolutionary progress assumed to be taking place, yet able to play a part in it."[26] Utopian visions provide an ideal which people can then struggle to reach.

What is decidedly missing from these definitions of utopia is any notion of, or room for, evolution and change within the vision. The vision may be part of a process of change, pushing us to strive and change, but the vision itself is static. Joyce Hertzler, among others, asserts this view of utopian visions as static ideals.

The equation of utopia with impossibility is emphasized by the argument that utopia is coming to an end. It is because utopia is a static state representing perfection as opposed to progress that Bellamy, Hertzka and Wells are described as pseudo-utopians; their utopias "were not so much high flights of the imagination as the calculated product of beneficent forces now at work." Because these utopias "are based in most cases upon proved potentialities, and depend upon normal evolutionary advance for attainment," they are not proper utopias at all.[27]

Given such limits on the form and content of utopian literature it is not surprising that such visions have come to be seen as dangerous and/or undesirable. Given the massive destruction of the two World Wars, the violence of totalitarian states against their citizens, the exploitation of the Third World countries, the continued discrimination against "minorities" across the globe, the globalization of the economy, and the technology which has been used with little foresight, people are warranted in their suspicion of dreams of a final perfect world. The Nazis' vision of the perfect world is a world without Jews; the Afrikaners' vision of the perfect world entails apartheid; the British Raj's vision required an oppressive system of colonialization. It is just such dreams that threaten to help us destroy ourselves. Not only are these visions problematic in themselves, but also since all such "utopian" proposals are fallible, it is important to consider how the proposed orders might fall apart. Will the people be prepared to cope with and adapt to the changes when they have been under such authoritarian systems? In order to deal with the negative possibilities of any vision it is necessary to promote critical intelligence and foresight. We are still dealing with the repercussions of the totalizing visions of the past.

This distrust of utopian visions, however, can be tempered if one begins to define utopian visions in terms of their function as inspiration and allow content and form to be more fluid. Common to definitions of utopia in terms of function is the idea that they are visions of optimism and hope that can inspire and help people to make changes. Utopian visions can be transformative, but for many this is still tied to a specific end-state. "The acceptable function of utopia is, then, the embodiment of an impossible ideal in the form of a description of a fictitious state of society, as inspiration to the continued march of progress."[28] However, even as inspiration, as long as this focus on specific final ends remains, utopian visions present a danger. As long as we seek transformation to a specific final end, there remains the risk that achieving the end, at any cost and by any means, will be seen as the only measure of success or progress. Visions that seek specific static ends run the risk of unleashing on the world, in an organized and devastating manner, nuclear destruction, sophisticated genetic engineering, and intentionally directed psychological manipulation. Albrecht Wellmer, in his essay "Models of Freedom," points to a similar concern.

> Freedom . . . is not the sort of thing that could ever be realized in a definitive or perfect sense; the project of modernity, therefore, is not the kind of project that could ever be "completed." The only way in which this project could ever be completed is through exhaustion or through the self-annihilation of humanity—a possibility which, as we know, is no longer inconceivable. The open-ended project of modernity implies the end of utopia, if utopia means "completion" in the sense of a definitive realization of an ideal or a telos of history. . . . This end of utopia would not be the blocking of utopian energies; it would rather be their redirection, their transformation, their pluralization; for no human life, no human passion, no human love seems to be conceivable without a utopian horizon.[29]

Utopian visions can avoid the problems of static totalitarian visions only when we no longer seek a final, static goal, but realize that it is the process of transformation itself that is our task. What is needed is to keep the possibility of change alive; what is needed is to introduce the notion of evolution and process into utopian visions. Levitas, drawing on the work of Tom Moylan, calls such visions critical utopias. With these utopian visions "utopia itself is presented ambiguously as imperfect, subject to difficulties, inconsistencies, faults, change. And utopia is not a necessary outcome of the present but a possible future, which may or may not be achieved."[30] These visions differ from previous visions in form, content, and possibly function. "In concentrating on action rather than system, it is more capable of performing the consciousness-raising function of representing and stimulating the will to transformation which is a key function of utopia."[31]

Claims to universality are problematic; final solutions are not acceptable.[32] There can be no static definition of utopia either. We need to implement this sense of process and change into visions of the future. "In conclusion then, a new definition of utopia is offered, which recognizes the common factor of the expression of desire. Utopia is the expression of the desire for a better way of being. . . . It allows for the form, function and content to change over time."[33] If we embrace this new model of utopia we can find the ongoing process exciting and develop an ability to try to adapt the changing world to our needs. The world becomes unending possibility, rather than simply an obstacle to be overcome. Critical engagement with the world allows us to begin to see new and more complex relationships between various aspects of existence and our horizons of experience begin to expand. As the horizon expands, the possibilities of the future become more numerous. While we must critically select and act on particular goals, at least we now realize these decisions have wide-ranging consequences. What we select makes a difference. As our possibilities increase, so too do our responsibilities. We must create both the conditions of our responsibility and participation and a method for fulfilling them. I think a framework for such visions can be found in a feminist informed reading of the work of John Dewey.

AN OVERVIEW

In what follows I offer a critique of two forms of the static/perfectible view of utopia—end-state and anarchists models of utopia—and I propose a pragmatist and feminist (process) model as an alternative. To help ground this discussion, I use feminist utopian novels which critically examine different schools of feminist thought while addressing the issue of male violence.[34] I have chosen to include these novels because I think literature can address the complexity of visions for a better future in a way philosophical discourse often falls short of doing. The novels can show people in the process of changing and show how things may go wrong along the way. Literature puts the philosophical ideal into action and plays with its possibilities—good and bad. Another factor in choosing these particular novels is that they are all considered feminist utopias in the general sense of believing that the subordination of women is wrong and they all focus on ridding the world of violence, especially male violence. As will be seen, however, their proposals vary greatly. I believe their differences reflect more than the diversity of feminist concerns and approaches. I believe they represent the three approaches of end-state, anarchistic, and process models of utopia. It is hoped that this common focus will aid the reader in comparing the three models of utopia.

I use the novel *The Gate to Women's Country,* by Sheri S. Tepper, for the end-state model, *Woman on the Edge of Time,* by Marge Piercy, for the anarchist model, and *Always Coming Home,* by Ursula K. Le Guin, and *The Wanderground,* by Sally Miller Gearhart, for the process model. I discuss both philosophical theory and utopian literature for, as Dewey says in *Art as Experience*:

> Words furnish a record of what has happened and give direction by request and command to particular future actions. Literature conveys the meaning of the past that is significant in present experience and is prophetic of the larger movement of the future. Only imaginative vision elicits the possibilities that are interwoven within the texture of the actual. The first stirrings of dissatisfaction and the first intimations of a better future are always found in works of art.[35]

I believe the pragmatist and feminist (process) model of utopia can help us envision, and so possibly achieve, a better future.

Chapter 2 addresses the end-state model of utopia. After looking at why end-state models have been adopted by some utopian writers, I explore some of the problems of perfection raised by many critics of utopian thought. These problems include boredom, mediocrity, loss of heroes, loss of character, loss of strength, and loss of courage. Then the difficulties of maintaining perfection are addressed. Are violence and/or manipulation necessary for achieving "perfection"? If harmony requires that diversity be minimized or eliminated, does this unduly narrow what will be possible in the future? Does the possibility of the utopian goal of perfection entail the end of utopian dreaming? If perfection is achieved, change can only qualify as degeneration. Dreams of progress can no longer exist and experimentation and discovery are at an end. Can this irony be addressed?

Chapter 2 also discusses the end-state model of utopia in terms of Tepper's *The Gate to Women's Country.* Tepper provides a critical view of the towns of Women's Country which seek to develop and instill a virtuous character in the populace. Control of the community comes less through education than through eugenics, but control of information is an essential component in the plan for engineering the desired social state. They act on the idea of breeding people who comply with the general will, and of breeding out those with what are identified as anti-social or undesirable tendencies. The people are intentionally transformed to fit the projected end-state and so those in charge ignore the need to develop critical intelligence and allow for change and growth.

Chapter 3 addresses the anarchist model of utopia. After looking at why this model is appealing to some utopian writers, this chapter focuses on three main areas that are vulnerable to criticism. The first problem is the tendency for anarchist visions to endorse, and rely for their success on a more or less spontaneous, immediate, and complete revolution—often violent in nature. Severing connections to past institutions, value systems, beliefs, and habits would leave people without the tools to make the choices of how they want to live. Second, for anarchy to work, people must realize that each individual's freedom to direct her own life is important and they must accept responsibility for safeguarding such freedom for everyone. This requires an informed and involved public, and tends to be time consuming—critics claim it is just too much work to expect from the "ordinary" citizen. Finally, a third concern is about the ability of anarchist visions to handle diversity. As was discussed before, the need to establish and maintain a small community where everyone feels accountable may involve undue pressure on minority groups to conform to some standard.

Chapter 3 also discusses the anarchist model of utopia in terms of Piercy's *Woman on the Edge of Time*. In this book, which forces us to critically view the complexity and ambiguity of our choices, we find a society based on the cooperative efforts of individuals in small communities and the cooperative efforts of such communities in a federation. Face-to-face accountability and reciprocity maintain social unity and cooperation. There is no control of individuals by an authority; people actively participate in social decision making, and there is no claim that any one way of working together is the final answer. Despite these positive aspects, it appears violence was necessary to achieve the society and is needed to maintain it. Furthermore, the arrangement of people in small communities, responsible for participating in all social decisions, requires a great deal of the citizens. This demand of participation and adaptability leads some to see it as necessary to restrict the freedom of, or do violence against, members of their community who challenge the social arrangements. Given the limitations and faults of the human creature, and the fact that the anarchist does not provide a convincing method for changing values, beliefs, and habits—it is just expected to happen as a result of the close-knit and reciprocal relationships each is involved in—the setup of small communities may do more to restrict some people's freedom than it does to open up the freedom of possibility for others.

Chapter 4 develops the process model of utopia using Dewey's model of democracy as a basis. I use this to develop a model of utopia that answers the critics of end-state and anarchist utopian models and that moves beyond these models. Dewey's vision of democracy is the embodiment of the experimental method, preparing us to interact with our world and guide it to a better future by immersing us in the method of critical intelligence. With Dewey, democracy is not participation by an inchoate public, nor is it a perfected end-state to be attained. It is the development of a method of living with regard to the past, present, and future. We learn to engage the world we are in, unmake what is problematic, and make it the world we want it to be. Dewey's faith in democracy will make it clear what the role of experimentation in social living is to be and will serve to point out what Dewey takes to be the necessary application of critical intelligence to how we choose to live. Experimentation requires critical intelligence, and critical intelligence requires active participants involved in the directing of their lives, therefore the role of education in preparing such citizens for active duty will also be examined.

Chapter 5 further explores this model and critiques and develops it from some feminist perspectives. I think that the model I develop from Dewey is inherently feminist and answers many of the criticisms feminist theorists have of traditional political theories, but there are still concerns to be addressed. I discuss the connections between pragmatism and feminism and develop Dewey's pragmatism from a feminist perspective. Inasmuch as feminist theorists challenge foundational beliefs of various political theories, they also challenge the utopian visions that grow out of these theories. Chapter 5 also discusses the connections between feminism and utopia and examines the process model of utopia in terms of Le Guin's *Always Coming Home* and Gearhart's *The Wanderground*. Both books stress the social embeddedness of individuals and the connectedness of every live creature and its environment. They both stress the importance of learning to live with the world and all its inhabitants. Both books embody Dewey's idea of lived experience in that they both stress an understanding of the relational nature of things in order to save the future from those who lack such understanding. The people of these societies recognize themselves as responsible agents in a changing world. They change and adapt their ends-in-view as they encounter different people and situations. They recognize the impact of means on ends, the relational nature of experience, and the connectedness of method and purpose. They do not present final homogeneous perfect end-states, but possible futures-in-process.

The concluding chapter brings together the discussion of utopian theory and literature and assesses whether the process model is successful in answering the criticisms made of the end-state and anarchist models. Furthermore, the process model is examined to decide if it is constructive in its own right. I hope to show that utopian theory can be a useful asset to political philosophy and that pragmatist and feminist utopian visions can help us all live better now.

NOTES

1. Some examples include Robert Schehr, *Dynamic Utopia: Establishing Intentional Communities as a New Social Movement* (Westport, Conn.: Bergin and Garvey, 1997)—"I will also discuss more recent efforts to resurrect the concept that, like Mannheim (1936), without some conceptualization of utopia without the cultivation of alternative perceptions of reality, society would be dead" (133); Marlene Barr and Nicholas Smith, eds., *Women and Utopia: Critical Interpretations* (New York: University Press of America, 1983)—"To conceive of utopia, then, is from the outset to reconstruct human culture" (1); and Russell Jacoby, *The End of Utopia: Politics and Culture in an Age of Apathy* (New York: Basic Books, 1999)—"The effort to envision other possibilities of life and society remains urgent and constitutes the essential precondition of doing something" (181). John Rawls' most recent book, *The Law of Peoples* (Cambridge, Mass.: Harvard University Press, 1999), proposes what he calls "a realistic utopia." "Our answer to the question of whether a reasonably just Society of Peoples is possible affects our attitudes toward the world as a whole. . . . If a reasonably just Society of Peoples whose members subordinate their power to reasonable aims is not possible, and human beings are largely amoral, if not incurably cynical and self-centered, one might ask, with Kant, whether it is worthwhile for human beings to live on the earth" (128).

2. Jacoby, *The End of Utopia*, xi.

3. Jacoby, *The End of Utopia*, 43.

4. Jacoby, *The End of Utopia*, 137.

5. William James, *Pragmatism* (Indianapolis: Hackett, 1981), 74.

6. Gregory Johnson ("The Situated Self and Utopian Thinking," *Hypatia*, forthcoming Summer 2002) makes a similar case from the perspective of postmodern philosophy. Using Seyla Benhabib, Johnson argues for "situated utopian thinking" which rejects traditional notions of universalism for what Benhabib calls "interactive universalism." "Interactive universalism acknowledges the plurality of modes of being human, and differences among humans, without endorsing all these pluralities and differences as morally and politically valid. While agreeing that normative disputes can be settled rationally, and that fairness, reciprocity and some procedure of universalizability are constituents, that is, necessary conditions of the novel standpoint, interactive universalism regards difference as a starting-point for reflection and action" (Benhabib 153). Johnson says, "It is a view of the utopian that enables us to engender critique from our embodied and embedded locations yet not be restricted to these embodied and embedded locations."

7. Angelika Bammer, *Partial Visions: Feminism and Utopianism* (New York: Routledge, 1991), 3.

8. For some good discussions of the definition of utopia see Ernst Bloch, *The Principle of Hope* (Cambridge, Mass.: MIT Press, 1986); J. C. Davis, *Utopia and the Ideal Society* (Cambridge: Cambridge University Press, 1981); Barbara Goodwin and Keith Taylor, eds., *The Politics of Utopia: A Study in Theory and Practice* (New York: St. Martin's Press, 1982); Krishan Kumar, *Utopia and Anti-Utopia in Modern Times* (New York: Basil Blackwell, 1987) and *Utopianism* (Minneapolis: University of Minnesota Press, 1991); Ruth Levitas, *The Concept of Utopia* (Syracuse, N.Y.: Syracuse University Press, 1990); Frank E. Manuel and Fritzie P. Manuel, *Utopian Thought in the Western World* (Cambridge: Belknap Press, 1979); Lewis Mumford, *The Story of Utopia* (New York: Boni & Liverright, 1922); Lyman Tower Sargent, *British and American Utopian Literature 1516–1985: An Annotated, Chronological Bibliography* (New York: Garland, 1988); and Lucy Sargisson, *Contemporary Feminist Utopianism* (London: Routledge, 1996).

9. Sargent, *British and American Utopian Literature,* xii.

10. Levitas, *The Concept of Utopia,* 1.

11. These fictional societies seek to demonstrate how theory can be instantiated in lived experience. It is in this sense that I refer to fictional societies as "practice."

12. For a good discussion of the definitions of feminism, and the variety in schools of thought, see Alison Jaggar, *Feminist Politics and Human Nature* (Totowa, N.J.: Rowman & Littlefield, 1988) and Rosemarie Putnam Tong's *Feminist Thought: A More Comprehensive Introduction* (Boulder, Colo.: Westview Press, 1998).

13. Different schools of feminist thought provide different perspectives on the ways in which theory has been distorted and the hopes for increased inclusivity.

14. It is important to note that I am not entering the debate about a feminist pragmatism and/or a pragmatist feminism. These distinctions are very usefully discussed in Charlene Haddock Seigfried's *Pragmatism and Feminism: Reweaving the Social Fabric* (Chicago: University of Chicago Press, 1996).

15. In my experience pragmatists reject the connection because they believe it reduces pragmatism to wishful thinking and utopian theorists reject the connection because they see pragmatism as purely instrumental.

16. John J. Stuhr, *Genealogical Pragmatism: Philosophy, Experience, and Community* (New York: SUNY Press, 1997), 246.

17. Richard J. Bernstein, "Community in the Pragmatist Tradition," in *The Revival of Pragmatism,* ed. Morris Dickstein (Durham, N.C.: Duke University Press, 1998), 149–150.

18. In his book *Dynamic Utopia,* Robert C. Schehr introduces a similar idea with regard to the sociological study of intentional communities. Schehr takes chaos theory as his starting point, though a pragmatist—C. S. Peirce—is also mentioned in his analysis. Schehr argues that chaos theory pushes us to see the need for a dynamic, non-linear, nondualistic view that accepts flux, difference, and uncertainty. He says, "Accepting flux, heterogeneity, and change as perpetual components of natural and social systems at least moves us in the direction of cultivating methods for managing difference. This would represent a far more beneficial line of theoretical and practical work than continuing a futile search for the torchbearers of democratic reform" (179).

19. John Dewey, "The Logic of Judgments of Practice," in *John Dewey: The Middle Works, Vol. 8: 1915,* ed. Jo Ann Boydston (Carbondale: Southern Illinois University Press, 1979), 19.

20. John Dewey, *The Public and Its Problems*, in *John Dewey: The Later Works, Vol. 2: 1925–1927*, ed. Jo Ann Boydston (Carbondale: Southern Illinois University Press, 1984), 256.

21. John Dewey, *Human Nature and Conduct*, in *John Dewey: The Middle Works, Vol. 14: 1922*, ed. Jo Ann Boydston (Carbondale: Southern Illinois University Press, 1983), 144–145.

22. For further reading on the history of utopian thought see the following: Davis, *Utopia and the Ideal Society*; Kumar, *Utopia and Anti-Utopia in Modern Times*; Manuel and Manuel, *Utopian Thought in the Western World*; and Mumford, *The Story of Utopia*.

23. Another important aspect of this book is a discussion of whether there is an innate or universal utopian impulse in human beings. While this is an interesting and important question, it is not my concern here.

24. Levitas, *Utopia*, 27.

25. Levitas, *Utopia*, 16.

26. Levitas, *Utopia*, 18.

27. Levitas, *Utopia*, 20.

28. Levitas, *Utopia*, 14.

29. Albrecht Wellmer, "Models of Freedom," *Philosophical Forum* (1990): 250–251.

30. Levitas, *Utopia*, 172.

31. Levitas, *Utopia*, 173.

32. Richard Rorty, in an essay titled "For a More Banal Politics" (*Harper's*, May 1992, 16–21), argues that with the decline of socialism it is time to give up grand political theory. "I hope we have reached a time when we can finally get rid of the conviction common to Plato and Marx, the conviction that there just must be large theoretical ways of finding out how to end injustice. I hope we can learn to get along without the conviction that there is something deep—such as the human soul, or human nature, or the will of God, or the shape of history—which provides a subject matter for grand, politically useful theory. We should accept the fact that from here on in we are going to have to be as crudely experimental as the new governments of Poland and Lithuania are being forced to be" (17). Hope for a better world remains, but not in grand visions of change such as end-state and anarchist visions. Rather, hope remains in embracing a process of continual experimentation and adaptation.

33. Levitas, *Utopia*, 8.

34. All of these novels are very rich and complex. I do not believe the authors are presenting these visions as the model of any particular school of thought, though they are clearly informed by different approaches to political theory, and by different schools of feminist thought in particular. Further, the authors problematize these visions as they go. They challenge us to think critically about the options being presented.

35. John Dewey, *Art as Experience*, in *John Dewey: The Later Works, Vol. 10: 1934*, ed. Jo Ann Boydston (Carbondale: Southern Illinois University Press, 1987), 348.

Chapter Two

The End-State Model of Utopia

Imagine a society in which all conflicts of conscience and conflicts of interest were abolished, a society in which all the obstacles to a decent life for all men had been removed, all the hindrances hindered, a society in which the resourcefulness of modern technology was put in the unfettered service of lessening labor and increasing and enriching leisure, a society in which the advances in biological and psychological science were used to correct the work of nature and improve the species, a society in which peace, abundance, and virtue permanently and universally obtained. Such a society answers to the traditional ends of utopianism. . . . Such a society . . . amplifies and elevates those things which utopianism, in its vision of perfection, has always stood for.[1]

The tradition of utopian thought, as described above, is inherently rationalistic, and prescribes that the final aim in the utopian vision is the rational direction of all action toward human perfection. This rationalistic view of the world posits that the world, and the live creatures in it, are directed toward a predetermined end or goal—that is, the good. Further, this rationalistic worldview implies that the absolute good exists, is identifiable, and can be fulfilled. Such visions require that one believe that there is an absolute good or best order of society that can be identified and achieved.

The focus, then, of such visions is on the final desired state, not on the process of change itself. Such visions focus on the ends and make no judgments concerning the means seen as necessary to achieve the desired end-state. The method and approach of such utopian visions is seldom an open-ended process, but rather the development of a rational plan by means of which it is hoped a desired end will be achieved—engineered perfection. I will refer to such visions as end-state utopian visions.

This rationalistic worldview tends to identify the absolute good with a perfect, complete, unchanging entity or state of being that can be discerned by examining the world, and our place in it, from a god's-eye view (which has

17

been the perspective of males in power). This end-state approach seeks to control the future so completely that any future individual participation will become meaningless and unnecessary. The belief is that by gaining control over nature, over the ordering of society, we will be able to achieve the right ordering of individuals in society and achieve a lasting harmony. It is this idea of rational control leading to final harmony that promotes the view of utopian visions as static, totalitarian nightmares. The end-state approach tends to be preoccupied with ends and indifferent to means, views individuals and society as a totality, makes dogmatic assumptions, is preoccupied with management, and neglects human variety.

Further, such visions tend to employ violence and/or manipulation as means to achieving and/or maintaining the envisioned end-state. This conflicts with the desired end of stability and peace and taints the ideal of "perfection." To the extent to which the means of violence and/or manipulation inform the end the resulting order will be corrupted—a common theme of dystopian novels such as *1984* and *Brave New World*. Further, if harmony requires that diversity be minimized or eliminated, future possibilities and human experience will be limited and narrowed. Because future possibilities are constrained by what is and has been, narrowing the present narrows the future. Finally, in an ironic twist, there is the possibility that the utopian goal of perfection entails the end of utopian dreaming. If perfection is achieved, any change can qualify only as degeneration. Dreams of progress can no longer exist and experimentation, discovery, and hope are at an end. If this irony is to be addressed there needs to be a model of utopia that incorporates change and variety without becoming authoritarian. If dreams of progress are to be constructive, there needs to be a constructive model of utopia that realizes problems, proposes solutions, and adjusts to needs rather than focusing solely on the ideal of perfectibility.

STATIC IMAGINATION

The end-state model of utopia rests on a view of human experience that is caught between a spectator model and a participatory (scientific) model. It has its foundations in a worldview that sees the world, and our experience in it, as a given over which we have no control. At the same time it is formulating a worldview, based on the methods of scientific experimentation, in which people can not only observe but also control and manipulate the world toward some chosen end. While it may be implicit in the methods of science that the process of experimentation is essentially hypothetical in nature and continuously ongoing, the old spectator model hinders the acceptance of such participation, uncertainty, and responsibility. Instead, in the end-state model of utopia, the notion that people can perfect the world—achieve some final static end-state—and no longer have to participate and experiment takes hold. If the world is not already perfect (or if by our own doing we have caused a fall from the perfect state), the end-state model gives evidence that we believe we can now achieve the perfect world and then return to our role as spectator. People eschew responsibility on this model and hope to just exist in a state of everlasting bliss.

Karl Popper discusses this dilemma by identifying two models he thinks influence this utopian approach. These are the model of historical determinism (identified with the old spectator model) and the method of science (identified with the emerging participatory model).[2] Popper describes the approach of historical determinism in the following way: the belief that if one contemplates history, one will discover certain natural laws which one then can use to predict how the future will shape up. On Popper's view, there are many things wrong with this approach. Most importantly, it perpetuates the "Myth of Destiny." Historical necessity subordinates the individual to its purposes. People become passive recipients, rather than the creators, of their fate. As long as prophets are esteemed, people will fail to use their critical powers. As long as the fatalistic view has a hold, people will consider themselves exempt from responsibility, and so without reason to resist, promote, or examine society's organization and functioning.

While historical determinism is bad enough on its own—teaching people to be passive spectators—it is worse when this faith in destiny is combined with the active approach of scientific engineering. When these two approaches are combined, historical determinism, by looking to the past to anticipate our destiny, gives one an end for which to strive. With an end in sight, the engineer, rather than just waiting for destiny to unfold, provides a means to achieve it. There is room to go wrong both in choosing an end and in the means of attaining it. Such an approach is likely to lead to a dictatorship which can suppress objections and new ideas. Also, if one changes the end, the whole process must begin again and no progress is made. There must be commitment to one unchanging ideal if such engineering is to work.

Popper criticizes Plato, among others, for combining historical determinism and social engineering to create what Popper considers to be a dangerous utopian vision. According to Popper, Plato has a vision of an ideal, stable, changeless state as the proper end-state of human society. Plato sees disunion and change as signs of corruption, decay, and degeneration.[3] His overriding need to achieve his envisioned end-state and to prevent its decay (though he recognizes the inevitability of its eventual degeneration) leads him to propose a totalitarian regime. Plato proposes a caste system through eugenics, and

censorship through selective education. In the Republic the individual is des-
tined by her talents to a certain role which she must fulfill for the sake of the
stability of the state.

> Society and the individual are thus interdependent. The one owes its existence to the
> other. Society owes its existence to human nature, and especially to its lack of self-
> sufficiency; and the individual owes his existence to society, since he is not self-
> sufficient. But within this relationship of interdependence, the superiority of the state
> over the individual manifests itself in various ways; for instance, in the fact that the
> seed of decay and disunion of a perfect state does not spring up in the state itself, but
> rather in its individuals.[4]

Given the overriding concern for a stable society, Plato sees the state as justified in limiting the individual and imposing a certain organization of society. Freedom requires an authoritarian state if freedom is defined as the end
of degeneration and change and the individual is seen as the source of this degeneration. Engineering schemes based on a vision of our destiny tend to require authoritarian control to achieve the end-state and so are all dangerous,
according to Popper, and will ultimately fail. What we need, in Popper's view,
is scientific objectivity.

What Popper means by scientific objectivity is that any assumption can be
subject to criticism and any hypotheses subject to revision. The scientific
method is necessarily public, intersubjective, and cooperative. Subjectivity
and prejudice will exist, of course, but with this method both the method and
results of the experiment are open to public scrutiny and debate. Practice will
tell success. Popper understands the scientific method to implicitly hold to a
critical attitude, the rejection of authority, and a tolerance for a plurality of
views.[5] On this model people accept the uncertainty of the future, examine
themselves and their society critically, and accept the responsibility for what
they make of themselves.

This new world view is very unsettling, however, and people seek stability. "There is a finality in utopian perfection which is not to be contradicted
by the onward, aimless, essentially anarchic march of science."[6] The scientific method is seen to threaten the very concepts of stability and order. So, in
the end-state utopian vision, we temper it. We employ the scientific method,
but only as a tool to achieve some predetermined, predestined, or natural order. We deny the spirit of the scientific model which implies that our destiny
depends on our actions and that no order is final or lasting, but rather transitory and changing. We combine the old view of historical determinism and
the new view of science and reach a compromise—a vision of an end-state
which we engineer and control. As long as the scientific model is being employed to achieve some specific end, though, it seems the questions and prob-

lems of end-state utopian dreams are going to accompany it. Any vision which forms a picture of the most desirable form of human association and explores means for its being attained and maintained must address the criticisms to which I will now turn.

THE DESIRABILITY OF PERFECTION

While the body of utopian literature is incredibly diverse (as are the norms of classification), there do appear to be some common concerns in the projects which come to be so classified, and some common objections raised against them. Utopian visions are visions of hope. They are vehicles by which one can explore a range of possible human conditions.[7] As such, there seem to be at least two questions all utopian writers must ask and/or address: (1) What is possible for human beings? (2) What is desirable for human existence?[8] It is in answering the second question that most critics of utopian writing and thinking find the project of drawing utopian visions dangerous. While these critics assume that the first (what is possible for human beings) is just a variable which will remain unknowable, they focus their complaints against the proposed vision of what is desirable. According to the critics, in attempting to reshape individuals and society to fit one view of what is desirable for humankind, or in determining wherein our perfection lies, all that one can hope to achieve is stagnation. Visions of utopian society are often isolated and homogeneous, uniform and stable; they entail no development or change.[9]

An interesting question here concerns the desirability of the utopian vision. In choosing what is the most desirable form of society, and subordinating all other considerations to such a vision, there is a great deal of room for things to go wrong. Will creativity and innovation be lost? Will the end of conflict entail the end of progress? Will harmony require the end of difference? Will the individual become a tool of the state? The literature of anti-utopian novels gives evidence of these concerns, and is enough to persuade many to condemn utopian visions altogether. To such critics, utopian visions are at best useless and at worst terrifyingly possible. "Once utopia is achieved, the problem of how man is to find new enterprises and purposes is left unresolved."[10]

I believe these critics raise important concerns about end-state utopian visions, but their critiques do not apply to all utopian possibilities. In the end-state utopian vision, there is an emphasis on goals—an instrumental approach—which can lead one to allow any means as permissible in light of the overriding nature of the end goal. As a result there arises the concern that such utopian visions result in the subordination of individual human beings to abstract aims of the "good life." Individuality, diversity, creativity, and innovation all can be used to achieve the end-state, but once achieved these same qualities come to be seen as destabilizing and potentially threatening to the new order. Even when attempts are made to incorporate novelty and development, "the difficulty is that the character of utopian reality, in which the author has included all the values he believes are important for men, does not readily allow either novelty or serious change to be convincingly portrayed."[11] To make order permanent rather than transitory, it appears to be necessary to remove such dynamic and potentially dangerous qualities from the people who are to inhabit the new order. In the interest of the "common good" or the "the greater interest of society," the individual is to be modified, controlled, or at least restricted. "To retain order, and whatever values are selected the freedom to create confusion, muddle, to make mistakes or to do the wrong thing must be eliminated."[12]

One example of such a vision can be found in Marion Zimmer Bradley's *The Ruins of Isis*.[13] Isis, originally known as Persephone, is a matriarchal planet where men are the property of women. Men are referred to as "it," their education is limited, and they serve the pleasure of women. The planet is ruled by the Matriarchate that keeps order and provides stability. While the Matriarchate has allowed a woman scientist and male assistant (who is a scientist as well) to come from Unity—a large federation of planets—to study some important ruins, they resist all overtures to join Unity. Joining Unity would mean having to treat their men as equals. They say, "Our history tells us that every society where men are admitted to equality soon comes under their domination. Males . . . are not content with equality; they cannot endure a society where they do not dominate. And every society dominated by men has come to accept male values and aggression, competition, and eventually, war. And this has destroyed every culture known in the Galaxy, one after another."[14] The Matriarchate attempts to maintain the peace of the planet by not allowing men to dominate. They keep the men subordinate. "The Persephone experiment, an attempt to build a culture which could resist decay, progress, and entropy, by indefinitely delaying or eliminating the stage at which males seized power from the primitive mother-right. Patrilineal cultures always signal the beginning of entropy and decay, and the death of a culture by aggression and war."[15]

Male violence is seen as the problem and the "necessary" steps are taken to prevent its emergence. However, change cannot be forestalled indefinitely. Influenced by the example of the male visitor from Unity, the men rebel. The attempts to suppress the rebellion fail and even the mysterious Beings who give guidance to Isis support the change as they come to realize that they had been given limited and distorted information by the women about the nature and abilities of men. The ruling women resist the changes that face them. The visiting woman saw the situation as "an old argument between majority rule, anarchy or tyranny, the age-old struggle between efficiency and personal liberty."

Most societies sacrificed something on both sides and accepted a form of participatory democracy; the tyrants sacrificed personal freedom, the anarchist sacrificed efficiency. Every form of government has its price. But governments changed. And this one, after a long period of changelessness, seemed to be changing.[16]

In the end, the men and women have to cooperate to deal with a natural disaster and save lives. A cooperative government is formed and social changes begin to emerge slowly. Change comes to Isis and reveals the ways in which all individuals on the planet had been controlled and restricted by the attempts to prevent this very change.

The story of Isis shows us that in exploring what is desirable for human beings it is necessary to arrive at some balance of individual and community needs. Such a balance must be struck by all utopian writing—fiction and non-fiction. It is in proposing different pictures of what such a balance might entail, and how it can be attained, that end-state utopian visions come to be seen as radical. It is these pictures people find discomforting. Most utopian pictures, such as the Matriarchate on Isis, threaten our sense of individual freedom and challenge the belief (often given voice to but seldom acted on) that the interests of individual communities, and indeed the world at large, will be best served by encouraging individual variety, nonconformity, and ingenuity. The end-state utopian vision is to be a model in which the individual has no cause to rebel or reason to struggle. This does not necessarily entail that the individual will not be creative (unless, of course, it is the case that creativity requires adversity and conflict, as will be discussed later), but it does point the way to some "body" limiting and directing the creative outlets of all other individuals and controlling the application of such innovations. It must all be done with regard to achieving the final end and maintaining the status quo once this vision is achieved. On Isis we see "a government ruled by custom and tradition, without crime and without rebellion, and without need of law or enforcement."

She did not know if she would care for such a world, but the problem of crime and enforcement was an enormous one on every world in the Unity. The women of the Matriarchate had solved it in their own way, which was, by and large, quite successful. They had, at least a right to complete their experiment without interference.[17]

Harmony is the overriding concern, and the aim of the end-state model of utopia is to achieve the conditions where the individual can "flourish within the limits of excellence."[18]

The "limits of excellence" include, among other things, an ideal physical environment which allows people to fulfill their highest capacities.
Most end-state utopian visions propose the end of conflict, need, and suffering through, at least in part, material abundance. Ideally, if more food
could be grown, more houses built, more energy supplied—if scarcity
were eliminated—the needy would vanish. Most end-state utopian visions proceed on the assumption that the problems of material need which
exist in society may possibly be satisfied with an increase in production. Some then argue that a condition of material abundance would entail
the end of conflict. The individual and the community would be in harmony. Without want, there would be no source of dissension or motive
to fight. With need and conflict eliminated, suffering, too, would be a
thing of the past.

Most criticisms of such attempts to resolve the tension between the interests of the individual and those of the community involve a sense of loss.
What is it that is lost in abundance and harmony that the critics feel it would
be better to retain? They claim that if suffering and hardship are eliminated
(or even greatly reduced), life will lose its meaning. For example, Plato finds
courage to be a necessary virtue, so the conditions which provide an opportunity for courage to be practiced also become necessary. Similarly, in *Brave
New World*, Aldous Huxley writes:

> I'm claiming the right to be unhappy. . . . Not to mention the right to grow old and
> ugly and impotent; the right to have syphilis and cancer; the right to have too little
> to eat; the right to be lousy; the right to live in constant apprehension of what may
> happen tomorrow; the right to catch typhoid; the right to be tortured by unspeakable
> pains of every kind.[19]

Without certain experiences, certain characters will be lost. On the theory that
one cannot know sweetness without tasting the bitter, cannot appreciate peace
without participating in conflict, cannot dream of the "good life" without living the opposite, many claim that tension is the necessary ground of individual existence and vitality. Without struggle and despair life will become bor-
ing and the future will offer nothing new to hope for. Life simply will not be
interesting in a utopian society.

William James gives voice to this view after visiting an intentional
community—the Assembly Grounds at Chautauqua Lake, New York. He describes the accomplishments of the community: sobriety, industry, prosperity,
cheerfulness, education, physical fitness, health, peace. "You have, in short, a
foretaste of what human society might be, were it all in the light, with no suffering and no dark corners." Yet, when he leaves the community, James experiences a sense of relief and a yearning for something savage.

This order is too tame, this culture is too second-rate, this goodness too uninspiring. This human drama without a villain or a pang; . . . this atrocious harmlessness of all things—I cannot abide with them. Let me take my chances again in the big outside worldly wilderness with all its sins and sufferings. There are the heights and depths, the precipices and the steep ideals, the gleams of the awful and the infinite; and there is more hope and help a thousand times than in this dead level and quintessence of every mediocrity.[20]

The claim is that "utopia does not allow the heights and depths of human possibility to be reached."[21] The assumption of the critics is that people grow and develop only by overcoming adversity and conquering obstacles. Without anything to overcome or conquer people, and so society, will stagnate.

It would appear that the end-state utopian vision frustrates the very conditions by which people gain the strength and wisdom to flourish. It settles for a monotonous mediocrity. Without need to push people's creativity it seems people will consistently be less than they are capable of being. Without something to defy it seems individuals will fail to develop wills of their own. Without suffering no one will foster virtues such as benevolence, charity, gratitude, and fortitude.[22] "Despite the authors' efforts to make their societies dynamic, the modern citizen of utopia, living in a world that has solved all its problems, has no purposes or goals beyond his own satisfaction."[23] In such a society there will be no great art or literature for the tragedy of human existence and the strength of human perseverance and triumph will no longer provide its subject matter. There will be no heroes, for the conditions of heroism will have been eliminated. The character and personality of the people who would populate a perfected end-state utopian society is found wanting. If adversity or conflict were reintroduced, would such people be capable of responding to it effectively? These are some of the concerns of critics.

The protest to the end-state model of utopia presented here is that suffering must be allowed to continue so the depths of human despair and desperation and the heights of human compassion and courage can be experienced and used to build character. The critics believe that the conditions of tragedy must be maintained so knowledge of the full range of human responses can be gained and developed. Are these necessary conditions of meaningful life? Utopian thinkers find the critics' position somewhat perverse. To prefer to maintain the status quo just so conflict, need, and suffering can continue to be experienced and studied requires a willful neglect of the perspective of those oppressed by conflict, need, and suffering. The critics' arguments that end-state utopian visions will lead to boredom, mediocrity, loss of heroes, loss of character, loss of strength, or loss of courage do not seem to provide any substantial reason for not experimenting to see if abundance and harmony would uplift or reduce the human condition.

Of course, in this whole discussion, there is an assumption on the part of the end-state utopian thinker that most important problems of society can be solved by material abundance. It is important, however, to ask what is being produced and how is it being distributed. If production is governed strictly by profit and does not look to changing needs, there may not be abundance of what is needed. Further, distribution is also a matter of human disposition. This disposition is certainly affected by the amount and quality of goods available, but it is not availability alone that will determine distribution. What is needed on the end-state model is to convince people to produce what is needed and to work out a distribution of wealth and goods by which none will be left wanting. In addition to greater abundance, what must change is people's disposition toward the material conditions of life. What any end-state utopian society needs are "virtuous" citizens who recognize an obligation to an equitable distribution of necessary goods. If it is the case that people are not naturally virtuous, or do not naturally exercise their virtue, how is the necessary virtuous nature to be instilled? This brings us to the first of the questions with which this section began: What is possible for human beings?

THE POSSIBILITY OF PERFECTION

Much of the discussion of, and many of the criticisms about, utopian literature focus on the question, "What is desirable for human existence?" Answers to the question "What is possible for human beings?" have their own important consequences, though. What one conceives as possible for human beings depends on how one conceives of human nature. Plans for a city, government, or world order based on a model that views human nature as essentially self-interested, suspicious, deceitful, greedy, power hungry, and unchanging will probably look very different from plans for a city, government, or world order based on a model that views human beings as cooperative, social, honest, caring, giving, and adaptive.

Are end-state utopian visions committed to any particular view of human nature? Are they committed to the belief that human nature is knowable, predictable, and malleable? If so, are they committed to intentionally forming some desired human nature? I recognize that this body of literature is much too large and diverse to be subject to any such generalization, but I think all utopian writers must address these questions about human nature in some way.

It would seem that the anti-utopian writer (who is mainly responding to the end-state model of utopia) typically draws a picture of human beings as basically individualistic and capricious, and so claims that human nature is ultimately unknowable and unpredictable.[24] Such critics claim society should recognize this and not try to draw blueprints of an ideal society. At most, it should try to prepare for the different, the unexpected, and the innovative. The end-state utopian writer, on the other hand, draws a picture of people as more communal and resolute, and claims that human nature is knowable, predictable, and malleable. On this view society should plan according to the needs and possibilities of this knowable and predictable nature; in some cases, it should plan to shape and direct this nature to fit some end which has already been deemed desirable.

In attempting to respond to the question of what is possible for human beings and human society, utopian writers often look to education for the answer. Education and/or social conditioning are a part of most utopian dreams. End-state utopian visions pose a picture of a different order and they rely on education as a means for attaining the actualization of their proposed order. I have found that most works of end-state utopian fiction have a changed human nature already fixed and in place when the story begins. People are often portrayed as "naturally" cooperative, peaceful, and loving. The possibility of changing human nature is simply assumed, nothing but beneficial effects are drawn from the new nature, and almost no clue as to how the change was actually brought about is given. For example, in Edward Bellamy's *Looking Backward* the literary device of sleeping through more than a century of progress and change is employed. In Charlotte Perkins Gilman's *Herland*, a war that takes most of the men away and a natural catastrophe which isolates the community result in a community of "a bunch of hysterical girls and some older slave women. . . . At first there was a period of sheer despair. . . . Some were for suicide, but not the majority."[25] They get on with the work of burying their dead and planting their crops until the miracle of asexual reproduction spontaneously occurs (a gift from the goddess). Most often one just chances upon (during travel or by misadventure) the already perfect and functioning society isolated somewhere on earth or in the heavens. This is part of what leaves critics frustrated and skeptical. Some writers of end-state utopian literature, however, try to fill in the method and content of such educational reforms. They give directions on how to shape human nature to fit their vision. Utopian planners such as Robert Owen drew up, and even implemented, plans for communities that included plans for education and modification of behavior. B. F. Skinner is very explicit on how to reinforce "desirable" behavior and how to discourage what is not wanted. Some fictional accounts exist as well—Aldous Huxley's *Island* discusses how certain behaviors have been modified and why (that is, how many children people are to have, whether to marry, how to have sex). Usually, when there is much detail provided on the shaping of human nature the book has a dystopian twist. It is this aspect of manipulation that people most fear. Such directive planning is downright dangerous because it usually results in a manipulative and authoritarian system in which the individual and difference will be lost.

Most end-state utopian visions seem committed to the view that the great bulk of "human nature" is acquired. One may be born with some very minimal "self," but it is one's material conditions, experience, and education which will give this "self" its form and content. Even Charles Fourier, who appears to want only to shape the community to fit the various individual natures present in people, ultimately admits that "in the Combined Order, after it is fully established, there will exist, by means of its system of education— unity of habit, of manner, customs, language, etc., together with general politeness, refinement and urbanity."[26] On most end-state visions it seems necessary to assume that human nature is basically plastic. On this view, then, what any given community should do is provide the conditions for the experience and education which will form individuals most suited to that community's needs and desires. In order to do this, one must decide what nature is desired and then one must gain knowledge of how to shape such a nature. On the end-state model, control of the community comes in controlling the habits and sentiments of the individuals who make it up. What must be done is to experiment in order to decide on the best set of habits and sentiments to instill, and to determine the best method for so changing human nature. Once the essential character of human nature is discovered, and properly studied, the engineer will be able to produce the desired habits and sentiments— whatever they may be. The idea is, as Skinner says, that "men can build a better world and, through it, better men."[27]

End-state utopian visions have provided a variety of alternative methods for attempting such engineering of human nature. The possibilities include the use of coercion (subtle and otherwise), terror, legal punishment, education, eugenics, morality, inducements, drugs, indoctrination, and psychological conditioning.[28] Intuitively, the most appealing of these is education. We tend to view education as a right or privilege, while force, coercion, and drugs are seen as restrictive and manipulative. Furthermore, while force and coercion require the maintenance of a constant threat, and drugs constant application, education has the benefit of perpetuating itself once begun. Assuming human nature is infinitely malleable, though, means one must carefully examine and direct what influences individuals in their development. A very careful and efficient method of education must be developed.[29] Only an irresponsible community would leave the formation of its citizens to chance. People must be educated to see themselves as part of a larger whole and learn to conform to the needs of the community. If people are so educated, happiness and harmony are expected to follow.

Conformity in agreement on the point of recognizing and acting on communal interests, however, does not necessarily entail the loss of individuality and difference. Rather, individuals can hold common beliefs that guide their actions for the common good, while still differing greatly with regard to personal interests, tastes, and points of view. By providing a framework for choice, the utopian education proposes to handle differences without conflict. People are asked only to give up seeing themselves as being in opposition to one another and to recognize their interdependence and mutuality. At times, however, this spirit of collectivity may seem to be more an installation of certain behavior into people than an inspiration of people to a certain conduct. Once people come to hold the necessary basic beliefs in common, though, so much stands to be gained that how the beliefs came to be held seems to some a relatively unimportant concern. If need, conflict, and suffering can be eliminated by bringing people to live in mutual charity and fellowship, many feel it is worth whatever cost such a transition requires.

The fear, of course, evident in dystopian and anti-utopian writing is that "education" will become unmitigated manipulation and "citizens" merely homogeneous obedient cogs. This is not usually the writer's plan, however. In most cases, education is not to manipulate or externally determine what individuals will be and how they will behave. Rather, it is a kind of conditioning of the individual which can take a number of forms. The most important aspect of any form of responsible social conditioning is to make it easier to be the kind of individual who can exist in harmony with the community—that is, to be virtuous.[30] It is easier to acquire a virtuous character (however this has been defined by the community) when there are few, or no, obstacles to performing virtuous acts. How to act is still the individual's choice; it has just been made easier to choose the virtuous act. As one starts to choose, at least occasionally, to act virtuously (that is, in accord with the community), the hope is that one will eventually come to want to do only what is virtuous. In this way new habits and sentiments will be formed as proper education liberates reason to make morally responsible decisions. It does not coerce or co-opt the decision. An excellent example of this way of thinking can be found in Jean Jacques Rousseau's *Emile*.

ROUSSEAU: UTOPIAN EDUCATION

The society which results from Rousseau's discussion in *On the Social Contract* places certain requirements and restraints on its citizens. Each citizen must feel obligated to others; he must have a sense of the general will and freely comply with it. Rousseau thinks that it is legitimate to force male citizens to see the reasonableness of what is in the interest of the community. This "persuasion" will be done most effectively through the education of the citizens. One finds in *Emile* that education is a necessary preparation for the citizens of the society proposed in *On the Social Contract*. It is education which is to bring freedom and obligation together.

Rousseau believes that the purposeful shaping of human nature is essential given the arbitrary and destructive condition human social and cultural development has brought upon human life. "Under existing conditions a man left to himself from birth would be more of a monster than the rest. Prejudice, authority, necessity, example, all the social conditions into which we are plunged, would stifle nature in him and put nothing in her place."[31] Since the social condition has perverted our nature and removed our freedom from us, education must give it back. Rousseau's is an education to develop citizens free from the constraints and influences of an arbitrary will—be it their own or someone else's. It is an education to develop the ideal citizen for the ideal society.

It is important to note that Rousseau's citizens are male. Rousseau's description of education for women, found in the chapter on Sophie, is an education to prepare her to be the helpmate of Emile, but not a citizen in her own right. Some proponents of Rousseau's political philosophy argue that this distinction between the education of men and women is just a result of the time period in which he was writing. I think, however, that the education of dependence Rousseau describes for women is one of the necessary prejudices his system requires. If women were educated to be citizens in their own right, the distinction between private and public spheres would be blurred and the ideal of an abstract, impartial general will would be threatened.[32]

Rousseau begins with the assumption that nature is good and that those things that have gone wrong are the result of human society gone wrong. Somehow people have chosen the wrong ends and/or ways of being human. The best place to start, then, to form the good citizen is with the uncorrupted infant. In the early years education does not require a process of positive formulation as much as it requires the educator to restrain influences that would alter what nature has put in the human infant. Rousseau believes one must try to keep children as uncorrupted as possible—that is, as free from societal influence as can be managed. This involves some seemingly directive actions, though, on the part of the educator.

The environment provided for the infant is a subtle (or not so subtle) form of direction. Breast-feeding, fresh air, cold-water baths, no swaddling—there is a whole list of prescriptions. Rousseau recognizes this as part of education. "As I said before, man's education begins at birth; before he can speak or understand he is learning. Experience precedes instruction."[33] Experience therefore should be chosen carefully. For Emile, experience should be directed so that no arbitrary fears, prejudices, or habits (moral and/or physical) will develop. It is just such arbitrary fears, prejudices, and habits which, according to Rousseau, make us inflexible and so unfree. To prevent their development is to keep the will free, or rather to make the formulation of a free will possible. The prevention of the formation of an arbitrary framework of judgment is necessary if there is to be real choice in the adult life of the citizen. (Sophie's development is not aimed at making her an independent, autonomous thinker, but rather the "complement" to Emile. She is taught dependence and not encouraged to think for herself. She will follow her husband's judgment.)

Childhood is the stage during which a sense of self is gained and the transition from child to potential moral being and citizen begins for boys. "Men, be kind to your fellow-men; this is your first duty, kind to every age and station, kind to all that is not foreign to humanity."[34] This is the only positive lesson one need teach children. Beyond this, Rousseau stresses the need to keep male children independent so that later participation in the general will is possible.

> Oh, man! live your own life and you will no longer be wretched. Keep to your appointed place in the order of nature and nothing can tear you from it. . . .Your freedom and your power extend as far and no further than your natural strength; anything more is but slavery, deceit, and trickery. Power itself is servile when it depends upon public opinion.[35]

One should not be dependent on the opinion or will of others; one should not be dependent on possessing power over and above one's needs or at another's expense. The general will requires each person be free from these particular dependencies. Proper education will not allow dependence on opinion or authority to enter into a child's life. One should not come to believe, however, that this entails being independent in the sense of being free from influence or obligation. Emile must feel obligated to others; one must realize the general will and comply.

The natural male child gains happiness in the enjoyment of liberty but, as Rousseau believes that this liberty is not absolute, limits, constraints, and obligations are part of this happiness. It is the educator who is responsible for achieving this melding of freedom and obligation. The tutor must provide an environment in which boys can do as they please and still never come to develop a restricted will. It must appear to be a process of self-education. Allow children to suffer; it leads to the knowledge that one is no different from other people and prepares one to deal more easily with future setbacks. Allow nature to keep desire in check. Give as little overt direction as possible. Early education should be focused "not on teaching virtue or truth, but in preserving the heart from vice and from the spirit of error."

Free from prejudices and free from habits, there would be nothing in him to coun-
teract the effect of your labours. In your hands he would soon become the wisest of
men; by doing nothing to begin with you would end with a prodigy of education.[36]

Preserve the unblemished state as long as possible—this "sleep of reason"—
and let the adult begin to show itself in the child. There is more than the
preservation of the natural child going on here, however.

During the "sleep of reason," much has already been done. The tutor has
shaped the passions, prejudices, habits, and desires of the pupil simply by
controlling the child's environment. When reason begins to show itself, the
more obviously directive work can begin. Proper direction must be given to
the use of this newly emerging reason; what has been developed thus far must
now be given a rational foundation.

There is no subjection so complete as that which preserves the forms of freedom; it
is then that the will is taken captive. Is not this poor child, without knowledge,
strength, or wisdom, entirely at your mercy? Are you not master of his whole environment so far as it affects him? Cannot you make him what you please? His work
and play, his pleasure and pain, are they not, unknown to him, under your control?
No doubt he ought only to do what he wants, but he ought only to want to do what
you want him to do.[37]

Has not the freedom of the individual been lost here? Rousseau would argue
that it has not. Emile, educated on this model, is aware only of freedom and
makes choices in light of this. All that has been done is to limit artificially
what the choices are, to make it easier to be virtuous. The tutor limits experiences so that reason has the "proper" subject matter. Nature places limits on
choices and so must humanity if it is to achieve better citizens, and thereby
improve society. What would frustrate freedom would be to disallow the
choosing, to give commands or ultimatums. Responsibility is learned through
making and acting on one's own choices.

Now, when Emile is aware that there are consequences which follow from
his choices, moral education can begin. By observation, not moralistic
preaching, the young adult becomes aware that one's individual needs are interdependent with the needs of others. People require one another for the satisfaction of their needs. No one can fulfill all their needs alone, nor are one's
desires formed in isolation. Emile becomes aware that his choices affect not
only his own possibilities, but his society's as well.

Rousseau's citizen has a duty, then, to be aware of the general well-
being, act in accord with it, and make sure others do so as well. There is
no greater sense of social obligation. So what of individual freedom? How

can citizens be free if there is a general will capable of setting aside their individual wills? Rousseau's answer is that freedom is attainable only if we teach citizens to be virtuous and love their country. "A man is virtuous," he tells us, "when his individual will is in conformity with the general will in all respects, and he spontaneously seeks to do what the people he loves wish him to do."[38] Given that people are inevitably educated and socialized, it makes sense to want to use this process as effectively and beneficially as possible. If the power to condition people is institutionalized, though, it can become a very dangerous power. Is the potential good that might come from such engineering worth the risk of the potential harm? Writers of dystopias show us the cost of such a system gone wrong and hope to convince us it is too great a risk to take.

By putting such stress on the process of education and/or socialization, Rousseau (and other utopian writers) creates a very powerful means for shaping individuals. The shaping he sees as necessary is such that the individual feels an obligation to society through the realization of individual interdependence and equality. Rousseau thinks that by showing individuals that ultimately there is no difference in vulnerability among people—that they are equal—rationality and feeling will then direct such people to form a community that is in the interest of all. Provided that they have been instilled with the correct sentiments, reason will lead to the formation of the general will where each is bound only to one's own will.

Prejudices, misinformation, and selective education—these are all part of Rousseau's process of socialization (as they are probably part of any such process). The difference with Rousseau, and most end-state utopian visions, is that these processes are effectively directed and intentionally formed. This makes them more prevalent, more deeply instilled and *potentially* more beneficial and/or more dangerous. Rousseau is producing male citizens who are capable of critical thought. These same citizens, however, have had their sentiments and prejudices "properly" instilled. They have been created with a certain image in mind.

> One who dares to undertake the founding of a people should feel that he is capable of changing human nature, so to speak; of transforming each individual, who by himself is a perfect and solitary whole, into a part of a larger whole from which this individual receives, in a sense, his life and his being; of altering man's constitution in order to strengthen it; of substituting a partial and moral existence for the physical and independent existence we have all received from nature. He must, in short, take away man's own force in order to give him forces that are foreign to him and that he cannot make use of without the help of others. The more these natural forces are dead and destroyed, and the acquired ones great and lasting, the more the institution as well is solid and perfect.[39]

A community with common, deeply instilled sentiments and prejudices may in the end be more dangerous than one where diversity in these areas is encouraged. Who will decide on and direct the program of education? Such engineering requires some kind of directive authority. This increases the chance of "experts" dominating and manipulating individuals. If the rational shaping of human nature goes awry, what kind of person will be left? What about when this process itself is perverted, intentionally or otherwise? Rousseau's own views on women show that even "experts" incorporate their biases and weaknesses as well as their strengths when providing directive guidance. People who have been intentionally shaped are likely to have deep-seated behaviors and beliefs which would be difficult to change or redirect. If it turned out the society had chosen to instill behaviors that were not harmonious with its ends, or if someone misdirected the process of shaping, then very restrictive measures would likely follow in an attempt to stay on course. Variety and freedom are definitely at risk here. Such shaping may ultimately limit possibilities more than it opens them up.

Rousseau's vision may be appealing to some, but one must ask what will happen when it goes awry. When choosing a form of association, one should consider the consequences of its ending. How will it begin to fall apart and in what condition will this leave the people? Even if there is a good chance that the social engineering will go as planned, and a good chance that the plan will prove to be desirable, there is still the chance that the system will eventually encounter external interference or temptations and experience some internal disruption. When the community begins to disintegrate, these intentionally shaped individuals have few resources on which to fall back. Their critical skills are not enough to overcome institutionalized bias. With their society gone awry, their experiences make no sense; their understanding may be too limited. In time they might be able to resolve their situation, but, more likely, such people will latch on to anyone who promises to rule them well. They will not be able to find in themselves the ability to rule themselves—the conditions for the ultimate loss of freedom to an arbitrary power. The engineering involved in the end-state model of utopia is far-reaching and all the consequences cannot be foreseen—good and bad. But given some of the potential dangers, caution is warranted. End-state visions are dangerous if they impede the development of critical thought and choice.

PERFECTION AS PROCESS

End-state utopian thinking involves visions of improving life—improving to the point of perfection. As discussed before, in the perfect society there will

be nothing left to dream about. If need, conflict, and suffering have successfully been eliminated, all suggestions for change in the society must be regarded as suspect. Change, at this point, is no longer seen as the necessary
means of improvement, but as the threat of the disintegration of stable, unchanging perfection.

However, we are changing and evolving creatures in a changing and evolving environment. We appear to be creatures that push for change just as hard
as we resist it. We have a tendency toward hope. Inasmuch as we "think
ahead" and make plans to shape our environment to fit our needs and wants
we exercise this hope. It helps us to survive.[40] If perfection means the end of
change, and so the end of hope, this could be a very difficult adjustment and
cost us more than we stand to gain. "Reality without real possibility is not
complete, the world without future-laden properties does not deserve a
glance, an art, a science. . . . Concrete utopia stands on the horizon of every
reality; real possibility surrounds the open dialectical tendencies and latencies
to the very last."[41]

We need visions that can incorporate change, hope, and dreams. Even if
such change is unnecessary its possibility could be constructive. Of course, it
could be destructive as well. That is why change came to be feared in the first
place; it was seen as destructive, debilitating, and destabilizing.[42] With this
assumption/premise in mind, if we are going to risk allowing change into the
end-state vision, it is likely that stricter controls are going to be seen as necessary. In order to protect and preserve the overriding goal of harmony an authoritarian system is a likely result.

Similarly, fear of difference and lack of diversity are problems for the end-
state vision. End-state utopian thinking involves visions of everlasting harmony. It has been thought by many that homogeneity is the necessary means
to this harmony. Difference in culture, religion, intelligence, sex, and color
are some common examples of differences which are seen as natural sources
of conflict. People tend to fear that which seems different from themselves;
they regard the dissimilar as a potential threat to be crushed or controlled. On
this view, then, to achieve harmony one must either start with basically similar people and/or cause them to be similar. Harmony on this model, though,
is rather empty.

We learn and grow (perhaps painfully) from difference. Experience expands by encountering divergent points of view and a variety of lifestyles.
Working to harmonize various views often results in new ideas and outlooks.
Even if it were possible to eliminate difference, it would be a loss. If fear
of difference results in a lack of diversity, possibilities are narrowed. However, diversity leads to comparison and blending of ideas. This often results
in change, or at least the desire, in some, for change. Inasmuch as change

threatens the stability of the end-state vision, it follows that diversity threatens the stability of the end-state vision. We should recognize, however, that though there may be gains in order and constancy, inasmuch as end-state visions require the squelching of diversity, these visions squelch human potential. As long as we are the finite and imperfect creatures we appear to be, we need visions that can incorporate and build on the diversity of people (perhaps on the diversity of all life), and encourage critical thought and choice.

THE END-STATE VISION OF WOMEN'S COUNTRY

In discussing the origin and implications of the end-state model of utopia, I have already alluded to several literary works that follow this model—Plato's *Republic*, Huxley's *Brave New World*, Gilman's *Herland*, Bellamy's *Looking Backward*, and Bradley's *The Ruins of Isis*. These works explore the assumption that by gaining control over nature and finding the proper arrangement of individuals, we can achieve a workable lasting, harmonious ordering of society. For a sustained discussion, I have chosen to use Sheri S. Tepper's *The Gate to Women's Country* as an example of an end-state utopian vision, in part because it is a feminist utopian novel both modeled on and critical of Plato's *Republic*, and because it focuses on ridding the world of violence, especially male violence. All of the novels discussed in this book address the issue of ending violence. Since the threat and reality of violence are often what push people to seek a more perfect world, it is important to see that only the process model of utopia is able to avoid using violence as a means.

The characters in Tepper's *The Gate to Women's Country* combine the fatalistic and scientific attitudes that Popper believes ultimately lead to repression and violence. Furthermore, the "Council" attempts to develop and instill a virtuous character in the populace. Control of the community comes less through education than through eugenics, but control of information is an essential component in the plan for engineering the desired social state. They try to breed people who comply with the general will, and breed out those with what are identified as anti-social or undesirable tendencies. As in Rousseau's educational plan, people are intentionally transformed to fit the projected end-state. This section examines the societal arrangement developed in Tepper's *The Gate to Women's Country* and shows how the critiques of end-state visions apply. The end-state model of utopia has certain problematic assumptions and implications. Such visions focus on a final desired end-state without questioning the value of the means involved in achieving the desired state; by gaining rational control over nature and the ordering of society it will be possible to achieve a lasting harmony—engineered perfection.

One example of such an attempt at engineering has to do with the shaping of human nature. On most end-state visions it seems necessary to assume that human nature is basically plastic. Since control of the community comes in controlling the habits and sentiments of the individuals who make it up, it is necessary to determine the best set of habits and sentiments to instill and to determine the best method for so changing human nature. As mentioned before, some of the most common methods of change employed in end-state utopian visions include the use of coercion, terror, legal punishment, education, eugenics, inducements, drugs, and psychological conditioning. This idea of rational control leading to final harmony causes many to see utopian visions as static, totalitarian nightmares. End-state visions tend to make dogmatic assumptions about people and human society and to impose their single-minded view on others in an authoritarian and restrictive manner.

WOMEN'S COUNTRY

The story of *The Gate to Women's Country* follows the life of a young woman, Stavia, from childhood and innocence to middle age and enforced membership on the ruling council of Marthatown—that is, a member of the "Damned Few." Women's Country consists of a group of cities almost entirely inhabited and run by women, but protected by male warriors who live in garrisons outside the gates of each city. This arrangement was developed after the Convulsion, which appears to have been a nuclear war. Only a few people survived and there was widespread environmental devastation. Among the survivors was a woman, Martha Evesdaughter, who "taught that the destruction had come about because of men's willingness—even eagerness—to fight, and she determined that this eagerness to fight must be bred out of our race, even though it might take a thousand years. She and the other women banded together and started a town, with a garrison outside."[43] This arrangement worked well; and as population increased, other cities were set up in the same way.

The culture of Women's Country is centered on a type of goddess worship of The Lady or Great Mother. There is a fatalism involved in this goddess worship and Stavia understood early on that "the Great Mother didn't bargain. The deity didn't change her mind for women's convenience. Her way was immutable. As the temple servers said, 'No sentimentality, no romance, no false hopes, no self-petting lies, merely that which is!' "[44] This Mother has certain rules—ordinances—which everyone must follow. While some find this restrictive, they have learned that if the ordinances are broken the peace and order of Women's Country will be threatened. So, no matter the difficulty

involved in obeying, it is understood that the good of everyone is on the line
and one must obey.

> We all have to do things we don't want to do. . . . All of us here in Women's Coun-
> try. Sometimes they are things that hurt us to do. We accept the hurt because the al-
> ternative would be worse. We have many reminders to keep us aware of that. The
> Council ceremonies. The play before summer carnival. The desolations are there to
> remind us of pain.[45]

In order to keep things running smoothly, the power to enforce the ordinances
is held by the Council. The Council originated with Martha and has always
been self-selective. In other words, people are not elected to the council by the
general populace, but are chosen by other council members. The Council
makes the economic and political decisions for the city. Some of the major areas of control are making trade agreements, determining the distribution of
goods, and directing educational programs. The Council is responsible for
maintaining stability. They do not appear to be in total control, however. The
garrisons exist to protect the cities from invasion by strangers and from attack
by other cities whose people might wish to gain their resources. As the garrisons are an integral part of Women's Country, their relationship is outlined
by the ordinances. They do not, however, *appear* to be subject to Council rule.

The main connection between the women and the men of the garrison is at
Carnival. This is a festival during which young women and men arrange to
meet and have sex. Such appointments must be arranged and approved of
ahead of time. The female children which result from such meetings remain
in Women's Country, but male children are given to their warrior fathers at
the age of five. This is an ordinance that cannot be broken. The male child
may visit his female relatives during Carnival up until the age of fifteen. At
this point he must choose either to become a warrior and remain with the garrison, or to return to Women's Country permanently.

Within the garrison there is a distinct warrior culture. It is considered hon-
orable among warriors to protect women and breed sons. It is believed that the
women earn the protective services of the men by providing them with sons
and food. The central monument of the garrison, and the focus of worship, is
a phallus—"an erection suitable for parade ground."[46] This symbol of male
power and virility is what defines the men's purpose as warrior and father. The
ordinances require that the warriors do not have doctors, and that their
weapons are such that they must fight at close range. "They must see their own
blood and the blood of their fellows, and they must care for their own dying
and see their pain. It's part of the choice they have to make."[47]

If they choose the life of the warrior, they must know the consequences.
They are not, however, as well informed as to the consequences of life in

Women's Country. The only books in the garrison library are romantic tales of battle and quest. All other education is denied to warriors, though the men who return to Women's Country can read and learn as much as the women do. The ordinances require each woman to have a science, a craft and an art so she can be useful to the community throughout her lifetime. The same is required of the men who return—servitors. Life in Women's Country is a demanding life, and the men who choose it are not aware of all its benefits or of its demands. They do not so much make a choice for Women's Country as they make a choice against penis worship and warrior life.

This arrangement between the cities of Women's Country and the corresponding garrisons seems to work well. There are, periodically, attempts by the garrison to overtake the cities, but they always fail. Most men in the garrison are content to let the women do all the work. They are well fed and clothed by the women's labor, and fighting is not too frequent. They get their sons and retain their independence. The entire arrangement, however, is a lie. Beneath the orderly and stable everyday existence of the women and servitors of the cities, and the men of the garrisons, the Council controls and manipulates everything.

In fact, no warriors father children. The ordinances require the breeding out of the violent tendencies of men and women. Old books, held in secret by the Council, describe domestic violence—mostly violence of men against women and children. The devastation is seen as evidence of the destructive tendencies of male power and aggression. The Council, therefore, controls who will reproduce—selecting the cooperative and gentle. While it is necessary to sterilize some women, the main focus is on controlling which men procreate. All of this is done without the people knowing it—only the Council knows.

Before Carnival the women who plan to have assignations must have an exam and be stamped as healthy and fit to become pregnant. When they go for their exam they go to a councilwoman, most of whom are medically trained. A contraceptive device is implanted in their arm during this exam. They are told, however, that this is a vitamin implant to help them be in good health and increase the odds of a successful pregnancy. After carnival, they have the implant removed and undergo a vaginal exam to check for infection—all under the guise of protecting the woman's health. During the exam, however, the woman is artificially inseminated with the sperm of those men who have returned to Women's Country over the years. What started as self-selection is now intentionally controlled and directed.[48]

The model the women follow is that of pre-Convulsion domestication of wild animals, such as sheep and cattle. The bulls who tended to be gentle and not to wander were selected as breeding stock. So now men who are gentle and cooperative are selected to breed. As a result, more boys return to Women's Country every year. Theoretically, such breeding will eventually result in the end of the warrior temperament and the end of the garrisons which will no longer be needed. As domestication of wild animals was seen to increase the odds of survival for both the animals and the people domesticating them, the Council sees a parallel need to domesticate men in order to secure the survival of everyone.

As violence has not yet been bred out, though, the Council uses other methods of control. The lack of education is one, but violence is another. When secrets are in danger, or a councilwoman threatened, violence is used as a defense. After Stavia has broken some of the ordinances and has unintentionally fed the fires of rebellion in the Marthatown garrison, the Council sees a violent weeding out of the men as necessary. They stage a threat to the town by another city's garrison, and the Marthatown garrison goes out to fight. The councilwomen of the various other cities have arranged that five garrisons will meet this one—no one from the Marthatown garrison will return. There is already a story prepared to explain the trap as warrior treachery. A myth is also developed and songs commissioned by the Council to celebrate the lost brothers, lovers, and sons as heroes. The truth must never be spoken. Only the women and servitors on the Council know—those that refer to themselves as the "Damned Few." "Those who kept things running. Those who did what had to be done."[49]

PROBLEMS OF THE VISION

The Gate to Women's Country is identified as an end-state vision because, as was mentioned earlier, it instantiates the idea of rational engineering and control leading to a lasting harmony. As an end-state vision, Women's Country tends to be authoritarian, has little tolerance for difference, and focuses narrowly on achieving certain traits rather than developing critical and adaptive capabilities. As discussed before, engineering schemes based on a vision of a desired final end-state are dangerous because they tend to require authoritarian control to achieve the end-state. Martha, a self-proclaimed prophet, set the goal of domesticating men and selected women with medical training to serve on the Council and implement this goal. These same women developed the goddess's ordinances to maintain order and to cover up their real methods of control. Selected mainly for their medical expertise, these women are nonetheless expected to serve as moral and political leaders. There is no discussion of why members of the medical profession should be given such dictatorial power over the lives of others. Tepper provides no argument or justification for the original selection of Council members besides their medical training. With such little justification for selecting members of the original Council, the future self-selection creates an arbitrary and tyrannical system that limits the possibilities of the community.

In Women's Country the members of the Council have complete power over the populace and control people's lives as they see fit. The lives of individual human beings are subordinated to a static view of the "good life." The Council, from the time of Martha, saw the domestication of men as an imperative to save the planet, the women, and the children. With this goal in mind, they have sought to control the habits and sentiments of individuals by maintaining the control of information and the control of breeding. In order to get a better community, a select few have defined, and seek to engineer, a better type of person.

The Council alone decides what a better type of person will be like and to what ends they will be directed. In Women's Country it is non-violence that has been defined as desirable.[50] This goal was formulated in the immediate aftermath of a nuclear war that nearly destroyed the planet and everything on it. In this context it is not unreasonable to seek to eliminate the root causes of such destructive capacities in the human creature. In fact, such a goal would seem mandated by our desire to survive. What is problematic, however, is the belief that one person (or set of persons) knows what is best for humanity and the belief that what is best will never change, even though conditions change. To assume that there is only one perspective (a god's-eye view), only one set of concerns, and only one solution is likely to lead to societal arrangements that attempt to achieve perfection and then forestall all future change or development. Such a static view denies the developmental nature of the world and the live creatures in it—a problem which will be addressed by the process model of utopia developed in chapters 4 and 5.

Given their singular static view, the council is so preoccupied with the managing of the society and with achieving their goal that they no longer see individuals as having worth apart from their social purpose and so are able to treat them as mere instruments for their larger task. Lured by the myth of destiny seen in the will of the Great Mother (the ordinances created by the first Council), that is by the belief that they have no choice, the members of the Council undertake to engineer a better world. Using the ordinances to excuse themselves from responsibility, the Council uses scientific engineering to achieve a chosen destiny.

Because this approach requires an unwavering commitment to act only in ways that promote the achievement of the chosen end, it can also lead to a form of authoritarian rule whereby the non-committed can be controlled or defused. In Women's Country the individual has become a tool of the state.

The women have their education and work prescribed for them with a minimum of choice on their part, others control their reproductive capacities without their knowledge, and they must give away any male offspring. The men of the garrisons appear to be mere pawns in the Council's hands. They are deceived about their role in reproduction and they are unknowingly sent off to die if they appear to challenge the order of things. Individuals are controlled for the sake of achieving and maintaining the end-state of a non-violent human race. Since the Council believes that human survival depends on achieving this non-violent, harmonious, stable state, their methods appear—at least to them—more than justified.

Not only is each individual limited by such an authoritarian arrangement, each person is further limited by the homogeneity sought by such an end-state vision. For example, the doctors of Women's Country take pride in having eliminated homosexuality.

Even in preconvulsion times it had been known that the so-called "gay syndrome" was caused by aberrant hormone levels during pregnancy. The women doctors now identified the condition as "hormonal reproductive maladaption," and corrected it before birth. There were very few actual HNRMs—called Hen Rams—either male or female, born in Women's Country, though there was still the occasional unsexed person or the omnisexed.[51]

There is an assumption that such difference is a maladaption which should be fixed. There is a desired norm and anything else is considered aberrant. We also see in the story that some people who just do not seem to fit city life have few choices—prostitution and/or a wandering existence. Not only do these "different" people miss out on some of the benefits of education, medication, and protection which the city can provide, the city misses out on the talents of those with unacceptable lifestyles. We learn and grow from difference. Experience expands by encountering divergent points of view and a variety of lifestyles. We need visions that can incorporate diversity and encourage critical thought and choice.

Any end-state achieved by the methods of manipulation, suppression, and authoritarian control will be tainted and limited by the very means of its achievement. If the Council were to succeed, there would not only be a populace of homogeneous non-violent men and women, but also a built-in elite who have grown accustomed to exercising power and control. While such an elite may not pose the danger of blowing up the world, they could pose the danger of limiting human potential and causing the stagnation or disintegration of human society. If one seeks to employ restrictive or oppressive means to achieve the end-state of a world without violence, the justification is usually that such a world would in turn be the means to further development—advances in art, science, and moral virtue. If the means employed to achieve the end-state of a non-violent world, however, cut off and limit the possibility of further growth, if they have the side effect of creating a world without difference, one must question the value of achieving the non-violent world.

A final problem is the belief that there is one overwhelmingly desirable trait and the resultant single-minded and narrow focus on developing and promulgating that one trait. Non-violence without intelligence or imagination may do little to sustain, much less improve, society. Non-violence without independence of thought or initiative may do little to promote the "good life." It is unlikely that the elimination or promotion of one behavior or trait will save the world. What is needed is critical intelligence that will enable people to understand their situatedness and guide their future with intelligent and flexible foresight.

As was discussed before, there is room for error both in choosing an end and in choosing the means of attaining it. If the Council has chosen a problematic end goal and/or problematic means for attaining their goal, their actions may result in limiting human potentiality and in limiting the possibilities of future survival and development. On the belief that survival requires a eugenics program aimed at the emergence of a non-violent human race, the Council deceives and manipulates the individuals of their society—for their own good and the good of the future. We know from the story that they have books on genetics that have survived the Convulsion, though how sophisticated or advanced this work is we are not told. They also have an anthropology book that describes how the Laplanders, tired of following the wild herds of reindeer, began to domesticate them by controlling which bulls bred. Only those that were gentle and did not wander were allowed to perpetuate their genes.

It is also clear that the medically trained women of Women's Country understand the need of genetic variety as they express concern about the possibility of bringing back a breed of dog with only two animals as a base. We can assume, then, that care is taken to maintain a good genetic pool among human beings, even though the chosen male breeding population started from a very few and is still relatively small. It would seem, however, that just as with the selective breeding of other animals, not only do the desired traits of individuals get passed on—in this case gentle, cooperative behavior and occasionally ESP—but so do some undesired or weak characteristics.

If breeding lines are very close the chances of physical problems increase. If one breeds animals for a selected characteristic—speed, color, size, temperament—it often results in animals with weak hips, bad hearts, poor eyesight, and little intelligence. One only has to look at the variety of dog breeds which have resulted from human selection and control to realize what power selective breeding can have. If one also looks at the many medical and mental problems these various breeds have, however, one also realizes the dangers of such narrowly focused selection.

Focusing on the end of breeding men who are cooperative and gentle may prove to be problematic in a similar way. Genetic variety may be lost, congenital conditions may develop and be perpetuated, unforeseen and undesirable traits may result. It could also turn out to be the case that some violent tendencies are necessary to human survival. In the book, we encounter a group of people living in the hills—Holylanders. Their culture is very patriarchal and violent. When this group holds Stavia captive she is almost killed. Her rescue requires violence and we find the servitors and some councilwomen capable of doing what is necessary to free her. While it is true that the Holylanders are dying out from inbreeding and exposure to radiation, there is a clear possibility that other groups of people have survived in other parts of the world and contact may eventually be possible. Would a *completely* nonviolent race be able to survive such contact? There will likely be suspicion between the strangers and Women's Country and, as Women's Country is fairly prosperous, it would be a likely target for takeover. Can they afford to be totally non-violent? Given the risk of repeating the "Convulsion," can they afford not to be?

Besides the possible danger of weakening their ability to defend themselves, selective breeding could result in internal stagnation and/or disintegration. Even with our relatively advanced genetic knowledge, there are often unexpected consequences in selective breeding. We have trouble identifying and singling out one trait for change. Focusing on ridding people of violent tendencies could also affect other desirable traits. Our capacity for critical thought, imagination, creativity, perseverance, and optimism all may be affected. We just do not know. We do not understand in any detail how these drives, outlooks, and abilities are connected. Even if our violent nature is problematic, its total elimination may prove equally troublesome in different ways.

WOMEN'S COUNTRY: A USEFUL UTOPIAN VISION?

Just as Rousseau's pupils—Emile and Sophie—have experienced selective education which has left them with intentionally formed behavior and beliefs, the people of Women's Country are being born with a selected basic character and then selectively educated. Both methods of systematic engineering put variety and freedom at risk. We are biological creatures who need genetic variety to survive and grow. The same seems to be true for our social and cultural development. The intentional shaping of human beings may limit possibilities more than it opens them, and it is a serious question whether it is worth the risk. With such intentionally shaped characters, the people of Women's Country may not be able to cope with the possibilities of change coming from external interference or internal disintegration. They will not be able to find in themselves the ability to rule themselves—the condition for the ultimate loss of freedom to an arbitrary power.

If their community begins to disintegrate, perhaps due to economic difficulty, these people will have a limited array of coping mechanisms. They may not be able to adapt to the new conditions, as they have not been encouraged to develop the capacities of critical thought and choice. Rather, they have been manipulated and controlled to fit a specific social plan. While this vision may serve well as a critique of current society and as a warning about the future we are moving toward (both the devastating possibilities of nuclear war and the increasingly sophisticated possibilities of genetic engineering), it does not serve well as a positive vision for shaping our possibilities. This seems to be part of Tepper's message.

Manipulating people into non-violence changes little—they must choose non-violence and understand what can be gained by such a choice if it is to be a worthwhile goal. Non-violence must not be seen as an ultimate or final end, but as a goal that will allow for further development of a variety of potentialities. As an end-state vision, the vision of Tepper's Women's Country does little to promote critical thought in its citizens or to prepare its people for further growth. Women's Country, as an end-state vision, embodies the problems of such visions. There is a fear of difference, a lack of diversity, a loss of autonomy, a fear of, or inability to cope with, change, and a resulting reliance on an authoritarian system. End-state utopian visions squelch human potential. The importance of critical intelligence and the need of a continued potential for growth are ignored by such visions.

If the end-state model of utopia cannot incorporate change, difference, and diversity and avoid becoming authoritarian, if it cannot encourage critical thought and choice in individuals, perhaps it is the project of end-state visions that should be given up. In its place we can develop a vision of utopia that sets up a model of perfection as process.

By perfectible, it is not meant that he is capable of being brought to perfection. But the word seems sufficiently adapted to express the faculty of being continually made better and receiving perpetual improvement. . . . If we could arrive at perfection, there would be an end to our improvement. There is however one thing of great importance that it does imply; every perfection or excellence that human beings are competent to conceive, human beings unless in cases that are palpably and unequivocally excluded by the structure of their frame, are competent to attain.[52]

On this model, to attain any particular excellence does not entail the cessation of striving. Instead, each achievement can be grasped as an ongoing task for the future.[53] This is the view developed in the process model of utopia in chapters 4 and 5.

NOTES

1. George Kateb, *Utopia and Its Enemies* (London: Collier-Macmillan, 1975), 17.

2. What I have labeled historical determinism, Popper calls historicism. Given the variety of uses and interpretations the term historicism has had, I have chosen not to use it. The concept Popper is trying to convey is some sense of historical necessity and/or destiny.

3. Karl Popper, *The Open Society and Its Enemies* (Princeton, N.J.: Princeton University Press, 1950), 22.

4. Popper, *Open Society*, 76.

5. Popper, *Open Society*, 423.

6. Krishan Kumar, *Utopianism* (Minneapolis: University of Minnesota Press, 1991), 55.

7. George Kateb, "Introduction," in *Utopia*, ed. George Kateb (New York: Atherton Press, 1971), 23.

8. Francis Golffing and Barbara Golffing, "An Essay on Utopian Possibility," in *Utopia*, ed. George Kateb (New York: Atherton Press, 1971), 29.

9. Ralf Dahrendorf, "Out of Utopia: Toward a Reorientation of Sociological Analysis," in *Utopia*, ed. George Kateb (New York: Atherton Press, 1971), 103–106.

10. Elisabeth Hansot, *Perfection and Progress: Two Modes of Utopian Thought* (Cambridge, Mass.: MIT Press, 1974), 200.

11. Hansot, *Perfection and Progress*, 198.

12. J. C. Davis, *Utopia and the Ideal Society* (Cambridge: Cambridge University Press, 1981), 388.

13. Bradley offers a complex analysis of sex discrimination among other things. Here I use it solely as an example of what can emerge in the name of the common good.

14. Marion Zimmer Bradley, *The Ruins of Isis* (New York: Pocket Books, 1978), 174.

15. Bradley, *The Ruins of Isis*, 174.

16. Bradley, *The Ruins of Isis*, 222.

17. Bradley, *The Ruins of Isis*, 207.

18. Kateb, *Utopia and Its Enemies*, 225.

19. Aldous Huxley, *Brave New World* (New York: Harper & Row, 1946), 246.

20. William James, "What Makes a Life Significant," in The *Writings of William James*, ed. John J. McDermott (Chicago: University of Chicago Press, 1976), 645–60.

21. Kateb, *Utopia*, 16–17.

22. Kateb, *Utopia and Its Enemies*, 134.

23. Hansot, *Perfection and Progress*, 112.

24. This is different from writers of dystopias who share the assumption, with utopian writers, that human nature can be shaped, but give a picture where something has gone wrong in the process of such shaping.

25. Charlotte Perkins Gilman, *Herland*. Introduction by Ann J. Lane (New York: Pantheon Books, 1979), 55.

26. Charles Fourier, *The Social Destiny of Man* (New York: Gordon Press, 1972), 154–155.

27. B. F. Skinner, "Freedom and the Control of Men," in *Utopia*, ed. George Kateb (New York: Atherton Press, 1971), 58.

28. Barbara Goodwin, *Social Science and Utopia: Nineteenth Century Models of Social Harmony* (Atlantic Highlands, N.J.: Humanities Press, 1978), 84.

29. Kateb, *Utopia and Its Enemies*, 155.

30. Kateb, *Utopia and Its Enemies*, 156.

31. Jean Jacques Rousseau, *Emile* (London: Everyman's Library, 1972), 5.

32. Sophie is to be pleasing and compliant, the perfect counterpart in marriage. She is to soothe and comfort Emile when he returns home from his work in the public sphere. Her childhood prepares her to be pliant and conform to his will, not to choose for herself. See the following for some interesting discussions of the status of women in Rousseau's educational and political theory: Helen Evans Misenheimer, *Rousseau on the Education of Women* (Washington, D.C.: University Press of America, 1981); Susan Moller Okin, "Rousseau's Natural Woman," *Journal of Politics* 41 (May 1979): 393–416; Penny Weiss, *Gendered Community: Rousseau, Sex, and Politics* (New York: New York University Press, 1993).

33. Rousseau, *Emile*, 29.

34. Rousseau, *Emile*, 43.

35. Rousseau, *Emile*, 47.

36. Rousseau, *Emile*, 58–59.

37. Rousseau, *Emile*, 85.

38. William Boyd, *The Education Theory of Jean Jacques Rousseau* (New York: Russell & Russell, 1963), 98.

39. Jean Jacques Rousseau, *On the Social Contract*, trans. Judith Masters (New York: St. Martin's Press, 1978), 68.

40. Lionel Tiger, *Optimism: The Biology of Hope* (New York: Simon & Schuster, 1979), 21.

41. Ernst Bloch, *The Principle of Hope*, trans. Neville Plaice, Stephen Plaice, and Paul Knight (Cambridge, Mass.: MIT Press, 1986), 223.

42. In *Quest for Certainty,* in *John Dewey: The Later Works, Vol. 4: 1929*, John Dewey notes:

Before the rise of experimental method, change was simply an inevitable evil; the world . . . of change, while an inferior realm compared with the changeless, was nevertheless there and had to be accepted practically as it happened to occur. . . . Goods, however, can be made secure in existence only through regulation of processes of change, a regulation dependent upon knowledge of their relations. While the abolition of fixed tendencies toward definite ends has been mourned by many as if it involved a despiritualization of nature, it is in fact a precondition of the projection of new ends and of the possibility of realizing them through intentional activity. Objects which are not fixed goals of nature and which have no inherent defining forms become candidates for receiving new qualities; means for serving new purposes. (82)

43. Sheri S. Tepper, *The Gate to Women's Country* (New York: Bantam Books, 1988), 301–302.

44. Tepper, *Women's Country*, 9.

45. Tepper, *Women's Country*, 11–12.

46. Tepper, *Women's Country*, 79.

47. Tepper, *Women's Country*, 128.

48. Some of the similarities with Plato's Republic are worth noting. As in the Republic, Tepper attempts to control people through breeding and the control of information—censorship and the creation of myths. In both books, there are carnival times when people think they are mating with whom they wish. In reality though, their true mates have been carefully chosen. In both books, a select few determine what information is fit for which people and these same few create songs and myths to encourage "proper" sentiments in the populace. There also appear to be three castes making up each society. As the Philosophers order and control everything in the Republic, so too the Council directs and decides the lives of others in Women's Country. Both societies maintain a warrior class and a class of artisans—all doing what they are suited to do. There are some differences, though. Where Plato, at least in theory, believed that both men and women would make up each class, Tepper has made the warrior class exclusively male. Furthermore, where Plato saw the warriors as an important and integral part of the society, Tepper sees them as dangerous and expendable.

49. Tepper, *Women's Country*, 313.

50. It is also considered valuable to possess telepathic abilities.

51. Tepper, *Women's Country*, 76.

52. William Godwin, *Enquiry Concerning Political Justice*, ed. Raymond A. Preston (New York: Alfred A. Knopf, 1926), xxix.

53. Bloch, *The Principle of Hope*, 188.

Chapter Three

The Anarchist Model of Utopia

The critical institution of Anarchy, a society without a ruler, is the local assembly, the free association of individuals for mutual aid and collective action. Freely generated and disbanded, such assemblies are a full and direct democracy, reaching decisions by consensus and free experimentation but not by the tyranny of the majority. . . .

The Anarchist thus no more advocates chaos than does the strictest authoritarian; but the Anarchist seeks order in diversity and agreement rather than in uniformity and control. *Moreover, order consists in change; a free society cannot be static. It must form a fluid organism, a natural unity that left unhampered, freely adjusts and grows in the face of new requirements and aspirations.* Anarchy is incompatible with constricting social forms or rigid and dogmatic thought.[1] (Emphasis added.)

This description of the anarchist vision appears to be a direct response to the criticisms of end-state utopian visions. Anarchist utopian visions reject control of individuals by an authority, avoid the centralization of power, and promote order that is compatible with creativity and diversity. Furthermore, the anarchist makes no claim about achieving a final, perfect balance of authority, individuals, control, and freedom but recognizes that arrangements of society will likely differ from one another due to a variety of factors: culture, physical environment, population size, food supply, different prioritizing of problems. "The methods of Anarchism . . . do not comprise an iron-clad program to be carried out under all circumstances. Methods must grow out of the economic needs of each place and time, and of the intellectual and temperamental requirements of the individual."[2]

In addition to there being differences among societies, anarchist societies will always be in a process of internal change. Anarchy is a kind of ongoing experiment. While it has certain principles to guide it, their application is flexible, and the outcome can never be fully predicted. If successful in achieving the goal of free and equal individuals living in harmony under conditions of voluntary control, anarchy will have opened up a whole host of new possibilities and new problems that cannot even be imagined in the present. It is just the first guiding principle in a never-ending experiment of trying to discover and to live out our full human potential.

Not knowing what an anarchist society would actually be like, and not being sure what would follow from such social organization, does not mean a meaningful critique of anarchist principles, methods, and goals cannot be made. I will focus on three areas that are vulnerable to such critique: the difficulties of revolution, the demands of freedom, the dubious promise of diversity. Despite these critiques, however, it is important to note that anarchist utopian visions avoid the dogmatism of end-state utopian visions, and by so doing are a marked improvement. They become both less restrictive and more workable than end-state visions and leave people in charge of their own fate. This notion of personal responsibility for oneself and the future of others can be daunting and/or inspiring. Although it is frightening to face oneself as creator, it can also be liberating. When a society is no longer tied to a sense of fatalism, real changes can be attempted and not be seen as destabilizing society and undermining perfection. Anarchist utopian visions have a greater possibility of effectiveness because they tend to view society as an ongoing experiment. Correspondingly, however, they have potential for being disaffecting and disempowering and this must be guarded against.

ANARCHIST IMAGINATION

Anarchists believe people, as individuals, are in the best position to govern themselves. With anarchy the individual is the heart of society and the only possible source of authority.

> With what delight must every well-informed friend of man-kind look forward to the auspicious period, the dissolution of political government, of the brute engine which has been the only perennial cause of the vices of mankind, and which . . . has mischiefs of various sorts incorporated with its substance, and no otherwise to be removed than by its utter annihilation![3]

The anarchist's complaint against government is that all forms of government, including democracy, eventually forget that the source of their authority is the individual, and they centralize power and decision making. People disempowered in this way have lost something anarchists consider essential to humanity, namely, freedom. The notion of freedom here has both negative and positive connotations. For the anarchist, though, the achievement of one kind of freedom depends on having the other. Their argument is that in order to have the positive freedom to direct one's life as one chooses, the social condition must be such that no external authority interferes with or artificially limits one's choices. Therefore, inasmuch as government exists people cannot be free.

Interestingly, this libertarian notion of freedom is a result of the same enlightenment notions that influence end-state utopian visions. Both of these models of utopia start from a common base—rational intellectualism and radical hope. Anarchists believe that rational individuals, making their own rational choices, will achieve a self-regulating harmony.[4] They combine this ideal of laissez-faire, however, with a belief in the moral, intellectual and social progress of human beings.[5] While individual liberty is for the most part inviolable, most anarchists do not see human nature as essentially individualistic. Freedom is power in association with others, not over and against them.[6] The individual and society need not be seen as inevitably being in conflict. The anarchist notion of laissez-faire does not depend on an invisible hand, but rather on thinking, feeling, committed individuals fully participating in governing themselves.

> The great mission of the Utopia is to make room for the possible as opposed to a passive acquiescence in the present actual state of affairs. It is symbolic thought which overcomes the natural inertia of man and endows him with . . . the ability constantly to reshape his human universe.[7]

Anarchists realize that progress, freedom, and harmony all require active participation and acceptance of responsibility for the social conditions—past, present, and future. Where the end-state utopian vision is caught between the hope that people can participate and change things and the spectator model belief that certain aspects of our nature and social condition are determined and inevitable, the anarchist utopian vision takes the full step into the participatory model.[8]

This libertarian model, combined with the view of individuals as active agents, leaves the future open-ended. One cannot predict how society will be structured at any time, nor can one prescribe how it should be structured. The anarchist model of utopia is not so much a blueprint (as end-state visions are) as a call to awaken consciousness to the possibilities of freedom. Anarchism is committed to the belief that freedom is a necessary condition to living a worthwhile life. This notion of freedom is vague, however, and no vision of its achievement is possible. Choices will present themselves at all points in time and there is no way to know how people, especially free and equal individuals, will choose.

> In short, anarchism is a philosophy based on the premise that men need freedom in order to solve urgent social problems, and begin to realize their potentialities for

happiness and creativity. Anarchists initiate their practical action by looking squarely at the time and place they live in, and deciding what can be done now to forward their goal: to find the next step to be taken, to take it, and encourage others to move ahead.[9]

One cannot dictate how others, in the present or in the future, should move ahead. One cannot even guess what might develop if people were to be truly free, self-directing agents.

While anarchist utopian visions may not be able to draw a picture of how things will turn out, they do make prescriptions for how they should proceed and what principles should govern their choices. "Anarchism, then, can be characterized as a social theory opposing coercion and advocating a community-centered life with great amounts of personal liberty. Social decision making is reduced and personal decision making is expanded. Life in an anarchist society would be a free life within a community."[10] Even individualistic anarchists (Max Stirner for example) must recognize the freedom of others and see that their own freedom is a condition of their community. Therefore everyone must be concerned with how individual liberty is to be balanced with community needs. If one abdicates this responsibility, one surrenders one's freedom as well.

> But I recognize no infallible authority, even in special questions; consequently, whatever respect I may have for the honesty and the sincerity of such or such an individual, I have no absolute faith in any person. Such a faith would be fatal to my reason, to my liberty, and even to the success of my undertakings; it would immediately transform me into a stupid slave, an instrument of the will and interests of others. . . . Each directs and is directed in his turn. Therefore there is no fixed and constant authority, but a continual exchange of mutual, temporary, and, above all, voluntary authority and subordination.[11]

Anarchist utopian visions suggest that people will voluntarily join communities because they see the benefit of organization and order. They will then become active participants in these communities in order to preserve their liberty. Participation in community decisions is at the heart of the anarchist model of utopia; self-management is the key to achieving order without authority. "Anarchism stands for a social order based on the free grouping of individuals for the purpose of producing real social wealth; an order that will guarantee to every human being free access to the earth and full enjoyment of the necessities of life, according to individual desires, tastes, and inclinations."[12] While anarchy may be a fluid notion, with no fixed end and changing methods, it always demands that individuals be active agents creating the possibilities of their own future.

Anarchism . . . leaves posterity free to develop its own particular systems, in harmony with its needs. Our most vivid imagination can not foresee the potentialities of a race set free from external restraints. How, then, can any one assume to map out a line of conduct for those to come? We, who pay dearly for every breath of pure, fresh air, must guard against the tendency to fetter the future. If we succeed in clearing the soil from the rubbish of the past and present, we will leave to posterity the greatest and safest heritage of all ages.[13]

Freedom is not easily acquired or easily carried. Anarchy asks a great deal of people.

THE COST OF FREEDOM

Critics of anarchism argue that while freedom may open up unknown beneficial possibilities, it has a price. If the price is revolution, it may be too high. Clearing away the rubbish of the past and present may destabilize the present and threaten the freedom of the future. With revolution, no one can predict what the future will bring. Since we cannot predict what freedom will bring either, why risk so much uncertainty in its name? Further, if the anarchist pictures of free society bear any resemblance to what might actually result from the changes they propose, then we should expect that freedom will continue to exact a price and continue to require sacrifice. It is not something any one or any group can achieve and be done with. It must be continually worked at and preserved.

Most anarchists see revolution as a necessary and positive good. Progress cannot be made, freedom cannot be gained, unless there occurs a total and complete change in people's beliefs, values, and habits. Furthermore, all vestiges of past institutions which are the result of or encourage old beliefs, values and habits must be destroyed.

A revolution is a swift overthrow, in a few years, of institutions which have taken centuries to root in the soil, and seem so fixed and immovable that even the most ardent reformers hardly dare to attack them in their writings. It is the fall, the crumbling away in a brief period, of all that up to that time composed the essence of social, religious, political, and economic life in a nation.[14]

Revolution is deep-seated change that makes it possible to arrive at a totally new societal arrangement.

Critics argue that such swift and complete revolution is not possible. People cannot purge themselves of old beliefs, values, and habits at will. Old ways cannot be erased from the social memory by declaring it is to be done. Even if people were to choose to try to start with a clear slate, their goals and methods would be influenced by their previous commitments. In order to prevent the corruption of the past influencing the possibilities of the future, some anarchists see the revolution as necessarily violent. "The only way to render any political power harmless, to pacify it and subdue it, is to destroy it."[15] In order to exterminate institutions of the past and put an end to old ways of thinking, they are willing to use violence.

> The revolution must of necessity be violent, even though violence is itself an evil. It must be violent because it would be folly to hope that the privileged classes will recognize the injustice of, the harm caused by, their privileged status, and will voluntarily renounce it. It must be violent because a transitional, revolutionary violence is the only way to put an end to the far greater, the permanent violence that keeps the majority of mankind in servitude.[16]

But even with violent change, old beliefs and habits are likely to reemerge.

On the anarchist vision, such violence is part of the necessary transition to build a new and better world. It is recognized, however, that if this violence is to be constructive it must have a vision of a free society as its guiding aim. "Destructive action is ever determined—not only its essence and the degree of its intensity, but likewise the means it uses—by the positive ideal which constitutes its initial inspiration, its soul."[17] It follows, then, that even a violent overthrow of institutions and a forcible attack on old beliefs, values, and habits falls short of achieving a fresh start. The positive ideal or utopian vision which guides the revolution to the future must be formulated in the corrupted present. It is likely to be tainted by old beliefs, values, and habits and so taint the future.

Tainted and incomplete as such revolution may be, however, some anarchists believe it is better than any of the alternatives or that it is the only alternative. In *The Wretched of the Earth,* Frantz Fanon discusses the inevitability of violent revolutions given the violent nature of colonization and argues that, given the international political situation (the Cold War), it is the most effective means of achieving independence. Even here, though, there is a warning that violence as a means of change is limited. Fanon concedes that independence won by violence changes nothing for 95 percent of the population. The leaders of the revolutions reap the benefits of the change and often take over the colonizer's role of exploiting the people and resources of the country. Another risk is that if it is violence that binds a group of people, once the common enemy is gone, the people will be left with no common focus and they are likely to lapse into inactivity and division. Others believe that given the impossibility of disconnecting ourselves from the past and present, it would be more productive to use some of what has come before and reform it in a positive way. "Revolution is only an essential part of evolution . . . no evolution is accomplished in nature without revolution. Periods of very slow changes are succeeded by periods of violent changes. Revolutions are as necessary for evolution as the slow changes which prepare them and succeed them."[18] On this model revolution is not always abrupt swift change, but the beginning of a long-term re-construction of humanity and society. I will call revolution on this model re-construction.

> No revolution can ever succeed as a factor of liberation unless the MEANS used to further it be identical in spirit and tendency with the PURPOSES to be achieved. Revolution is the negation of the existing, a violent protest against man's inhumanity to man with all the thousand and one slaveries it involves. It is the destroyer of dominant values upon which a complex system of injustice, oppression, and wrong has been built up by ignorance and brutality. It is the herald of NEW VALUES, ushering in a transformation of the basic relations of man to man, and of man to society. It is not a mere reformer, patching up some social evils; not a mere changer of forms and institutions; not only a re-distributor of social well-being. It is all that, yet more, much more, It is, first and foremost, the TRANSVALUATOR, the bearer of new values. It is the great TEACHER of the NEW ETHICS, inspiring man with a new concept of life and its manifestations in social relationships. It is the mental and spiritual regenerator.[19]

Such re-construction is no less radical than violent revolution, but as it acknowledges and works with past and present beliefs, values, and habits in order to change them I believe it has more of a chance of being effective. As individuals we are born into and brought up within a family, a society, a culture. While it is not possible to escape this influence, neither is it necessary to simply acquiesce. One can resist, challenge, and change a practice most effectively from within the structures of that practice. One must acknowledge, though not accept, the structures that promote and sustain the status quo even when one acts to change one's own, and other people's, habits.

> For the world of human freedom cannot be built by the established societies, no matter how much they may streamline and rationalize their dominion. Their class structure, and the perfected controls required to sustain it, generate needs, satisfactions, and values which reproduce the servitude of the human existence. This "voluntary" servitude . . . which justifies the benevolent master, can be broken only through a political practice which reaches the roots of containment and contentment in the infrastructure of man, a political practice of methodological disengagement from and refusal of the Establishment, aiming at a radical transvaluation of values. Such a practice involves a break with the familiar, the routine ways of seeing, hearing, feeling, understanding things so that the organism may become receptive to the potential forms of a nonaggressive, nonexploitative world.[20]

The break with the past required in re-construction is described as a transvaluation of values. This is different from a complete and violent revolution—a wiping out of the past. There is still a push to see things differently, but it does not require that people try to change so quickly or so completely. The model of re-construction acknowledges our cultural embeddedness at the same time that it allows us to challenge this culture. I think this may be a more positive and constructive approach to changing society than violent revolution, and its possible methods will be examined later in this chapter.

If these methods prove effective and re-construction is achievable, such change is only the beginning of the hard work society must face. This leads us to the second critique of anarchism—it is too demanding and people would prefer to sacrifice some freedom to a governmental authority than to work so hard or so constantly. Critics argue that unbounded freedom, with no central or overarching authority, must result in conflicts which the parties involved cannot resolve. With no concept of legitimate authority embedded in the society, everyone will try to do just as he or she pleases and the result will be chaos. Such inevitable disorder, the critics argue, leaves people less free than if they would accept the need and positive good of having an arbiter and give that person, or body of persons, the power needed to enforce their decisions. While such an authority may limit every individual's power somewhat, the critics of anarchy argue that the establishment of such authority is the only way to secure people from the inevitable and perpetual conflict which will constrain their actions if there is no such authority, and is the only way to keep them from being bullied by those more powerful than themselves.

This liberal critique of anarchism has its effect. It is most damaging to individualistic anarchists who hold in common with liberal theorists the belief that people are rational individuals who look to their own self-interest first and foremost (for some theorists exclusively). Thomas Hobbes' notion of people sprung up like mushrooms—unconnected individuals whose interests exclude rather than include the interests of others—is very problematic and few anarchists agree with it (as do few liberals when you look carefully). Rather, even individualistic anarchists recognize that people depend on one another to a certain extent and have interests in common.

> Individualists do not oppose all co-operation between men. While they agree with Ibsen that "he is strongest who stands most as one," they see the value of cooperation to satisfy some of their needs. There is nothing contradictory in this, for only he who is strong enough to stand alone is capable of forming a genuinely free association with others. But such an association is not an end in itself. It lasts only as long as those who form it find it useful to them. It is not a sacred thing towards which its members have duties. It is their creation and servant—nothing more.[21]

Individualistic anarchists are forced to admit that at the very least individuals must decide that individuals should and will be, for the most part, left alone.

They must come to some agreement, as a group, on how this society of individuals will function on a day-to-day level and how such temporary associations will come and go. They need a fundamental framework that they all agree to that allows the group to function. One argument offered by individualistic anarchists is that all individuals are rational and the necessary framework will be obvious to each and no communal discussion is needed. This idea of rationality leading to one obvious form of harmonious social organization is the same idea that guides end-state utopian visions and has been critiqued in chapter 2. Belief in the obvious correctness of any particular vision or order can lead one to promote or implement the order with little regard for the means involved. The individual may be subordinated to the order. Ultimately, the freedom the anarchist seeks would be lost. There is, however, another form of anarchism which may have an answer to the liberal critique and which does not fall prey to the rationalist critique presented before. It is not without its problems, though.

This second form of anarchism also assumes individuals are rational beings. On this theory, though, reason leads people to recognize and accept that they, as individuals, are naturally social beings and not atomistic individuals. With this communal notion of human nature, reason is employed to arrive at a form of social organization based on cooperation, not competition. "The essential principle of anarchism is that mankind has reached a stage of development at which it is possible to abolish the old relationship of master-man (capitalist-proletarian) and substitute a relationship of egalitarian co-operation."[22] With communal anarchy, individuals' interests become more inclusive than exclusive because they are no longer essentially competitive and society and the individual are no longer seen as being in conflict, for they are no longer seen as separate entities.

Most communal or collectivist anarchists agree that for a community to function on their anarchist model and have a workable day-to-day existence, there must be a limit to the size of the communities. (These communities may or may not join in a larger federation of communities for purposes of trade.) It is argued that for anarchism to work, for society to function without a governmental authority, the community needs to be small enough for there to be some face-to-face accountability to eliminate free riders and to make consensual decision making a practical possibility. Such a community, it is argued by critics, would be very inefficient. On the economic side, the limit on size would mean less division of labor, fewer material resources, less production. This will mean fewer products and less choice among products. This lack of competition will eventually lead to inferior quality, which will in turn cause a lack of trust and a break in the cohesiveness of the community. But if people are held accountable for the quality of what they produce by their neighbors, who use the product to produce something which they in turn will use themselves, there are already two built-in controls, namely pride in product and the desire to receive good quality products. "Do unto others as you would have them do unto you" has an immediate and direct meaning in such a community.

Such a community, however, depends on people having a sense of pride and being willing to make a point of holding people accountable for their work. Communal anarchy, then, depends on a transvaluation of values occurring; it requires the re-construction discussed earlier. How is such a transvaluation or re-construction to take place? Many anarchists believe that people are more likely to have the necessary incentive to participate in decision making and quality control when they perceive a direct connection between the issue at stake and their personal lives (especially in economic terms). What about the more complex questions of economics and the more abstract social and political questions? People will need to have a certain level of awareness and sense of interconnectedness for this to work. Each person will have to realize that her own freedom is tied up with the freedom of everyone else; each person will have to be willing to safeguard the freedom of all. Without this interest participation will drop off and consensual decision making will be replaced by majority or minority rule and those who do not participate no longer will feel a sense of responsibility or accountability. Those who do participate will begin to feel justified in making decisions for others and start to feel privileged and powerful—not the basis for a community of free individuals. How can the sense of freedom which incites all to remain active agents in community life be attained and/or maintained?

THE POSSIBILITY OF FREEDOM AND ITS MAINTENANCE

Freedom requires people to participate in their society. Such participation can result only when an increased awareness of our interconnectedness and a changed view of how people should relate to one another are in place. In other words, as the desired transvaluation of values is accomplished by the re-construction of society along anarchist lines, people will become aware of their freedom and awaken to govern themselves.

> As long as man is held in the trammels of obedience, and habituated to look to some foreign guidance for the direction of his conduct, his understanding and the vigor of his mind will sleep. Do I desire to raise him to the energy of which he is capable? I must teach him to feel himself, to bow to no authority, to examine the principles he entertains, and render to his mind the reason of his conduct.[23]

Most anarchists further assume that this transvaluation will occur by changing the economic market place. The ideal of a truly free market with no government controls or interference is the libertarian ideal. The anarchists critique the capitalist market as it has been implemented for having led to exploitation and destructive competition. Most anarchists believe that by putting an end to the exploitation present in the current market system, destructive competition will be ended and the obstacles to cooperation will be removed. Many anarchists believe that a market where interconnections are promoted and recognized will lead to cooperative and healthy competition—a more socialistic model. Authority will no longer be necessary to coordinate competing liberties and desires because people will see that their interests need not exclude the interests of others. Conflict will disappear and things will just work out.

The belief that values will change simply by restructuring the material and economic side of life is too simplistic. While this may be a necessary condition of re-constructing society along anarchist lines, it is not sufficient. It must be accompanied by intellectual persuasion. If people have been conditioned to be managed and controlled, and have become accustomed to obeying an authority, these habits, if they cannot be wiped out by revolution, must be changed. This changing of beliefs, values, and habits must occur simultaneously with the material restructuring rather than be expected to follow from the material restructuring. If this is not done the material restructuring is likely to undergo severe setbacks as people are unprepared to deal with the changes and will revert to exploitative tactics.

> The social revolution means much more than the reorganization of conditions only: it means the establishment of new human values and social relationships, a changed attitude of man to man, as of one free and independent to his equal; it means a different spirit in individual and collective life, and that spirit cannot be born overnight. It is a spirit to be cultivated, to be nurtured, and reared, as the most delicate flower is, for indeed it is the flower of a new and beautiful existence.[24]

How is such a change in attitude to be accomplished? Can it be sustained once it blooms?

The transvaluation of values is necessary if social order and stability are to be possible with anarchy. The means of changing social attitudes, however, must involve more than material restructuring, but cannot include any centralized direction or power. People must direct themselves and power must be diffuse. Since this transvaluation is necessary, and is part of the transition to an anarchic society, its means of achievement must be compatible with liberty and equality. With no centralized power, how will full participation and accountability be encouraged? How will decisions be enforced? The answer is to be found in the character of community itself.

A useful analysis of community and the possibilities of anarchy can be found in Michael Taylor's *Community, Anarchy, and Liberty*. He defines community as a group of people who share a set of core characteristics, participate in direct and complex relationships with one another, and have a system of symmetric reciprocity. He argues that such community is the only way social order and stability can be achieved and maintained in the absence of a governmental authority. The classical liberal theory suggests people must surrender some of their liberty to a central powerful authority in order to gain the security of their person and their goods. The communal anarchist offers an alternative of diffuse power and authority which can secure persons and their goods without running the risk of the individuals' liberty being disregarded or infringed upon by a central power.

The asymmetric relationship of a sovereign and its subjects is more dangerous on the anarchist's view than a symmetrical threat of each against everyone. "Anyone who is invested with power, by an invariable social law will inevitably become the oppressor and exploiter of society."[25] Even if Hobbes' description of life in the state of nature were right (it will be solitary, poor, nasty, brutish and short), it would never warrant, from the anarchist's point of view, the surrender of liberty and power to an authority. But the anarchist does not agree with Hobbes' picture of the state of nature anyway.

The anarchist equivalent to Hobbes' state of nature is simply the condition of human society without a political authority. Even without such authority, though, the anarchist conceives of society existing. People are connected and working in common, not atomistic individuals at war with each other. The anarchist expects conflict between individuals, and even more probably between family and communal groups. Where Hobbes thinks life would be better if it were more secure, the anarchist would agree. The more stable and secure the society, the more productive and enriching human life can become. While Hobbes' answer of giving one person the power and authority to force people to respect one another's goods and behave in certain ways may seem a stabilizing arrangement in the short run, the anarchist believes such power must be eliminated in the long run. "All political government must necessarily become despotic because all government tends to become centralized in the hands of the few, who breed corruption among themselves and in a very short time disconnect themselves from the body of the people."[26] In the long run such imbalance of power restricts freedom and will lead to oppression and chaos. They have another answer—the diffusion of power.

If every individual is recognized as her own authority, her own sovereign, will there not be a war of each against all? Not necessarily. As each individual is connected to others by virtue of being born into a family and then choosing to befriend others, they will consider others (at least a limited number of others) when formulating their goals and deciding how best to accomplish them. The fact that they participate in multifaceted relationships acts as a temper on their egoistic self-interest and safeguards the interests of others. Such relationships must be encouraged then. People should be made to feel as connected as possible within their community and then in relation to other communities. One is less likely to fight within a community, or to wage war with another community, if they view people of that community as connected to themselves. It is important that such connections be made between communities as the likelihood of war between groups may increase as each group becomes internally more unified—they may see others as more of a threat to their own solidarity and unity. The building of such connections can be accomplished through blood relationships and/or developing mutual projects.

To reaffirm and strengthen voluntary relationships (those outside of family ties), the notion of reciprocity comes into play. Since actual physical equality of power may be difficult to maintain, mutual interest and reciprocity must be encouraged to maintain an equilibrium. On such a model different individuals are involved in the same project or in projects that help make each other possible. If this is done it no longer makes sense to try to undermine someone else as it is the same as undermining yourself. It makes no sense to produce something of inferior quality because at some point an inferior product will come back to you. On the level of social relations it can only make sense to be supportive of the others in your community—financially and emotionally—because you are involved in a direct relationship with them, depend on them for the success of your own projects, and feel a bond to them.

Such intertwining makes it in no one's interest to harm another, allow another to suffer misfortune unaided, or simply to be disinterested. As long as one is interested in survival, one must be interested in promoting the welfare of others, interested in promoting their liberty and equality. Such intertwining leads to the transvaluation of values. Even if your motivation for helping others is that you would want to be helped yourself if you suffered misfortune, anarchists believe that the day-to-day behavior of helping others and being concerned with others will bring about an actual valuing of others for their own sake.

If some individuals do not experience the necessary transvaluation, do not come to appreciate and be concerned with the liberty and equality of everyone, and try to freeload in an anarchist society, there are available to the community means of censure and control that do not require a central authority. Given the complexity of relationships in the community, and the direct kind of accountability which results from the reciprocity of those relationships, methods of ridicule, gossip, shame, disapproval, ostracism, withdrawal of reciprocal aid, and threat of expulsion can all be used with a high probability of success. These controls will lead people to either change their behavior or leave. If they change their behavior, in the

anarchist view, they will eventually experience the necessary transvaluation of value. According to Taylor, these techniques require a relatively
small group of people with little turnover intertwined by many-sided relationships and held together by some set of shared beliefs.[27] While the economic relations of a community can be arranged to encourage certain kinds
of relationships and can maintain an effective control through reciprocity,
such arrangements need not engender any set of shared beliefs. What beliefs need to be shared and how will they be instilled?

Perhaps one example is that for anarchy to work all need to share the belief that equality is preferable to inequality. As inequality in wealth or power
is a threat to the freedom of all, and there is no authority to maintain equality
among individuals, it would be important that all agree that a societal arrangement which results in equality is to be preferred. Inasmuch as equality requires placing limitations on individual liberty—no one is free to acquire as
much as one can, or to make decisions for others—it is not likely to be voluntarily adhered to by individuals prior to their experiencing the anarchist
transvaluation of values.[28] Somehow they must be brought to the position
where they will voluntarily surrender the liberty to be unequal because they
see that such liberty is destructive of community and therefore destructive of
their own ultimate liberty.[29] Even if the belief that equality is preferable is
shared, some kind of measure of control will need to be available to the community to persuade people to live up to their belief and to protect against renegades taking advantage of the society.

Taylor suggests that in a properly formed community possessing more than
others will make one uncomfortable and embarrassed. If this does not happen
on its own the community can apply the pressure of public opinion and the
threat of the withdrawal of reciprocal advantages and/or expulsion.[30] For
these methods to be effective, however, there must be some shared belief
about what is shameful, embarrassing, or wrong and why. Shared values are
necessary for the controls to work and yet the controls are supposed to safeguard against those who do not share the values of the community. For example, in her novel *The Dispossessed: An Ambiguous Utopia,* Ursula K. Le
Guin describes an anarchist society on the planet Annares. This society was
founded by a woman named Odo. Annares does not have government in any
traditional sense. There is a coordinating system called Production and Distribution Coordination (PDC). However, the root of the society is found in de-
centralization and free cooperation. Individuals choose their work placements
and schedules and coordinate this with their syndicate, which in turn coordi-
nates with PDC. No one is forced into a job. Public opinion is the force that
makes this work. Le Guin discusses what happens to a person who will not
cooperate in the anarchist community of Annares:

Well, he moves on. The others get tired of him, you know. They make fun of him, or they get rough with him, beat him up; in a small community they might agree to take his name off the meals listing, so he has to cook and eat all by himself; that is humiliating. So he moves on, and stays in another place for a while, and then maybe moves on again. Some do it all their lives. Nuchnibi, they're called.[31]

Later, one of her characters protests against the limitations imposed by fear of public opinion.

The social conscience completely dominates the individual conscience, instead of striking a balance with it. We don't cooperate — we *obey*. We fear being outcast, being called lazy, dysfunctional, egoizing. We fear our neighbor's opinion more than we respect our own freedom of choice. You don't believe me, Tak, but try, just try stepping over the line, just in imagination, and see how you feel. . . . We force a man outside the sphere of our approval, and then condemn him for it. We've made laws, laws of conventional behavior, built walls all around ourselves, and we can't see them, because they're part of our thinking.[32]

We must care about "our neighbor's opinion" for this to work. But clearly one could see the wandering life as a positive good, not a punishment. The fear of wandering must exist before it can be an effective control. Inasmuch as the controls and safeguards depend on people sharing certain values, the values cannot be instilled by way of these controls and safeguards. The values must precede any attempt to use these controls and so must have some other source.

ANARCHIST EDUCATION

Living on the model of communal anarchy requires that people come to value one another's liberty and respect one another as equals. Some anarchists believe that this shift in values can be achieved simply by restructuring the material conditions of life, and by developing and living within reciprocal social arrangements on the model of communal anarchy. As I have argued, this will not work because you need the changes in values, beliefs, and habits to accompany, not follow, the material restructuring of society. If the transvaluation does not occur simultaneously, the anarchist society is likely to be riddled with free-riders and plundered by anti-social renegades. Since all the safeguards anarchists propose to protect against such anti-social acts also require the transvaluation of values to have taken root, the transvaluation must have its source somewhere other than in the re-structuring of material and social relations and the abolition of authority. Education is an obvious candidate for effecting the necessary changes in values, beliefs, and habits.

Although education seems a good tool for effecting the changes in values, beliefs, and habits, it is a problematic means for the anarchist—at least education as it is structured at present. These new values, beliefs, and habits cannot be imposed by an authority, on the anarchist's argument, but must result from communal discussion and debate. Anarchist education, then, would have to be such that it encouraged free and critical thought, imaginative and creative problem solving, participation, and mutual respect. It would not work to effect the transvaluation of values if it were modeled on the system of an authority imparting knowledge to passive recipients. Nor can it be controlled by the state.

> The injuries that result from a system of national education are, in the first place, that all public establishments include in them the idea of permanence. They endeavour it may be to secure and to diffuse whatever of advantage to society is already known, but they forget that more remains to be known. . . . They actively restrain the flights of mind and fix it in the belief of exploded errors. It has commonly been observed of universities and extensive establishments for the purpose of education that the knowledge taught there is a century behind the knowledge which exists among the unshackled and unprejudiced members of the same political community. The moment any scheme of proceeding gains a permanent establishment it becomes impressed as one of its characteristic features with an aversion to change.[33]

To do away with the problem of authority it is often proposed that education must be removed from state control and put in the hands of individual families. Individuals will see to the education of the youth as it is in their own interest to do so. Their own success is seen as being bound up with the possible success of the future so they are motivated to take this task seriously.

There are some problems to consider, though. Will everyone have the resources to give the education the future needs? Will there be equal access to books and computers? What about variety of experience? If home education is the norm, where is socialization handled? Who in the family is responsible for overseeing education? Will this affect their "other" job? These problems aside, will a sufficient number of parents have the motivation and ability to take on the task of educating children? It would be a beneficial system in that it requires the adults to keep up with their own education in order to be prepared to teach, but as they have jobs in the economic sphere, and must be participating in the political arena, can they be expected to come home and be effective teachers? The participatory model of education—which needs to be developed and employed if the citizens are to be prepared to be effective citizens in an anarchic society—is taxing, though invigorating, for both student and teacher. I do not think it is realistic to expect teaching to be something done to relax after dinner.[34]

Even if the anarchists can answer these questions and overcome these problems, it appears that for education to be able to effect the changes in values, beliefs, and habits necessary for anarchy to work, it must itself be based on these desired values, beliefs, and habits. People must see that their own good is connected with the good of the future and be willing to act in ways consistent with this belief. If effective education must presuppose the transvaluation, it cannot be its source. The anarchist tries to get out of such circles by proposing complete and immediate revolution. For reasons discussed earlier I think this is problematic. Anarchist visions tend to endorse, and rely on for their success, a more or less spontaneous, immediate, and complete revolution—often violent in nature. Most anarchists claim that "reform is always a compromise with the past, but the progress accomplished by revolution is always a promise of future progress."[35] Admittedly reform is problematic in its own right and often makes it difficult to get at the root causes of problems, but if one could achieve the complete revolution anarchists dream of (a problem in itself), it would leave people empty, without direction, and vulnerable. Severing, too abruptly or too completely, connections to past institutions, value systems, beliefs, and habits leaves people without the tools to make the choices of how they want to live. People are unlikely to be able to handle such total rebirth; they need some base from which to work. A vision of the future, if it is to have practical import, must take the past into account and frame its own possibilities within these "constraints." Visions of the future can work to change habits, beliefs, values, and institutions but not to wipe them out. People cannot be disconnected from their past and made anew. The anarchist vision lacks a developed method of change.

FREEDOM AS THE PRECONDITION OF PROGRESS

On the anarchist view we cannot even begin to explore what the "good life" is until everyone is free and equal. People have been perverted by society as it has been structured, so we have no way of knowing what we may be capable of. The first step, then, is to restructure society, dismantle authority, and then see what we are made of. There is nothing in the act of dismantling authority, however, that guarantees we will be, or regard each other as, free and equal individuals. The anarchist does not provide a convincing method for changing values, beliefs, and habits to accompany the new absence of authority. My fear is that without such a method, the removal of authority may do more to restrict some people's freedom, and make them less equal, than does the presence of a governmental authority. This problem is compounded by the fact that for anarchy to work, people must realize that each individual's freedom to direct her own life is important and they must accept responsibility for safeguarding such freedom for everyone. This level of involvement requires a great deal of work and may ask too much of people.

On most models this will require that consensual decision-making procedures be implemented in making any social decisions. This not only tends to be time consuming in itself, it requires an informed and involved public. Some critics argue that it is easier, and in the long run "better," to give up some freedom and so have the time to do the things one likes. For example, if one gives to someone else the authority to decide where the new highway will go, then he or she can have time to go camping. If freedom requires full-time participation in social decision making, it asks too much. It is inconvenient. When the camping area is threatened by the new highway plans, however, those affected will realize their freedom has been curtailed. Anarchists argue that it is not the highway plans that curtail freedom, but the fact that the people chose not to participate (or more often were not allowed to participate) in deciding where the highway would go. Freedom does demand participation, and this leads to the question of whether such activism can reasonably be expected of people.

Another problem with the anarchist's version of freedom relates to the ability of anarchist visions to handle diversity. Most anarchists claim that they seek and promote diversity as an antidote to authority. "The strongest bulwark of authority is uniformity; the least divergence from it is the greatest crime."[36] They may seek order in diversity rather than uniformity, but given some of the non-authoritarian methods of control such visions tend to employ, I am skeptical about the success of anarchism on this score. Most anarchist visions rely on establishing small communities which may or may not join in a voluntary federation. At the level of each community, because of its size, each person feels directly accountable to the others. On this view, free-riders can be handled by instilling a sense of shame for not doing their part, reducing benefits of those who do not pull their weight, and threatening expulsion.

It is argued that such techniques do not interfere with a person's freedom, that they have a choice, and it is believed that these techniques are less insidious than a centralized authority directing economic activity. These same techniques, however, can easily be extended to those who, while good economic participants in the community, challenge it in other ways. If they dress differently, have a different religious belief than most, are in a minority group as far as sexual preference, race, or gender, they may feel undue pressure to conform to the standard of the majority or the most powerful. While this may not be an inevitable consequence of community life it is something that needs to be considered. Absence of authority is not enough to ensure freedom and diversity among a group of people.[37]

The anarchists argue that "the further a society progresses, the more clearly the individual becomes the antithesis of the group."[38] That is, the more free and equal people are in society the greater the differentiation among people will be and this will be good. The anarchist claims that while anarchy may require small communities it does not require uniformity, but rather flourishes on the challenge of reaching consensus through diversity. "The sharing of wealth would not produce a uniformity of life, simply because there is no uniformity of desire. Uniformity is an unintelligent nightmare; there can be no uniformity in a free human society. Uniformity can only be created by the tyranny of a totalitarian regime."[39] The anarchist believes diversity and difference can be controlled, power and authority cannot.

I agree that the anarchists have developed effective methods of handling diversity, assuming the necessary transvaluation has occurred, which do not rely on the existence of a political authority—ridicule, gossip, shame, disapproval, ostracism, withdrawal of reciprocal aid, and threat of expulsion. This is good in that it avoids the risks that accompany the existence of such an authority. The methods which replace the political authority, however, involve other risks.

Ideally, the citizens of the anarchist utopian community have experienced the necessary transvaluation of values and realize that everyone must safeguard the freedom of everyone else and that all are equal. With such people for citizens there should be no oppressed class or group because not only would it not be in anyone's interest to discriminate against someone because of their looks or beliefs, they would realize it would be against their interests to limit arbitrarily another's freedom because this would arbitrarily limit their own. I would argue, however, that since we cannot gain newly made people through revolution, the first citizens of the anarchist society will be tainted by prejudice and have limits to their tolerance. This is likely to infuse any education plan and be very hard to eradicate. Inasmuch as the citizens of the anarchist utopian community are imperfect human beings, with limitations and faults, it is likely that their shortcomings will be perpetuated as well as their rational insights.

Not being purely rational or impartial creatures, it may happen that some people, though they realize it is not in their interests to do so (they understand that it is irrational), will feel threatened by the freedom someone has to be different. Whether it is that they think differently or dress differently, it may happen that those who are different in some way make the "rest" insecure. This insecurity may lead the "rest" of society to try to reform those who are different. If this does not succeed they may see these people as anti-social renegades and turn to the techniques of shame, gossip, ostracism, and expulsion to remove the threat. Again in *The Dispossessed,* Le Guin describes an anarchist method of control.

You can't crush ideas by suppressing them. You can only crush them by ignoring
them. By refusing to think, refusing to change. And that's precisely what our society
is doing! Sabul uses you where he can, and where he can't, he prevents you from pub-
lishing, from teaching, even from working. Right? In other words he has power over
you. Where does he get it from? Not from vested authority, there isn't any. . . . He gets
it from the innate cowardice of the average human mind. Public opinion! . . . The un-
admitted, inadmissible government that rules the Odonian Society by stifling the individual mind.[40]

While it may not be inevitable that an attempt to realize the anarchist utopian
vision will result in such a closed society, there is enough of a risk to warrant
concern. Just as with Jean Jacques Rousseau's scheme of education and society (see chapter 2), while it may be possible to achieve great freedom for people, the accompanying risk of degenerating into tyranny is too great to be ignored. Anarchy needs to be tempered with methods of transition and social
control that limit the likelihood of this potential problem. John Dewey's theory of democracy and education may be able to help reduce this risk.

THE ANARCHIST VISION OF MATTAPOISETT

Anarchist utopian visions avoid the dogmatism of end-state utopian visions,
and by so doing are a marked improvement. As discussed, however, anarchist
visions of utopia still employ problematic means and can have troubling out-
comes. While the anarchist model rejects control of individuals by an authority, avoids the centralization of power, and attempts to promote order that is
compatible with diversity, nonetheless problems arise in the implementation
of such visions. While anarchy is a kind of ongoing experiment, with methods adapting to changing situations and different circumstances, certain principles or methods tend to guide such visions and lead to problems.

First, most anarchist visions reject reform as a compromise with the present that changes nothing and call, instead, for revolution. One problem with
revolution is that if it severs connections to the past too abruptly, or too completely, people are left without any framework or tools with which to make
the choices of how they want to live. Second, anarchist visions require people to realize that the freedom to direct their own lives is important and
that they must accept responsibility for their lives by participating in social
decision-making procedures. One must stay informed and involved. However, such activism takes time and effort, and there is a question as to whether
people can reasonably be expected to participate as much as the anarchist
model requires. Finally, there is a question as to how successful anarchist visions are at sustaining and handling diversity. Most anarchist visions rely on

the formation of small communities with face-to-face accountability and shame to handle the problems of free-riders. These same techniques, however, can be extended to bring pressure on those who are seen as different to conform to some majority standard.

Anarchist utopian visions have a greater possibility of effectiveness than end-state visions because they tend to view society as an ongoing experiment and the people in it as developmental creatures. However, they are potentially disaffecting and disempowering. In discussing the basic beliefs behind, and difficulties of, the anarchist model of utopia, I have already referred to several passages from *The Dispossessed*. In this book, Le Guin explores the difficulties of revolution, the demands of freedom, and the dubious promise of diversity which are all part of the anarchist vision. *The Dispossessed* provides an interesting and useful picture of an anarchist experiment that not only points to advantages that anarchist society may have, but also highlights the difficulties of such visions. Now I will turn to Marge Piercy's *Woman on the Edge of Time*. This book also faces the problems and costs of revolution, the demands of freedom, and the problems of constructively sustaining diversity. However, *Woman on the Edge of Time* not only presents a vision of an anarchist society of the future, but, as with Sheri S. Tepper's *The Gate to Women's Country,* also focuses on the dangers of and need to get beyond violence, especially male violence.

In *Woman on the Edge of Time,* the anarchists of Mattapoisett are one of many communities existing in a possible future. Through the story we see how they breed and raise children to fit their community, how they participate in "government," how they approach education and work. Despite the very positive picture Piercy paints of this anarchist future, it turns out that violence was necessary to achieve this future and is necessary now both within the communities of Mattapoisett and in fighting off an alternate future. People are pulled in many directions at once by the demands of freedom—among interests, relationships, duties—finding little time for themselves. Diversity is handled by eliminating differences of skin color, by making everyone darker. While the physical traits of the races are mixed up, cultures are kept distinct. Each community, while genetically mixed, is culturally pure.

The remainder of this chapter will examine the societal arrangement developed in *Woman on the Edge of Time* and discuss what can be gained from such a vision. Mattapoisian society is based on the cooperative efforts of individuals in small communities and the cooperative efforts of such communities in a federation. Face-to-face accountability and reciprocity maintain social unity and cooperation. There is no control of individuals by an authority; people actively participate in social decision making, and there is no claim that any one way of working together is the final answer. The people of

Mattapoisett see themselves and their social arrangement as one possible arrangement and as part of an ongoing experiment in learning how to live together without dominance and destruction. Despite these positive aspects of Mattapoisett, there are ways in which the critiques of anarchist visions developed earlier in this chapter are relevant and are raised by the author.

First, the problems and costs of revolution are not absent from this possible future—violence was/is needed to arrive at this society, is necessary to maintain it, and may be resulting in people developing a callous attitude toward participating in violent acts. Secondly, the demands of freedom are evident in Mattapoisett. The experimental and changing nature of the society asks a great deal of people. Each person is expected to remain a responsible and active member of the community, being part of and keeping up with its every decision and change. It is in trying to cope with this very demand of activism and adaptation that the third critique, the difficulty of sustaining difference, comes to apply. In order to be the responsible and flexible citizens required by this anarchist vision, people are raised with a sense of their social responsibility and connectedness. This also requires, however, discouraging behavior that is considered negative or harmful. The pressures that can be brought to bear in the small community may do more to restrict some people's freedom than it does to open up the freedom of possibility for others.

MATTAPOISETT

Woman on the Edge of Time follows the life of Connie Ramos. She is a Chicana, living in New York. She has been in and out of several relationships (one marriage), the only healthy one being with a pickpocket, Claud, who died in prison as a result of a medical experiment he "volunteered" for. She has had one nearly fatal abortion and one child, Angelina. After Claud died, Connie spent several weeks drinking and doing drugs. During this time she hit Angelina for ruining her one pair of shoes. Angelina—then four years old—fell against a doorframe and broke her wrist. Connie immediately took her to the hospital and explained what had happened. Her daughter was taken away from her and she was sent to a mental hospital. Committed by her brother, she believed herself sick for harming her child and worked with the doctors to recover.

Released and on welfare, she savors her freedom, but misses her daughter. She spends time with her niece Dolly and Dolly's daughter, Nita. Dolly, who works as a prostitute, becomes pregnant by her pimp, Geraldo. When Geraldo finds out, he wants to force Dolly to have an abortion. When she objects, he beats her. Dolly comes to hide at Connie's apartment, but Geraldo brings a "doctor" to Connie's to perform the abortion. During a physical struggle Connie smashes a bottle into Geraldo's face and breaks his nose. Connie is hit and knocked unconscious. She wakes up in a hospital, strapped down to a table. Geraldo tells the doctors that Connie just went crazy and attacked him and Dolly. She is committed again. This time, however, she is chosen to be part of a special experiment aimed at controlling the violent. A device is implanted into her brain which apparently causes pain and releases drugs whenever she gets angry or violent—whenever she dares to feel.

It is this implantation that so concerns the citizens of the future—at least of one possible future. It turns out that Connie has a mind that is open and receptive to a kind of time travel. She is contacted by Luciente, a person from Mattapoisett—Massachusetts in the year 2137. This contact is really a call for help. Mattapoisett is only one of several possible futures. It will not come to be unless people in Connie's present start making changes. Connie travels to one other future, by accident, where cyborgs and people are hardly distinguishable and women are kept as caged animals. It appears that if the "scientists" working on Connie are allowed to continue, such techniques will become a common method of control and part of everyday life and this future will be the result. The people of Mattapoisett are at war with this cyborg race and have engaged in time travel to help in the war. It is intimated that if Connie could end the experiment in which she is involved, this would be one step in stopping the alternate future from coming to be and increase the odds that Mattapoisett's society would come to be. As people actually die in this war of futures, there is a real interest for the people of Mattapoisett, and its corresponding communities, to see to it that the other future is not a likely possibility.

Being in the hospital, Connie chooses to cross over to Mattapoisett more often than Luciente crosses into New York. Surprisingly, she finds village life. She remarks that it is no better than the village she left in Mexico—dirt, animals, poverty. Where is the technology and the resulting prosperity people expect of the future?

> She saw . . . a river, little no account buildings, strange structures like long-legged birds with sails that turned in the wind, a few large terracotta and yellow buildings and one blue dome, irregular buildings, none bigger than a supermarket of her day. . . . No skyscrapers, no spaceports, no traffic jam in the sky. "You sure we went in the right direction? Into the future?"[41]

While it is not clear how many villages are involved in the future federation, it is clear that all are small. Each village is about six hundred people. Each region, with an undisclosed number of villages, does its best to be self-sufficient—especially in terms of food production. They can control the weather to some extent to help with crops, but they do not interfere often as it requires agreement from all regions. The need to plan and make decisions cooperatively is seen as central in this society.

> "We have limited resources. We plan cooperatively. We can afford to waste . . . nothing. You might say our—you'd say religion?—ideas make us see ourselves as partners with water, air, birds, fish, trees.
>
> "We learned a lot from societies people used to call primitive. Primitive technically. But socially sophisticated. . . . We tried to learn from cultures that dealt well with handling conflict, promoting cooperation, coming of age, growing a sense of community, getting sick, aging, going mad, dying—."[42]

The government of Mattapoisett is run on a one-year rotation and representatives are chosen by lot. It works so that a new representative serves three months with the predecessor, six months alone, and three months with the incoming representative. Meetings are held in small rooms to increase the face-to-face nature of discussion, leadership rotates daily, and there is a five-minute limit on speeches to encourage people to stay focused on the present issue. Allocation of resources is the main task of these representatives. Questions of population size and diversity are also discussed, but such decisions require the whole community's input.

> "Grasp, political decisions—like whether to raise or lower population—go a different route. We talk locally and then choose a rep to speak our posit on area hookup. Then we all sit in holi simulcast and the rep from each group speaks their village posit. Then we go back into local meeting to fuse our final word. Then the reps argue more before everybody. Then we vote."[43]

The demands of such a system can take their toll. With all these meetings, and all this arguing, solidarity is maintained by requiring the winners to feed and give presents to the losers. They also celebrate a Thanksmaking day when one asks forgiveness from people offended during the year and then they all feast together. When there is a problem among several individuals of a community, a "worming" is held to relieve the tension and sort out the root of the problem. Each person criticizes the others and they work out a plan for changing what offends. Depending on the severity of the problem, they may be sent into temporary wandering or endure enforced invisibility for a time. The distance often reduces the tension and is seen by the individuals involved as shameful and a nuisance. Maintaining solidarity within and between communities is important for the society to work.

> "First, they need not like each other to behave civilly. Second, we believe many actions fail because of inner tensions. To get revenge against someone an individual thinks wronged per, individuals have offered up nations to conquest. Individuals

have devoted whole lives to pursuing vengeance. People have chosen defeat sooner than victory with credit going to an enemy. The social fabric means a lot to us."[44]

One strong element in building and maintaining social unity is the method of parenting. Children are mixed and grown in the brooder. The Mattapoisians believe that the power to give birth is a power and women had to give it up to achieve equality and cooperation and so that men could become more human through the mothering experience.[45] Men are even equipped to breast-feed. Three people, of any sex, choose to mother together and are assigned a child when one is available. No one can be born until someone dies. These three co-mother until the child chooses to leave for naming. Around the age of fifteen, the child goes out into the wilderness to search for a name. When the child returns there can be no real contact with the mothers for three months. This breaks the bonds of individual dependencies and establishes the child as a full member of the community. Particular ties are supplanted by more general social ties. This method of parenting does not discourage personal ties, but rather uses them to build a cohesive community.

The desired social unity, or cohesive community, is not threatened by racial differences in this future. Darker genes have been bred throughout all people everywhere, so no stance of "purity" is possible. Yet, it is not the case that everyone is the same.

"At grandcil—grand council—decisions were made forty years back to breed a high proportion of darker-skinned people and to mix the genes well through the population. At the same time, we decided to hold on to separate cultural identities. But we broke the bond between genes and culture, broke it forever. We want there to be no chance of racism again. But we don't want the melting pot where everybody ends up with thin gruel. We want diversity, for strangeness breeds richness."[46]

Difference is seen as a positive good, not an obstacle to be overcome. While people are brought up within a culture, they are not bound to it except by choice. One may leave and join another community, though it happens that most people are most comfortable where they are brought up. Other than competition for resources, which is settled collaboratively and amicably, friction between communities is not discussed. As people within communities recognize their interdependence and build bonds, it is expected that communities will accept their interdependence and build relations as they function in a larger federation."[47]

Sexuality has been freed of present constraints as well. There are no genders, just people.[48] People choose sweetfriends from either sex, any "race," any age. People are also often involved with more than one person at a time. Any jealousy that might arise from such multiple commitments is handled by wormings. Sweetfriends are not encouraged to mother together, however, as this might bind people too tightly. So, between co-mothers (coms) and sweetfriends, any one

person has many close personal ties to others. When one adds on the working relationships and relationships developed on councils and in meetings, one cannot
harm another without expecting to see the effects of such harm on someone close
to them. This is reciprocity in action to maintain social unity and cooperation.

This reciprocity is further reinforced through education and work. Mattapoisians believe that education and work go hand in hand. They learn by doing. "Most of what children must learn, they learn by doing. . . . They play farm-
ing and cooking and repair and fishing and diving and manufacture and plant
breeding and baby tending. When children aren't kept out of the real work, they
don't have the same need for imitation things."[49] When a person chooses a special area of interest, he or she signs on with those people in the community, or
sometimes those in other communities, involved in that area. They apprentice.
One does not "get" an education and then go to work. Learning goes on throughout one's life as interests develop or work requires. Another important part of education is learning to control one's body, feelings, and states of consciousness.
All of this helps people stay connected to themselves and to others.[50] When this
"inknowing" is not in place a person disintegrates. Some people choose to disintegrate to find themselves again or find new selves.

> "Our madhouses are places where people retreat when they want to go down into
> themselves—to collapse, carry on, see visions, hear voices of prophecy, bang on the
> walls, relive infancy—getting in touch with the buried self and the inner mind. We
> all lose parts of ourselves. We all make choices that go bad. . . . How can another
> person decide that it is time for me to disintegrate, to reintegrate myself?"[51]

"Going mad" is part of growing—not a disease to be punished or cured.

There are healers, however, in Mattapoisett who often help guide people
back to integration, help criminals atone, and assist in reconciliation after
wormings. Healers heal and maintain the social fabric by healing individual
lives. The individual life is made possible and full by the social life, and the
social life is maintained by and through the commitment of individuals.
"'Connie, we are born screaming Ow and I! The gift is in growing to care, to
connect, to cooperate. Everything we learn aims to make us feel strong in ourselves, connected to all living. At home.'"[52] People who do not grow to see
themselves as connected to all living things are considered sick. Healers,
therefore, are important instruments for maintaining social cohesiveness.

PROBLEMS OF THE VISION

There is much to admire in Mattapoisett. This anarchist vision does seem to
have answered most of the critiques of end-state visions. There is no control

of individuals by an authority—people decide for themselves how to direct and live their lives within the social structures of their community. There is no central power—consensual decision making and community deliberation are attempted instead. There is an order that is compatible with creativity and diversity—or so it appears. Free and equal individuals live in harmony under conditions of voluntary control. Furthermore, there is no claim that this social arrangement has achieved a final, perfect balance of authority, individuals, control, and freedom, but rather sees itself as one possible arrangement and as part of an ongoing experiment. There are some trouble spots, though. The problems of revolution and violence, the demands of freedom, and the difficulties of handling diversity all present challenges for Mattapoisian society.

One potential trouble spot for the vision of Mattapoisett is the violence necessary to arrive at and maintain the society. It appears that there was a thirty-year war and great ecological destruction that led to Mattapoisett (revolutionary action was taking place even before the war). If it is fear, the drive to survive, that binds these people together and has led them to change their beliefs and practices, it is possible that once the threat of violence or lack of resources is removed the motivation to be a responsible member of the community may lose its strength. Yet it appears violence is/was/will be the only alternative for the people of Mattapoisett.

"Power is violence. When did it get destroyed peacefully? We all fight when we're back to the wall—or to tear down a wall. You know we kill people who choose twice to hurt others. We don't think it's right to kill them. Only convenient. Nobody wants to stand guard over another."[53]

This convenience of killing does lead to replacing power with power. The society which results from violent means does run the risk of being corrupted by its means. The time travel experiment is attempted in order to persuade people of the present (or Mattapoisett's past) to change what is happening. They seek to encourage people to revolt against their situation, violently if necessary. "'You of your time. You individually may fail to understand us or to struggle in your own life and time. You of your time may fail to struggle together. . . . We must fight to come to exist, to remain in existence, to be the future that happens. That's why we reached you.'"[54] Connie does revolt for the sake of Mattapoisett—she kills in the hope of an uncertain future. In the end she poisons four of the doctors involved in the implantation project.

She washed her hands in the bathroom, she washed them again and again. "I just killed six people," she said to the mirror, but she washed her hands because she was terrified of the poison. "I murdered them dead. Because they are the violence-prone. Theirs is the money and the power, theirs the poisons that slow the mind and dull the heart. Theirs are the powers of life and death. I killed them.

Because it is war. . . . I'm a dead woman now too. I know it. But I did fight them.
I'm not ashamed. I tried."[55]

The violence of the revolution may result in people developing a callous attitude toward participation in violent acts. Is this the kind of citizen who can
make Mattapoisett a truly free and open society?

The problem of violence aside, the commitment to an anarchist vision does
engage people in an ongoing experiment of living. They are involved in and
responsible for their lives. While things may not always be decided as one
would like, each person is comfortable in the knowledge that all opinions are
heard and considered. Each person is also aware that how things are done in
her village is not the only or best way of doing things. Different villages, with
different cultures, have different rituals, practices, and organization. Interaction between communities, then, can lead to growth and change (though it is
not expected that it will ever lead to sameness). Each community is fluid and
flexible, responding to the needs and interests of the individuals who make it
up. When Connie objects to the ritual of naming—sending the child alone
into the wilderness—Luciente explains its purpose and suggests that if the ritual ever proves problematic or unsatisfactory it will be changed.

"We haven't misplaced a child yet. You're right, accidents happen. . . . But why try to
control everything? Grasp, we think control interferes with pleasure and communing—
and we care about both. . . . Comprend, we sweat out our rituals together. We change
them, we're all the time changing them! But they body our sense of good."[56]

If the rituals that embody a community's sense of good are all the time changing, it would appear that a community's sense of good may also be continually changing. How will people keep up? Will there not be a lag time between
a community's sense of good and people's habits or practices? Given the experimental and changing nature of the society, how can one expect people to
put in the necessary time and effort to stay involved and make this arrangement work?[57] The demands of freedom are ever present in Mattapoisett; as a
community it asks a great deal of people. Each person is expected to remain
a responsible and active member of the community, being part of and keeping up with its every decision and change. Anarchism, in general, asks a great
deal of people and does not provide a reliable means for them to succeed.
Everyday life presents special problems for anarchist communities because
they rely on individuals to participate and decide for themselves. It is in trying to keep up with the demands of the freedom and fluidity of life in Mattapoisett, that the threat to difference enters Mattapoisian life.

It is simply expected that people will have the motivation to be responsible
members of the community, whatever its sense of good. In Mattapoisett there

is a trust and interdependence that allows people to share resources. One-of-a kind items, such as artwork, travel between villages and individuals. Bikes are used and left at the destination for another to use. Rare clothing is borrowed for special occasions, as is jewelry. People possess little, but have a great variety of things available to them as a result. For the most part this sharing works. There are, however, those who take advantage of this trust. There are those who do not share the common sense of good, and the citizens of Mattapoisett struggle with such people. They see them as weak.

In Mattapoisett people are, of course, raised with a sense of their social responsibility and connectedness. This system requires more than promoting positive social ideals, however; it also involves discouraging behavior that is considered negative or harmful. The sense of good must be developed and those that stray from it discouraged.

> "At four, Dawn was timid. We worried. Me, my coms. We all struggled to bring per out."
> "But you say you respect difference."
> "Different strengths we respect. Not weakness. What is the use of not actively engaging in life?"[58]

When another child has trouble choosing one direction in his life, the frustrated and worried co-mothers try to shame him into committing.

> Person drove me wild! I would yell and bluster and my child would sulk and withdraw. . . . I could not grasp such trying on of subjects and roles was learning also. When Peony began to think seriously of shelf diving, I bound per into making a commit. I obsessed Peony into being ashamed of flightiness—which was excessive curiosity. I didn't do this alone. Others reacted the same way. Including the head of the children's house."[59]

There appear to be limits to the society's ability to cope with certain behavior insofar as it threatens the common good. Timidity and indecisiveness are two examples; violent behavior is another. While violence is not as common in Mattapoisett as it is in Connie's time, social conditions having eliminated most preconditions of a violent nature, it does still occasionally happen that a person does do something violent. (The possibility that people are still occasionally violent within their community, because they are involved in violence both in achieving and maintaining their community, is not considered.) For the first offense it is asked if the act was intentional and if the person is willing to take responsibility for the act. Healing is attempted and/or a sentence such as exile, or space service is given. Atonement can be gained by volunteering for something dangerous. If there is a second occurrence of violence, execution is seen as the only option. "'Second time someone uses violence, we give up. We don't want to watch each other or to imprison each other. We aren't willing to live with people who choose to use violence. We execute them.'"[60]

Another rather unreconciled group appears to be the wanderers—people without a village. Without the social bonds needed to work within the system, they seem to create a society of their own.

> Then there were the people without villages called politely drifters and impolitely puffs. . . . Unlike the other guests, drifters often sat apart. People seemed uncomfortable with them. Sometimes they seemed to know each other, and when Connie passed near them, she heard a slang she did not recognize.[61]

It is not clear whether these wanderers respect the customs of the various villages or how the villages respond if they violate these customs and threaten the order. It seems that people will respond to community criticism and sanctions only if they agree with the community's standards. As discussed before, the controls employed in the anarchist vision will be effective only if there has been a transvaluation of values. How will these controls work to effect the necessary changes? What help will they be when dealing with those who do not share in this transvaluation?

> "Ever hear of being lazy? Suppose I just don't want to get up in the morning?"
> "Then I must do your work on top of my own if I'm in your base. Or in your family, I must do your defense or your childcare. I'll come to mind that. Who wants to be resented? Such people are asked to leave and they may wander from village to village sourer and more self-pitying as they go. We sadden at it. . . . Sometimes a healer like my old friend Diana can help. . . . A healer can go back with you and help you grow again. It's going down and then climbing a hard path. But many heal well."[62]

It would seem that to heal well means to accept and take on for oneself the community's sense of good. Anyone who makes a choice to live by another standard cannot be healed and cannot be handled by the community. Such people can "choose" the wandering life but they are considered a problem.

One solution to this problem that is being considered in the community is to begin breeding for desired social traits. There is an ongoing debate between these Shapers and the Mixers.

> "The Shapers want to intervene genetically. . . . Now we only spot problems, watch for birth defects, genes linked with disease susceptibility."
> "The Shapers want to breed for selected traits . . . We three are all Mixers. That's the other side. We don't think people can know objectively how people should become. We think it's a power surge."[63]

The Shapers are reminiscent of end-state tactics discussed in chapter 2 and all the problems of Tepper's *The Gate to Women's Country* follow with these methods. There is a risk that the anarchist vision will degenerate into an end-state vision. This degeneration will occur because, although the people see that each person's interests and possibilities are intricately connected to the interests and possibilities of others, they do not yet understand that it is diversity not homogeneity, critical intelligence not conformity, that opens up the greatest number and most interesting of possibilities. Without people immersed in critical intelligence, conformity will be seen as necessary to gain any workable order.

MATTAPOISETT: A USEFUL UTOPIAN VISION?

Given the difficulties of achieving a transvaluation of values, of getting people to agree on or accept a common sense of good, it is possible that the anarchist society of Mattapoisett will degenerate into a tyranny of eugenics through the Shapers or psychological manipulation through the healers. More and more people may be branded as sick or as social renegades—difference may come to seem more and more threatening. We know the people of Mattapoisett still experience jealousy, possessiveness, and hatred. They are not drawn as altruistic or perfect people. Given the limitations and faults of the human creature, and the fact that the anarchist does not provide a convincing method for changing values, beliefs, and habits, the small communities set up may do more to restrict some people's freedom than it does to open up the freedom of possibility for others.

Ideally the citizens of the anarchist utopian community have experienced the necessary transvaluation of values and realize that everyone must safeguard the freedom of everyone else. With such people for citizens there should be no oppressed class or group because they realize it would be counter to their interests to limit arbitrarily another's freedom as it arbitrarily limits their own. Inasmuch as the citizens of the anarchist utopian community are imperfect creatures, though, it may happen that some people, although they realize it is not in their interest to do so, will feel threatened by the freedom someone has to be different. If this happens, the community may fall back on the techniques of shame, gossip, ostracism, expulsion, or eugenics to remove those who are perceived as the threat or challenge.

While it may not be inevitable that an attempt to realize the anarchist utopian vision will result in such a homogeneous closed society, there is enough of a risk to warrant concern.[64] Even though the citizens of the anarchist vision have been given opportunity to develop and exercise their critical abilities, and are expected to adapt to change and guide their future with foresight and understanding, the vision provides no method for developing such citizens—no process of transition. The return to small face-to-face communities required in the anarchist vision poses a threat to freedom and diversity because the vision does not provide a convincing method for changing values, beliefs, and habits. Dewey's theory of democracy and education may be able to provide the needed process of transition and help reduce the risk of such a vision decaying into a finished, static, closed end-state.

NOTES

1. Paul Berman, "Introduction," in *Quotations from the Anarchist,* ed. Paul Berman (New York: Praeger Publisher, 1972), 8–9.

2. Emma Goldman, "Anarchism: What It Really Stands For," in *Anarchism,* ed. Robert Hoffman (New York: Atherton Press, 1970), 46.

3. William Godwin, *Enquiry Concerning Political Justice,* ed. Raymond A. Preston (New York: Alfred A. Knopf, 1926), 71.

4. Judith Shklar, *After Utopia: The Decline of Political Faith* (Princeton, N.J.: Princeton University Press, 1957), 4, 8.

5. William Ernest Hocking, "The Philosophical Anarchist," in *Anarchism,* ed. Robert Hoffman (New York: Atherton Press, 1970), 116.

6. Giovanni Baldelli, *Social Anarchism* (Chicago: Aldine Atherton, 1971), 73.

7. Ernst Cassirer, *An Introduction to a Philosophy of Human Culture* (New Haven, Conn.: Yale University Press, 1944), 6.

8. Evidence of this can be found in anarchists' critiques of Marx's concept of historical materialism. They do not agree that anything is inevitably unfolding.

9. David Thoreau Wieck, "Essentials of Anarchism," in *Anarchism,* ed. Robert Hoffman (New York: Atherton Press, 1970), 97.

10. Lyman Tower Sargent, "William Morris and the Anarchist Tradition," in *Socialism and the Literary Artistry,* eds. Florence S. Boos and Carole G. Silver (Columbia: University of Missouri Press, 1990), 64.

11. Mikhail Bakunin, *Statism and Anarchy* (Cambridge: Cambridge University Press, 1990), 313.

12. Emma Goldman, *Anarchism and Other Essays* (New York: Kennikat Press, 1910), 60.

13. Goldman, *Anarchism and Other Essays,* 49.

14. P. A. Kropotkin, *The Great French Revolution 1789–1793* (New York: Vanguard Press, 1909), 2–3.

15. Bakunin, *Statism and Anarchy,* 150.

16. Errico Malatesta, "Umanita Nova," in *Quotations from the Anarchists,* ed. Paul Berman (New York: Praeger Publisher, 1972), 109.

17. Mikhail Bakunin, "Protestation of the Alliance," in *Quotations from the Anarchists,* ed. Paul Berman (New York: Praeger Publisher, 1972), 108.

18. P. A. Kropotkin, *Revolutionary Studies* (London: Office of the Commonweal, 1892), 9–10.

19. Emma Goldman, *My Further Disillusionment in Russia* (New York: Doubleday, Page, & Co., 1924), 175.

20. Herbert Marcuse, *An Essay on Liberation* (Boston: Beacon Press, 1969), 6.

21. S. E. Parker, *Individualist Anarchism: An Outline* (London: S. E. Parker, 1965), 3.

22. Herbert Read, *Anarchy and Order* (London: Faber & Faber, 1954), 92.

23. William Godwin, quoted in Paul Eltzbacher, *Anarchism: Exponents of the Anarchist Philosophy* (New York: Libertarian Book Club, 1960), 27.

24. Alexander Berkman, *What Is Communist Anarchism?* (New York: Dover, 1972), 232–233.

25. Bakunin, *Statism,* 134.

26. Lucy Parsons, "Interview with the New York *World*," in *Quotations from the Anarchists,* ed. Paul Berman (New York: Praeger, 1972), 49.

27. Michael Taylor, *Community, Anarchy, and Liberty* (Cambridge: Cambridge University Press, 1982), 91–93, 129.

28. Taylor, *Community,* 96, 101.

29. While it is admittedly very hard to achieve this kind of surrender of privilege, even being asked to imagine such a state can have the effect of making people think more critically about their relative privilege and act more responsibly with regard to it.

30. Taylor, *Community,* 104, 111.

31. Ursula K. Le Guin, *The Dispossessed: An Ambiguous Utopia* (New York: Harper Paperback, 1974), 150–151.

32. Le Guin, *Dispossessed,* 330–331.

33. Godwin, *Enquiry Concerning Political Justice,* 139.

34. While it may be that anarchist critiques of education and suggestions for positive reform have influenced education theory, they don't succeed in providing the needed tool of transvaluation.

35. Kropotkin, *The Great French Revolution,* 577.

36. Emma Goldman, "The Place of the Individual in Society," in *Quotations from the Anarchists,* ed. Paul Berman (New York: Praeger, 1972), 39.

37. Even in the supposedly egalitarian (though not necessarily anarchistic) Owenite communities, where equality between the sexes was theoretically promoted, narrative accounts from women within such communities show a double standard and a double burden. Women were expected to maintain their role as domestic support for men, but now on a community-wide scale. There was no support or tolerance for women with different views and aspirations and many women left disillusioned. Carol A. Kolmerton, *Women in Utopia: The Ideology of Gender in the American Owenite Communities* (Bloomington: Indiana University Press, 1990).

38. Herbert Read, *Anarchy and Order* (London: Faber & Faber, 1954), 38.

39. Read, *Anarchy and Order,* 88.

40. Le Guin, *Dispossessed,* 165.

41. Marge Piercy, *Woman on the Edge of Time* (New York: Fawcett Crest, 1976), 68.

42. Piercy, *Woman,* 125.

43. Piercy, *Woman,* 154.

44. Piercy, *Woman,* 207–208.

45. To further stress and maintain the equality, there are no sexually identifying pronouns in the language of the future. All people are referred to by name or as "per" or "person." Sex is irrelevant and hard for Connie to determine.

46. Piercy, *Woman*, 103–104.

47. There is no historical or experiential reason to assume that strong local ties will lead to strong translocal ties.

48. Feminists do not agree on whether the elimination of differences between the sexes is a good solution to anything. Some, including Carolyn G. Heilbrun, Andrea Dworkin, and Monique Wittig, believe that there is something to be gained in recognizing gender as a socialized division and doing away with it. Others—Mary Daly, Adrienne Rich, and Sally Miller Gearhart, for example—believe that some of the differences are important and think that we should be concentrating on developing certain female differences rather than working at a merging of the sexes.

49. Piercy, *Woman*, 136–137.

50. This connection includes learning to communicate with animals. Certain animal sign languages have been developed. Some people, with special callings, serve as earth and animal advocates.

51. Piercy, *Woman*, 66.

52. Piercy, *Woman*, 248.

53. Piercy, *Woman*, 370.

54. Piercy, *Woman*, 197–198.

55. Piercy, *Woman*, 375.

56. Piercy, *Woman*, 117.

57. Such fluidity is necessary for any non-dogmatic espousal of the good that is, in principle, tied to changing conditions and circumstances. The difficulty of maintaining people capable of coping with such change will be seen to be a critique of Dewey as well. While Dewey does not offer any final solution to the problem, he does recognize the difficulty and provides, in his educational theory, a method for promoting and sustaining in individuals the necessary effort. The anarchists, on the other hand, appear to just hope that a transformed character will be able to keep up.

58. Piercy, *Woman*, 182.

59. Piercy, *Woman*, 310.

60. Piercy, *Woman*, 209.

61. Piercy, *Woman*, 272.

62. Piercy, *Woman*, 101.

63. Piercy, *Woman*, 226.

64. All utopian proposals are fallible, and it is important to consider how the proposed orders might fall apart and to prepare people to cope with and adapt to the changes. It is in order to deal with the negative possibilities of any vision that it is necessary to promote critical intelligence and foresight.

Chapter Four

Dewey's Democracy:
A Process Model of Utopia

The very heart of political democracy is adjudication of social differences by discussion and exchange of views. This method provides a rough approximation to the method of effecting change by means of experimental inquiry and test: the scientific method. The very foundation of the democratic procedure is dependence upon experimental production of social change; an experimentation directed by working principles that are tested and developed in the very process of being tried out in action.[1]

John Dewey's model of democracy requires that we recognize that the unfolding of the future is not determined separate from us, but is intricately connected with us. It requires that we recognize how our participation affects what the future can be. It requires that we recognize that there is no end-state at which we must work to arrive, but a multiple of possible future states which we seek and try out. John Dewey's vision of democracy prepares us to interact with our world and guide it to a better future by immersing us in what he calls the method of critical intelligence. With Dewey, democracy is not participation by an inchoate public, nor is it a perfected end-state to be attained. It is the development of critical intelligence and a method of living with regard to the past, present, and future.

Dewey's dream of democracy, as a method of living by which individuals are fully engaged in the experience that is their lives, is what I take to be the basis of a new and different model of utopia. As discussed in chapter 1, many people resist the connection of pragmatism and utopian thought. As I have explained, I think they are correct to resist connecting Dewey's work with traditional end-state utopian thinking. However, I think his work provides the basis for a new process model of utopia. This chapter will explore Dewey's beliefs about human experience and show how these beliefs develop into his theory of democracy. Dewey's faith in democracy makes it clear what the role of experimentation in social living is to be and serves to point out what Dewey takes to be the necessary application of critical intelligence to how we choose to live. Experimentation requires critical intelligence, and critical intelligence requires active participants involved in directing their lives, therefore the role of education in preparing such citizens for active duty will also be examined.

Dewey's process model of democracy is compatible with feminist theory and can provide the foundation for community without resorting to authoritarian control. Dewey's vision dismantles hierarchies and dualisms and embraces diversity and change rather than seeing diversity and change as threatening to social order and progress. Diversity and change are seen as the challenge for us to participate in the world we live in; they are a necessary part of any world of actual human experience. We learn that "to cooperate by giving differences a chance to show themselves because of the belief that the expression of difference is not only a right of the other persons but is a means of enriching one's own life-experience, is inherent in the democratic personal way of life."[2] Embracing the expression of difference and accommodating change lead to a flexible and workable social order that deals with conflict constructively and addresses problems pragmatically.

INTELLIGENT IMAGINATION

Dewey believes that we must try to "make a future such as we desire." The conditions of such futures, however, are present in and limited by what is now, and our task is to apply critical intelligence and imagination to our present situation and make the possible the actual. "The mode in which the inevitable comes to pass is through effort. Consciously or unconsciously, we all strive to make the kind of world that we like. And although . . . we may regard criticism of the past as futile, there is every reason for doing all that we can to make a future such as we desire."[3] This ongoing process of making the future is what Dewey calls lived experience. Dewey believes that it is in the process of striving for the future that the living organism gives meaning and purpose to the present and the past. As human creatures, we create expectations which guide our present actions and desires; we provide the order and purpose out of which the future emerges. This notion of lived experience is central to understanding Dewey's thought and is the key to developing a process model of utopia.

Lived experience, as opposed to received experience, is characterized by an intense participatory relationship between the environment and the live creature. Critical engagement with the world gives the experience structure and provides one's perception of the world intentional direction. The experience is ordered and controlled by specific aspects of the future one envisions. This enables one to live the experience and integrate it into another more complete experience, which in turn will become the ground for yet another experience, and so on. Lived experience is dynamic and has a cumulating effect. It becomes part of what we bring to all other experiences in our lives, and its intensity affects how we see and feel about all that we perceive and how we perceive it. It affects past as well as future perceptions.

Lived experience reveals the dynamic ordering which underlies all that we do—its rhythm—and so deepens our awareness of the relational nature of ourselves as human creatures with other live creatures and with our environment. This awareness enables us to organize our experience such that it may be possible to make obstacles into opportunities, problems into possibilities, and move our experience forward toward a goal in a satisfying and fulfilling way. "For whenever each step forward is at the same time a summing up and fulfillment of what precedes, and every consummation carries expectation tensely forward, there is rhythm."[4] Without an awareness of the relational nature of ourselves and our environment, it is not possible to act with foresight or understanding. One must discern the rhythm of experience if there is to be any hope of moving experience forward in a satisfying and fulfilling way. Once rhythm is discerned, new possibilities emerge and it becomes possible to see the old and familiar in a new light and so see connections not previously seen. The future opens up as unending possibility which we can choose to organize and direct for our purposes.

Dewey believes that, as human creatures, we seem to have a habit or impulse to direct our actions toward a future goal; he calls this impulse mind. Because humans are sentient social creatures, we are mindful and we decide, individually and collectively, at what purposes we want our future to aim. We draw pictures of the futures we desire. Given this future orientation, we can critically engage and examine our experience in the world to make it better. According to Dewey, to fail to engage in this critical examination is to live at the level of received experience rather than to move to the level of lived experience. To live at the level of received experience is to remain a passive spectator. Lived experience, however, is dynamic and cumulative, and prepares us to make and embrace the future as on ongoing experiment.

Insofar as we are concerned with making a better future, this engagement must involve imagination. "All conscious experience must be imaginative to the degree that the past is used to interpret the present and its bearing toward the future."[5] Envisioning the future as a guide in the present is to achieve that very integrative standpoint which Dewey calls lived experience. Visions of the future help organize and structure our present experiences to some purpose; imagination helps organize experience by providing it with a goal. Dewey calls such goals ends-in-view.

Dewey's model of experience is a process model that builds on the premise that human beings are interactive, relational creatures. We are born physically dependent and remain socially interdependent. He further believes that we are finite developmental creatures who must grow and adapt to both our changing physical and changing social environments in order to survive. This means there can be no set goals, no predetermined unchanging goods or ends. Instead, there is a continuous chain of ends-in-view becoming means for new ends-in-view which become means for new ends-in-view.

As the present carries us forward to some end-in-view, that future end-in-view will become, itself, a present which will be carried forward to another end-in-view, and so on. There is no disjunction of means and ends. As each end-in-view achieved eventually becomes the means for achieving new ends-in-view, it is important to select carefully the ends we, as individuals and collectively, want to achieve. As human creatures engaged in individual and social development, we must critically examine the ends-in-view we choose to achieve as what we choose to achieve now defines what we will be able to achieve in the future. We must recognize the indeterminate nature of the future and realize the impact of our individual and societal choices upon it. We must accept responsibility for creating the future, develop a critical method of directing it, and not wait for it to unfold separately from us. For example, on Dewey's account it is important to directly and consciously address problems of population, pollution, and international relations, since they will not just dissolve of their own accord, and how they are addressed determines both our future problems and possibilities. The laissez-faire model of liberalism is not what Dewey has in mind.

Since the future is an ongoing process in which we participate and through which we develop, we can and should give it intelligent direction by forming it to some end-in-view. For this purpose, Dewey calls for the application of the scientific method to social problems. In fact, according to Dewey, "what is needed is intelligent examination of the consequences that are actually effected by inherited institutions and customs, in order that there may be intelligent consideration of the ways in which they are to be intentionally modified in behalf of generation of different consequences."[6] In other words, people need to engage in empirical, sociological, psychological studies of specific society's habits, customs and institutions. We need to understand how they came to be instantiated, discern what purpose they were developed to serve, and evaluate their success at solving the problem, or satisfying the need they were developed to meet. Then, with a concurrent examination of present situations and needs, it can be decided if the habits, customs, and institutions should be maintained as they are or modified in some way. It should be noted that, as opposed to the anarchist model, a radical revolution in customs, habits, and institutions is not a realistic option for Dewey. Some may be phased out over time, but given their internalized nature, the strength they possess to guide action and ways of thinking, and their widespread influence, it is not possible to remove their influence in any direct and immediate way. Instead, Dewey chooses to redirect or adapt them to new purposes. While this may eventually change the character of the customs, habits, and institutions drastically, it does so through gradual transformation, not radical revolution.

We must examine what purposes our customs, habits, and institutions can most successfully serve in the present so we can begin to experiment with adapting them to fit our current needs and purposes. Dewey's view of the scientific method or experimental process is not a positivistic view, or a view of technology achieving mastery and control. Science does not provide some objective "truth" to which we must surrender. According to Dewey's view of science we participate in and direct experimentation in light of our own purposes and goals. For Dewey, science becomes a tool to aid us in directing our future. To not experiment, in fact, would be to surrender to aimless action or to already extant centers of power and domination. "We *use* our past experience to construct new and better ones in the future. The very fact of experience thus includes the process by which it directs itself in its own betterment."[7]

We should expand and use our knowledge to enrich our imagination and give direction to our ideas. "We have more knowledge than we try to put to use, and until we try more systematically we shall not know what are the important gaps in our sciences judged from the point of view of their moral and humane use."[8] We are developmental social creatures, participants in a culture. We can, through critical intelligent investigation of our situation and values, promote our continued development and growth. Applying the method of intelligence to social problems requires us to engage in an interpretation of society, an articulation of its problems, and a process of proposing solutions.

> The point is to live well. Dewey thought we can do this best by developing the intelligent elements within our personal and collective experience in such a way that our practices and institutions become more fulfilling. We can modify who we are and what we do in such a way that we increase our satisfactions and create the conditions for future satisfactions. Being intelligent is not an end in itself; living well is the point. But intelligence is the best way to enhance our practices and institutions so that we might live well.[9]

We are put in a position to give society intelligent direction. This process of engagement requires us to understand society as it is, see how it might be different, and propose solutions to what is problematic. Imagination helps us envision alternate social orders which we might want to try out. These proposed solutions should then be tested, expecting that not all will be satisfactory.[10]

Such imaginative exercises—dramatic rehearsals—are part of the embodiment of Dewey's critical method, that is, the method of intelligence. This social experimentation should not be seen as a quest for certain and final closure, but instead as embracing the open-ended and uncertain nature of our experience in the world. "Deliberation is rational in the degree in which forethought flexibly remakes old aims and habits, institutes perception and love of new ends and acts."[11] We cannot predict the future, which is uncertain and unknowable, but we can prepare ourselves to handle a variety of possibilities. If we are immersed in the method of critical intelligence we can be better prepared to make the most out of what is. "The task of critical intelligence is to explore and develop experience—not to terminate it."[12] This is the activity of critical intelligence, and it is crucial if we are to have any meaningful lived experience.

THE POSSIBILITIES OF IMAGINED ENDS

Lack of vision results in a lack of direction, a lack of guiding aims. Without aims lived experience is not possible—only disjointed experience which may or may not lead to fulfilling culmination—and is rarely cumulative. We must have ends-in-view to ground experience and so make experimentation possible and fruitful. If intelligent imagination is to develop experience into a cumulative whole rather than terminate it, though, there are constraints on the kinds of futures it should envision.

There are certain ends-in-view which will prove to be unacceptable. If one imagines a final, complete, and perfect end-state, the possibilities of the future are as unduly limited as they are in a state of undirected trial and error. If one sees the present as simply part of an inevitable unfolding to some already determined end, the possibilities of the future are closed off. There is no expectation of anything beyond, or other than, the attainment of the end-state. Such restriction and finality close off the future as they close off experimentation, limit participation, and put an end to the process of cumulative lived experience.

A process model of utopia, however, will answer these difficulties. Dewey embraces the process nature of existence itself. "Dewey rejects, therefore, the idea that potentiality implies a fixed or predetermined end in any absolute sense; potentiality simply refers to 'a characteristic of change.'"[13] Because Dewey's view of human experience is developmental, ends-in-view must be seen as dynamic, not final; means must be seen as part of a continuum of ends-in-view, not as separate and purely instrumental. Present ends-in-view must be recognized as the means to future ends-in-view and present means must be chosen on the grounds of whether they are capable of issuing ends-in-view that will provide the basis for furthering experience. "Pragmatism is therefore grounded on an interpretation of nature in which consequences and possibilities are regarded as real factors of the world, and the present moment involves the issue of the future."[14]

A process model of utopia can avoid prescribing unchanging ends, and become an impetus for continued growth. "When the utopia points to ideal life without becoming a plan, that is, a lifeless machine applied to living matter, it truly becomes the realisation of progress."[15] Such a model provides descriptions of future states which, though they may never actually be arrived at, serve to structure what goes on in our present actions. With such visions imagination gives form and content to our present and our future. According to Dewey, imagination gives direction to the future and in so doing helps control and organize the present. It provides us with ends-in-view which we must critically reflect on, choose among, try out, and reflect on and revise again continuously.

It is with the switch from structuring our experience in regard to ends to structuring it in terms of ends-in-view that real possibilities begin to emerge and a different model of utopia begins to unfold—a model that has less chance of becoming totalitarian or authoritarian. "The terminal outcome when anticipated . . . becomes an end-in-view, an aim, purpose, a prediction usable as a plan in shaping the course of events. . . . They are projections of possible consequences . . . They are not objects of contemplative possession and use, but are intellectual and regulative means."[16] When we structure our experience in regard to final ends, rather than ends-in-view, there is an increased risk that our participation will be subjugated to the needs of the end. When the end is privileged it comes to be regarded as the real goal of experience, its attainment the only meaningful experience. This makes it possible for the end to become detached from our needs and allows it to control our aims and actions. When we structure our experience in terms of ends-in-view, though, our participation is more likely to remain primary, and particular ends-in-view will be sought only as they satisfy our needs. The model of ends-in-view requires our continual application of critical intelligence, and so the ends-in-view are not as likely to take on a life of their own. They are the tools we use to shape and direct the conditions of the present, not to achieve a specific final end, but to mold the past, present, and future into meaningful experience. With ends-in-view our choices regulate the future, rather than the reverse.

REALIZING THE POSSIBLE

Our choice of an end-in-view organizes our experience, mediating between what is and what might be. Such activity of choice is what Dewey calls the capacity of mind. Mind is an inherent tendency to organize and direct the world as we encounter it.

> Acting with an aim is all one with acting intelligently. To foresee a terminus of an act is to have a basis upon which to observe, to select, and to order objects and our own capacities. To do these things means to have mind. . . . To have a mind to do a thing is to foresee a future possibility; it is to have a plan for its accomplishment; it is to note the means which make the plan capable of execution and the obstructions in the way. . . . Mind is capacity to refer present conditions to future results, and future consequences to present conditions.[17]

Dewey's concept of mind is one of dynamic organization of the past, present, and future. Mind, as a capacity of sentient social beings, must take into account its embeddedness in a present and past and imagine future possibilities. Mind is the capacity that enables us to give structure and meaning to our experience; it makes it possible for us to move beyond received experience to lived experience.

According to Dewey, mind is an impulse to carry all experience toward significant integration—to structure our experience in regard to some goal or some end-in-view. Significance and sense result from this activity of mind, that is, from the organization made possible by these ends-in-view. Experience is the result of this process of structuring as much as, or more than, it is the "stuff" being structured. "Mind appears in experience as ability to respond to present stimuli on the basis of anticipation of future possible consequences, and with a view to controlling the kind of consequences that are to take place."[18] Mind, our ability to organize experience, is constituted by context not found free floating in a vacuum. Our social situation guides our understanding and forms our interests, and our understanding and interests structure our experience.

Our social situation is not something that simply happens to us, however. We appropriate and integrate our environment into experience. Whatever our situation, we participate in its future development. It does not develop separately from us. Our activity partially defines our social situation, and our social situation goes a long way to guiding our activity. There is an interplay of the determinate and indeterminate by which we realize the potential of the future. We are a perspective, influenced by our experience, through which we organize our participation and structure the community so that future experience is meaningful to us. "Meaning is a contextually determined social process which is structural but creative and dramatic and in which participation rather than decoding or autonomous self-realization is the key idea."[19] Meaning is not fixed, but rather emerges from our chosen aims.

Ends-in-view result from the interests we develop in our social context, and these interests will be diverse and changing. While we need some shared purposes, Dewey believes we must be careful not to close off the future by striving for homogeneity.

> The American nation is itself complex and compound. Strictly speaking it is interracial and international in its make-up. It is composed of a multitude of peoples speaking different tongues, inheriting diverse traditions, cherishing varying ideals of life. . . . Our unity cannot be a homogeneous thing . . . it must be a unity created by drawing out and composing into a harmonious whole the best, the most characteristic which each contributing race and people has to offer.[20]

Development from and of our past determines what we will see as possible and desirable for the future. What we imagine as desirable future possibilities determines how we will organize ourselves in the present and how we organize ourselves in the present will determine what is possible for the future. As the present will be the past for the future we should work to make the present as full, varied, and rich as possible. Our interests are informed by our present and past conditions, and discovered by imaginative views of what might be. It is very important, therefore, that we begin to consciously direct our imaginative views of what our future will be. We must learn to consciously direct and expand our interests and imagination.

Conscious deliberation about our ever-changing situation and interests should lead us to select specific ends-in-view. Ends-in-view provide the direction and order necessary to understand the present and to achieve the future. "The end is then an end-in-view and is in constant and cumulative reenactment at each stage of forward movement. It is no longer a terminal point, external to the conditions that have led up to it; it is the continually developing meaning of present tendencies—the very things which as directed we call 'means.'"[21] Ends-in-view provide the direction necessary to achieve future possibilities by intelligently directing the tendencies of present conditions. It is important, therefore, to select such guiding goals carefully.

This means we must become active participants in our present society, utilizing what is and has been for some consciously chosen and critically examined end-in-view. As we begin to modify the present, we must continually reevaluate both the end-in-view being sought and the methods being employed. If either fails to be satisfactory (what this entails will be discussed later), new ends-in-view must be sought or the methods of achievement altered. We must apply the method of intelligence to our choice of the future. The method of intelligence, applied to society, welcomes the problematic and the changing. Society becomes "something to be modified, to be intentionally controlled. It is material to act upon so as to transform it into new objects which better answer our needs . . . it exists at any particular time as a challenge, rather than a completion; it provides possible starting points and opportunities rather than final ends."[22]

Social living is an ongoing process, not a perfected life. No harmony is lasting. Each satisfying moment passes over into a new need for which we must alter our world and/or ourselves to meet. Our interests change; our ends-in-view change; we change. Dewey sees the future as something that is always new and expected in anticipation, not received as fulfilled prediction.

> There are two sorts of possible worlds in which esthetic experience would not occur. In a world of mere flux, change would not be cumulative; it would not move toward a close. Stability and rest would have no being. Equally is it true, however, that a world that is finished, ended, would have no traits of suspense and crises, and would offer no opportunity for resolution. Where everything is already complete, there is no fulfillment. . . . The moment of passage from disturbance into harmony is that of intensest life. In a finished world, sleep and waking could not be distinguished.[23]

With mere flux there is no experience; with completion there is no vivacity. We seek continuity and stability in our experience, though; we try to make sense out of it. In fact, according to Dewey, these are the controlling impulses (the impulse of mind) of our social life. This order which we seek to make sense of, however, is dynamic and precarious and Dewey warns that we should avoid trying to make it static and certain. How, then, can the qualities of continuity and stability be achieved without putting an end to lived experience? How can our impulse to organize be reconciled with this ongoing process of change? If we begin to participate in the change, direct and control the change, we will find stability and satisfaction in the constant modification itself. Lived experience will be found in the continuous process of reordering our lives according to the cumulative effects of various changes.

DEWEY REJECTS END-STATE AND ANARCHIST VISIONS

If it is imagination which examines our experience and discovers and refines our interests, and our interests which lead us to select specific ends-in-view, and these selected ends-in-view which shape the future, we must examine our imaginative visions critically and choose our goals carefully if we are to achieve a better and/or desirable future. The vision which Dewey chooses is democracy. It is not the specific political organization of democracy that Dewey has in mind, however. For Dewey:

> Democracy is belief in the ability of human experience to generate the aims and methods by which further experience will grow in ordered richness. Every other form of moral and social faith rests upon the idea that experience must be subjected at some point or other to some form of external control; to some "authority" alleged to exist outside the processes of experience. Democracy is the faith that the process of experience is more important than any special result attained, so that special results achieved are of ultimate value only as they are used to enrich and order the ongoing process. . . . All ends and values that are cut off from the ongoing process become arrests, fixations. They strive to fixate what has been gained instead of using it to open the road and point the way to new and better experiences.[24]

He sees democracy as a way of life—a condition of participation with corresponding responsibilities. It is a method for directing the future. It is an open-ended process, capable of being reformed and redirected. It is lived experience. Democracy is the experimental method—the method of intelligence—applied to social concerns.

According to Dewey, we make and unmake the world, first in our dreams and then in our lives. We can always imagine things as somehow different or better. With such visions we are able to articulate our desires, formulate hypotheses about how to achieve our desires, and commit ourselves to bringing about the changes we foresee without committing ourselves to a fixed end. Without such flexible visions, our world has no purpose and, on Dewey's account, with no purpose we can have no deep experience in life—no lived experience. Visions of the future help shape our present and past into meaningful experience by ordering them to some purpose. Flexible visions of the future guide our present actions by providing us with an aim to pursue without closing off possibility.

As live creatures, in an organic environment, we constantly seek to modify our environment to satisfy our needs. Methods of undirected trial and error have eventually given way to intelligent direction and control, as demonstrated by the methods of science. While this evolution has been accepted in regard to biological needs, it has been denied in regard to social needs, resulting in a gap of understanding. We still arrange society by simple methods of trial and error, not seeking causal links or an understanding of the relational nature of live creatures and their environment. According to Dewey, democracy takes the necessary step toward intelligent direction and control in the social sciences.

Ideal democracy is a method of living in the present with regard to the future. Democracy tries out institutions and modifies them as needs and interests change, not expecting a final form of society to eventually emerge, but embracing the potentiality of intentionally directed change. "As a society becomes more enlightened, it realizes that it is responsible *not* to transmit and conserve the whole of its existing achievements, but only such as make for a better future society."[25]

The quality of a society depends on its aims. How does Dewey propose that the people judge the quality of a society? What standards and/or values are applicable? Since Dewey is not prescribing, in democracy, an end-state with concrete definable goals, it is difficult to ascertain if one has "got it right." It is even difficult to compare one societal arrangement with another and determine which is "better." While it may appear that this leaves societal organization and values too vague to be of practical use, I do not think this is the case. The method of democracy does not leave us without guidelines. Dewey provides at least five criteria which, as I will discuss in the next section, show us that the experimental method, which democracy is to embody, puts value on free and open participation by all people in a society. This means authoritarian, dictatorial, totalitarian regimes will not qualify. Further, I believe Dewey would find that visions of anarchy, and/or of complete and final end states, will fail to appreciate and encourage our continued participation in the formation of the future.

Dewey agrees with many of the objectives of the anarchist vision as it was discussed in the previous chapter. In his book *The Public and Its Problems,* Dewey supports the building of smaller communities where there is face-to-face interaction and accountability. What he calls a Great Community, which will be discussed more later, depends on there being smaller communities where people can learn how to communicate and sympathize with others. He would also support the anarchist's stress on recognizing and living up to our interdependence. "The Great Society was marked by extensive webs of interdependence; the Great Community would be marked by a shared understanding of the consequences of this interdependence."[26] It is only with some shared understanding of our interconnectedness that community can be built and experience carried into the future with some purpose and direction.

With anarchy, however, there is too much radical change. Experience is disrupted by revolution rather than carried forward. One problem with revolution is the risk that it will result in a reactionary move to authoritarian, totalitarian rule. Dewey says:

> We should also note that a period of uncertainty and insecurity, accompanied as it is by more or less unsettlement and disturbance, creates a feeling that anything would be better than what exists, together with desire for order and stability upon almost any terms—the latter being a reason why revolutions are so regularly followed by reaction, and explain the fact that Lenin expressed by saying revolutions are authoritative, though not for the reason he gave.[27]

A second problem with the anarchist's method is that it is not one of con-trolled and directed change in that is does not pay enough attention to the past except as something to be done away with. Constructive experimentation is not possible as there is little or no studied accumulation of information and past experiences, but rather a cry for revolution and a break with the past. Without the past as a guide to what is possible any attempt to change things can be only guesswork, not constructive experimentation. On Dewey's view, to choose revolution as the means of change is to rely on undirected trial and error alone to work things out. But where the method of change by simple trial and error is employed there can be no effectual participation since it is more a matter of chance than directed intelligence. Instead, Dewey proposes a pragmatic theory of social change.

> A pragmatic social theory, Dewey told the Chinese, was neither radical nor con-servative in the means it proposed for social change, for it abandoned the quest of either wholesale change or wholesale social preservation. The theory looked for "particular kinds of solutions by particular methods for particular problems which arise on particular occasions." For the instrumentalist, progress toward desired ends, even revolutionary ends, was an incremental process of experimental problem solving. . . . "Reconstruction," not revolution, was the byword of Deweyan politics.[28]

While Dewey may agree with many of the goals set out by anarchist theorists, he does not agree with their means of revolution. It is important to note that Dewey is careful not to judge people for using revolutionary tactics. When visiting China, Turkey, Japan, Mexico, and the Soviet Union he was aware that the individual circumstances of these different people had created differ-ent needs, problems, and methods of resolution. He believes that only the people involved and affected can make the decisions of means and ends. He does, however, caution that violence as a means will affect any end achieved. As was discussed in chapter 3, violence often replaces one power structure with another, without changing much for the majority of the people. Violence can also do more to alienate people from one another, rather than bind them together, and can result in a loss of compassion and respect for other live crea-tures. Violence is an option, but one should act with an awareness of how it limits the potential for future growth. As means and ends are inseparable for Dewey, he attempts to set out the means he finds consistent with the goals found in anarchist visions. What he sets out is what he interchangeably calls the method of intelligence, the method of democracy, or critical intelli-gence.[29]

While Dewey finds some ground for agreement with the anarchists he has more trouble with those theorists who propose final end-states. With a vision of a final end-state the problem is that there is no future beyond the final state

imagined, and so there is no continuum of experience in which our participation carries us forward. No change is necessary, in fact no beneficial change
can be imagined beyond the end-state, so experimentation and growth are at
an end. Such ends become arrests and fixations and fail to move experience
forward. While such imagined end-states may appear to provide us with an
aim to pursue, a purpose to help shape our experience into some meaningful
future, they ultimately lead to a dead end.

> The doctrine of fixed ends not only diverts attention from examination of conse-
> quences and the intelligent creation of purpose, but, since means and ends are two
> ways of regarding the same actuality, it also renders men careless in their inspection
> of existing conditions. . . . The result is failure. Discouragement follows, assuaged
> perhaps by the thought that in any case the end is too ideal, too noble and remote, to
> be capable of realization. We fall back on the consoling thought that our moral ideals
> are too good for this world and that we must accustom ourselves to a gap between
> aim and execution.[30]

Imagining fixed ends will serve only to put an end to the material of imagination, make experience appear disjointed, and encourage us to be apathetic
and accept received experience.

We cannot achieve our most desirable world because, Dewey argues, we
live in a changing world, so our desires are not static. Neither, then, is our experience. Given the developmental and processive nature of experience,
change will occur. "Plato proposed a planned society, Dewey a society engaged in continuous planning."[31] Change is part of our experience, and we
must direct it toward our own enrichment or else let it constrain our possibilities. "An immense difference divides the plann*ed* society from a *continuously* plann*ing* society. The former requires fixed blue-prints imposed from
above and therefore involving reliance upon physical and psychological force
to secure conformity to them. The latter means the release of intelligence
through the wisest form of cooperative give-and-take."[32] The release of intelligence, good or enriching experience, is that which promotes growth.

> Not perfecting as a final goal, but the ever-enduring process of perfecting, maturing,
> refining is the aim in living. Honesty, industry, temperance, justice, like health,
> wealth and learning, are not goods to be possessed as they would be if they expressed
> fixed ends to be attained. They are directions of change in the quality of experience.
> Growth itself is the only moral "end."[33]

Dewey's notion of growth as the only moral "end" stems from his notion of
the human being as a developmental creature in a developing world. While
this is a vague ideal, it is an important one. It imparts the idea of seeking conditions that promote further development rather than seeking an ultimate or

perfect way of being. It embodies the concept of process as the only possible "end," pushing us to realize that it is our goals that inform and direct the process and that, ideally, as long as we keep forming pictures of the future there is no "end."[34]

Given the process nature of our existence, Dewey believes that we will always keep dreaming. There will always be a future to envision. Rather than surrender to undirected trial and error, or imagine final end-states, we should imagine guiding aims—what Dewey calls ends-in-view. Such aims can give intelligent direction and order to our present action without being committed to a fixed end *if* we engage in the method of intelligence. Such ends-in-view can create the future without closing it off. Such ends-in-view can help us grow. How will we judge if an end-in-view is a good or satisfactory end-in-view? How will we judge whether it promotes growth?

JUDGING FUTURE POSSIBILITIES

Although the notion of growth is a vague ideal, Dewey does provide some criteria for judging ends-in-view and making decisions about what to pursue and by what means. As we have seen, end-state and anarchist visions do not promote growth. I suggest that Dewey provides five criteria by which we can judge ends-in-view.

First, as developmental creatures, we must realize that our participation affects what the future can and will be. The future is not determined, but develops through the choices and actions of the live creatures in the world. The participation required by such a developmental process model, however, requires that people be educated for it—involved in the critical task. The first criterion, then, that Dewey would apply in judging whether an end-in-view is satisfactory relates to education. Does the end-in-view promote education and participation? Are the people prepared to participate in decision making and goal formation?

By education Dewey means much more than school, books, and teachers. It includes all aspects of socialization—especially overt doing. We need to be immersed in a task. It is in doing and making that we learn to apply a critical attitude to what is to be done and how we plan to do it. We must first ask if the aim of the task is worthwhile. What is its cumulative effect likely to be? Then we must examine what means will be employed to reach the end-in-view. Are they acceptable? Finally, we must decide whether one or both of the end-in-view and the means are desirable and propose alternatives to be examined. In doing something we come to employ the critical method of experimentation (the method of intelligence) which we need to develop in order to direct and guide our social context to a better future. We become entrenched in the method of intelligence

and learn to employ intelligent imagination to grasp our present and future possibilities. Through participation we begin to form the critical and flexible habits
of mind needed to participate in the method of democracy.

This brings us to the second criterion for judging ends-in-view. As participation requires that we be schooled in the method of experimentation, we
come to realize that there are constraints on the hypotheses we can form and
the tests we can carry out. We do not exist in a vacuum of understanding, beliefs, or knowledge. We can imagine the future only after consideration of the
actuality of the present and the past, or it will be pure fantasy. With the use of
intelligent imagination and present knowledge we are more likely to propose
workable or achievable aims—good ends-in-view. These ends-in-view arise
from our embeddedness in the present—"based upon a consideration for what
is already going on; upon the resources and difficulties of the situation. . . .
They are . . . the expression of mind in foresight, observation, and choice of
the better among alternative possibilities."[35] This second criterion, then,
amounts to asking how realistic the chosen ends-in-view are.

If one achieves the critical/experimental attitude, and recognizes the limits
and possibilities of any particular situation, there is a third criterion by which
to judge the end-in-view—flexibility. Both our minds and the temporary ends
must be flexible. One must not get so set on a way of seeing things that al-
terations become impossible. One must continually observe and examine any
given situation and adjust both ends-in-view and means to be more suitable.
"A good aim surveys the present state of experience of pupils, and forming a
tentative plan of treatment, keeps the plan constantly in view and yet modifies it as conditions develop. The aim, in short, is experimental, and hence
constantly growing as it is tested in action."[36] One must avoid making dogmatic claims and learn to treat results as information to further a hypothesis
which is provisional and proves nothing with absolute certainty. With a new
end-in-view, or under different conditions, things might appear to work quite
differently, and we must be prepared to see the variations.

A fourth criterion is that an end-in-view should free activity. A good end-
in-view is not focused solely on an object or state of affairs to be attained, but
equally on the development of those abilities necessary to attain the object or
state of affairs. In other words, means and ends-in-view must be fully integrated and given equal consideration. Dewey gives the example of shooting
a rabbit. Wanting to hit the rabbit and wanting to shoot straight are integrated
desires. And if one wants to eat the rabbit, the shooting becomes part of a
larger activity, not an end in itself. Further, if one achieves the activity of
shooting straight one can transfer this activity to other objects and so be able
to achieve a variety of ends-in-view. Such activity becomes what Dewey calls
an *active end* and helps make lived experience possible.[37] Such an end-in-

view makes many ends-in-view possible, not just the end-in-view originally sought. When we seek ends-in-view which require the development of abilities, not just achieve states, we open up a wide range of possibilities for moving forward.

A fifth criterion is that an end-in-view should open up possibilities rather than close them off.[38] It should promote plurality. Ends-in-view which isolate people from one another, put interests in conflict, or constrain capacities of development make for a poor quality of society as they limit the possibilities of the future. "The wider and the richer the social relationships into which an individual enters, the more fully are his powers evoked, and the more fully is he brought to recognize the possibilities latent in them."[39] The more varied one's experiences, the more one can grow. As one recognizes the connections and inevitable interdependence with a variety of live creatures and environments, the wider the possibilities of lived experience become. "Associated living was living that fostered the growth of the individuality of all the members of a society, and a social practice was 'to be judged good when it contributes positively to free intercourse, to unhampered exchange of ideas, to mutual respect and friendship and love.'"[40]

If one instead restricts or narrows experience, denies connections with the multiplicity of life forms with which one co-exists, lived experience and growth will be limited and become more limited with each coming generation.

> A small social group with fixed habits, a clan, a gang, a narrow sect, a dogmatic party, will restrict the formation of critical powers—i.e., of conscientiousness or moral thoughtfulness. But an individual who really becomes a member of modern society, with its multiple occupations, its easy intercourse, its free mobility, its rich resources of art and science, will have only too many opportunities for reflective judgment and personal valuation and preference. The very habits . . . of personal criticism of the existing order, and of private projection of a better order . . . are themselves effects of a variable and complex social order.[41]

On Dewey's view, plurality is a necessary condition of growth and a positive projection of the future. As developmental creatures, we use the variety of experience to expand ourselves. The perspectives that we embody as individuals need to encounter and learn to communicate with other perspectives for growth to be possible. Our social embeddedness should push us to be reflective thinkers. If it does not, if it in fact narrows our perspective and constrains our critical powers, there is something problematic in the social arrangement. Such a society does not qualify as Dewey's notion of associated living.

Associated living promotes diversity, interaction, and communication. It requires active participation from the individuals involved in the society and constantly pushes these individuals to grow out of fixed habits into flexible and adaptive habits. "Because the need of preparation for a continually developing life is great, it is imperative that every energy should be bent to making the present experience as rich and significant as possible. Then as the present merges insensibly into the future, the future is taken care of."[42] An enriching society will promote diversity within a shared context and thereby expand the limits of the future.

> A democracy is more than a form of government; it is primarily a mode of associated living, of conjoint communicated experience . . . so that each has to refer his own action to that of others, and to consider the action of others to give point and direction to his own. . . . These more numerous and more varied points of contact denote a greater diversity of stimuli to which an individual has to respond; they consequently put a premium on variation in his actions.[43]

Good ends-in-view push us to accept our interrelatedness and plurality, which in turn pushes us to enlarge our visions—to look further beyond ourselves and see a plurality of possible ends-in-view, possible futures. Good ends-in-view push us to grow.

People must be prepared to accept and utilize this realization of plurality, to give difference a chance, or they will be overwhelmed by it rather than able to utilize it. Only if their capacity of imagination is enlarged and enriched will they be able to cope—only if mind is expanded. As discussed before, mind is the capacity to organize and understand things in terms of a social context. The more pluralistic the society, the more coordination and guidance are necessary. We must form critical and flexible habits of mind so we can guide, expand, and develop the present toward good ends-in-view and enrich the future. This requires a theory of democratic education.

> Democracy has to be born anew every generation, and education is its midwife. Moreover, it is only education which can guarantee widespread community of interest and aim. In a complex society, ability to understand and sympathize with the operations and lot of others is a condition of common purpose which only education can procure. The external differences of pursuit and experience are so very great in our complicated industrial civilization, that men will not see across and through the walls which separate them, unless they have been trained to do so.[44]

We need and can use the plurality and complexity of modern society to promote growth. But this will not happen unless we learn to promote critical and flexible habits of mind. The formation of critical and flexible habits of mind, which makes the formation of good ends-in-view possible, is the task of education.

EDUCATION AND EXPERIMENTATION

Dewey's model of democracy depends on education to form critical and flexible habits of mind. To ask if education is possible is to ask:

> Is it possible to apply intelligence intentionally and systematically to the regulation of life? Is human nature such that it has the capacity for being led along directed paths into any assured realization of all its desirable capacities? Are there any who are wise enough to educate? Are there ends and principles upon which they may depend in attempting the controlled development of others? And, on the other side, is human nature such that it lends itself to, that it is capable of, education into personal and social excellence?[45]

To answer in the negative is to surrender to fate. To answer in the affirmative is to take up the utopian task of shaping the future. It is important to remember that, for Dewey, shaping the future does not involve the execution of some all-encompassing plan, but rather the preparation of individuals for political and social participation.

> Through the making of human beings, of men and women generous in aspiration, liberal in thought, cultivated in taste, and equipped with knowledge and competent method, society itself is constantly remade, and with this remaking the world itself is re-created . . . I do not believe that anyone can accurately predict what the future will bring forth or set up adequate ideals of future society. But in the degree in which education develops individuals into mastery of their own capacities, we must trust these individuals to meet issues as they arise, and to remake the social condition they face into something worthier of man and of life.[46]

Use education to create socially responsible citizens embedded in the method of intelligence and experimentation—this is Dewey's "utopian" plan. He does not prescribe any particular content for education. He does not draw a complete picture of the citizens such education will produce. What he does do is describe education as the means for the development of individuals committed to the method of intelligence—observation, reflection, flexible judgment, and vision.

The only utopian "story" I have found written by Dewey is an essay titled "Dewey Outlines Utopian Schools," which appeared in the *New York Times* on April 23, 1933. In this story he writes from the point of view of a visitor to Utopia. He presents children and adults interacting to gain and develop specific skills, general knowledge, and most importantly a positive and inquisitive attitude toward life. Creativity and inquiry are encouraged. There is hope that by eliminating fear of embarrassment, self-consciousness, and constraint on imagination, they can then work on developing confidence, open-mindedness, and a willingness to tackle problems. Education in Dewey's "utopia" is based on a deep faith in human capacities.[47]

Dewey sees education as a means to encourage the formation of "free men who have learned to think, feel, and act so they can choose their own ends reflectively, with understanding of their nature and consequences. There is no deliberate direction imposed by teachers or others in authority."[48] Dewey does not lay out a master plan for education, but expects that organization and curriculum of schools will change with time, place, and needs as should any institutions if they are to be responsive to our continued growth and development. He says:

> Schools must (1) form proper political habits and ideas; (2) foster the various forms of economic and commercial skill and ability; and (3) develop the traits and disposition of character, intellectual and moral, which fit men and women for self-government, economic self-support and industrial progress; namely, initiative and inventiveness, independence of judgment, ability to think scientifically and to cooperate for common purposes socially. To realize these ends, the mass of citizens must be educated for intellectual participation in the political, economic, and cultural growth of the country, and not simply certain leaders.[49]

He challenges us to begin to experiment with education, "to transform American schools into instruments for the further democratization of American society."[50] It is to be the means of shaping citizens for a changing social order. Its methods and purposes, then, should be critically examined and directed at making "a future such as we desire." Education should be approached as an urgent ongoing experiment.

Because the experimental method is inherently an ongoing process, the means involved in education are as, or more, important than any of the transitory ends we seek to achieve through it. The means inform the ends-in-view and must be consistent with them. Dewey, sensitive to this, criticizes most utopian visions for having a tendency to be rather sketchy on the means of implementation, to require violent overthrow of existing orders, or to rely on manipulation—any one of which Dewey would take exception with. First, as an experiment requires a plan of implementation, preferably one that is flexible and adjusts to contingencies that arise, any vision which does not provide such a plan cannot be seen as consistent with Dewey's method.

Second, any experiment which involves a radical overthrow, violent or otherwise, is not as helpful as controlled change. In order to know which variables are essential to the new situation their effect must be subject to some kind of individual verification. Incremental change would be preferable for Dewey, accompanied by constant evaluation of progress, recognition of changes in purpose, and the willingness to make needed adjustments. Education is an important part of any such change as it "has the potential to bring about the most deep-rooted and far-ranging changes in society, outstripping that of violent revolution, which leaves old habits, such as sexism and racism, unchanged."[51]

Third, if manipulation is necessary, there is the fear that people will become obedient cogs rather than the participating agents necessary for the experimental method to work. The use of the word manipulation seems to imply that some specific behavior is sought and that this, as a goal, is unacceptable. But does not any vision, including Dewey's, have need of some behavior which it must seek to instill? This is often the role given to education, and in Dewey's case it is to instill critical and flexible habits of mind which are to enable us to achieve harmony out of difference.

So what will education consist of for Dewey? How will it form critical and flexible habits of mind? He defines it as the "development of intelligence as a method of action." He says, as do many utopian thinkers, that "it holds the key to orderly social reconstruction."[52] Given that people are inevitably educated and socialized, it makes sense to want to use this process as effectively and beneficially as possible. "Mere activity, blind striving, gets nothing forward. Regulation of conditions . . . is possible only by doing, yet only by doing which has intelligent direction."[53] This implies that education, as an important activity of society, should be intelligently directed. How will this "direction," if it seeks to develop a specific method of action, avoid becoming "manipulation"?

Utopian thinkers usually claim that human nature is a determined and knowable element of human existence and society, not a developmental and changing element of the world. Further, it seems they either make the claim that it is predictable, and we can thereby arrange society to fit it, or they claim human nature is infinitely malleable and we can shape it to fit some preestablished vision of society. In the latter case, education is the manipulative means for forming any specific nature. What must be done is to experiment in order to decide on the best set of habits to develop, and then to determine the best method for developing them. I think this concept of social engineering entails a belief that there is something essential, stable, and knowable about human nature which, when properly studied, allows the engineer to produce the desired habits—whatever they may be. Dewey, who states that we are changing developmental creatures, must escape this essentialist view if he seeks to develop his method of intelligence.

How far is Dewey willing to play with "human nature"? While he argues that we are developmental creatures, does he assume, for the purposes of experimentation, that human nature is a fixed variable, or is it as much a subject of inquiry as the external environment? "But the alleged unchangeableness of human nature cannot be admitted. For while certain needs in human nature are constant, the consequences they produce (because of the existing state of culture—of science, morals, religion, art, industry, legal rules) react back into the original components of human nature to shape them into new forms. The total pattern is thereby modified."[54] Dewey talks about nature, the world and its objects, taking shape in us, taking on form and content only with the live creature's assignment of purposes and problems. The same seems to apply to human nature. Human nature changes with the assignment of different purposes and problems. Given this, it is important to ask who or what formulates the purposes and problems we as "individuals" apparently assign to the world and/or ourselves. He says that "no mechanically exact science of an individual is possible."

> An individual is a history unique in character. But constituents of an individual are known when they are regarded not as qualitative, but as statistical constants derived from a series of operations.
>
> This fact has an obvious bearing on freedom. . . . Freedom is an actuality when the recognition of relations, the stable element, is combined with the uncertain element, in the knowledge which makes foresight possible and secures intentional preparation for probable consequences. We are free in the degree in which we act knowing what we are about.[55]

If we recognize that human nature is neither definitely fixed (and therefore not absolutely predictable) nor infinitely malleable, we will not attempt to control it by domination, but rather through a process of understanding or guidance.

For Dewey, human nature is "essentially" social. This is supported by biology. We are born dependent and in need of education if we are to survive. This means we have needs that constrain our nature but that we are also influenced and formed by the cultures, traditions, and habits in which we are immersed. For Dewey, education should build on our social nature and needs to help us understand our interconnectedness with others and encourage and enable us to create and sustain a flourishing community. "Dewey shows how values can arise and can be inculcated through thoughtful reflection on the conditions of human development. This is done by first recognizing and then appreciating aspects of this process, devising ways to raise to consciousness in all members of society these connections of self with others, and developing means to bring them about."[56]

I think Dewey would find the mistake of many utopian thinkers in their essentialist view, not in their desire to experiment with nature—human and otherwise.

> Unlike many postmodernists, pragmatists believe that mind always involves social control, which can therefore never be bad in itself, though a worse rather than a bet-

ter means of control can be employed and thought control can be used for bad ends. Minds are not disembodied spirits or merely the imagined accompaniment of firing neurons. Instead, they are "the organized habits of intelligent response . . . acquired by putting things to use in connections with the way other persons use things. The control is inescapable; it saturates disposition."[57]

Education is instrumental for Dewey, but it does not serve some predetermined end. Rather it creates an intelligent responsive disposition. It serves to promote the conditions of continued growth and development. "When the school introduces and trains each child of society into membership within such a little community, saturating him with the spirit of service, and providing him with the instruments of effective self-direction, we shall have the deepest and best guarantee of a larger society which is worthy, lovely, and harmonious."[58] Education is to provide the means of self-direction and the instruments of critical experimentation, not to instill specific beliefs or behavior. It does not seek to develop a specific plan of action, but to form the ability in each of us to develop various plans to try out. Education serves anticipation rather than prediction. Our nature is material to act on just as the external world is. Equally, our nature "is a challenge, rather than a completion; it provides possible starting points and opportunities rather than final ends."[59]

THE NEED TO DREAM THE POSSIBLE

Of course, even with socially responsible citizens embedded in the method of intelligence, not all resulting visions will be "acceptable." Some solutions will work better than others, be more satisfactory in one circumstance than in another; some, while helpful, will give rise to new or different problematic situations. This is inherent in the process of experimentation, though, and is not a sufficient reason to reject Dewey's model of democracy as a possible basis for a constructive process model of utopia.

> Since a hypothesis is itself instrumental to inquiry, its verification cannot constitute the whole significance of inquiry.
>
> Hypotheses which have later been rejected have often proved serviceable in discovery of new facts, and thus advanced knowledge. A poor tool is often better than none at all.[60]

We must try to do something. Old ideas often hang on because we have nothing with which to replace them. Here, imagination must fill in and try on new possibilities and critical intelligence must evaluate how well they work.

As we envision the future, we direct the development of our social experience. "Interest and aims, concern and purpose, are necessarily connected. Such words as aim, intent, end, emphasize the *results* which are wanted and striven for. . . . Interest, concern, mean that self and world are engaged with each other in a developing situation."[61] The world, and our experience in it, is a developing situation. Every part of the development must be critically examined. We give shape to what is, and potential to what will be. There can be no disjunction between present and future, means and ends, self and society. We must realize the importance of our participation and accept the responsibility for the futures we choose to pursue. We must realize that the futures pursued direct present activity and that the futures pursued will be the present grounds for the future's future. We must open up our imaginations and examine their content if we are to open up the possibilities of how we will be, if we are to "help get rid of the useless lumber that blocks our highways of thought, and strive to make straight and open the paths that lead to the future."[62]

With Dewey's democracy we learn to critically engage the world we are in, unmake what is problematic, and make it the world we want it to be. "Deliberation . . . is to resolve entanglements in existing activity, restore continuity, recover harmony, utilize loose impulse and redirect habit. . . . Deliberation has its beginning in troubled activity and its conclusion in choice of a course of action which straightens it out."[63] This critical engagement with the world is an endless process of development; it is the capacity for growth. "Democracy has many meanings, but if it has a moral meaning, it is found in resolving that the supreme test of all political institutions and industrial arrangements shall be the contribution they make to the all-around growth of every member of society."[64] This ideal of democracy not only appreciates and encourages our participation in the formation of the future, it requires it. For Dewey, "the good society was, like the good self, a diverse yet harmonious, growing yet unified whole, a fully participatory democracy in which the powers and capacities of the individuals that comprised it were harmonized by their cooperative activities into a community that permitted the full and free expression of individuality."[65]

While Dewey's vision of democracy may seem naively optimistic, its mere expression helps to open up possibilities for the future. Dewey's faith in democracy requires that we have faith in ourselves. It requires that we develop our capacities of critical intelligence and imagination so that we can hope to make a better future. "Dewey was a 'meliorist' — one who believed that although perfection might forever elude us, yet we can by action guided by free creative intelligence make the world better than it is."[66]

Critical reflection and imagination hold the key to making a better future. This method of critical intelligence is just that — a method. As a method it does not, in itself, imply any particular result, but rather a continuum of means and ends. "Democratic ends demand democratic methods for their realization." We must "realize that democracy can be served only by the slow day by day adoption and contagious diffusion in every phase of our common life of methods that are identical with the ends to be reached and that recourse to monistic, wholesale, absolutist procedures is a betrayal of human freedom no matter in what guise it presents itself."[67] There are some means and ends which are incompatible with the spirit of the method. For instance, it is inconsistent to employ the means of revolution or to arrive at fixed and final answers or end-states when employing the method of critical intelligence because such means and ends do not lead to continued growth.[68] Nor does the method of intelligence allow for dogmatic claims or final solutions.

Dewey's vision of democracy helps us imagine certain possibilities for the future. A participatory democracy, inhabited by people with critical and flexible habits of mind, appears to be the necessary ground for a process model of utopia. This may change as individuals and society grow and change, but Dewey seems committed to the belief that this is the necessary next stage in our social evolution. He lays out a vague picture of what this next stage will look like, why we need to strive for it, and how it might be achieved in *The Public and Its Problems*.

DEWEY'S COMMUNITY

While it is the case that Dewey believes democracy to be an ongoing process without a fixed or final end, it is not the case, as we have seen, that he makes no judgments about better and worse forms of association. For Dewey, it is an important fact that as human beings we are born to and dependent on other human beings. We are, from the beginning, associated but it is important to judge the quality of this association.

> There is no sense in asking how individuals come to be associated. They exist and operate in association. . . .
> There is, however, an intelligible question about human association:—Not the question how individuals or singular beings come to be connected, but how they come to be connected in just those ways which give human communities traits so different from those which mark assemblies of electrons, unions of trees in forests, swarms of insects. . . .When we consider the difference we at once come upon the fact that the consequences of conjoint action take on a new value when they are observed. . . . Individuals still do the thinking, desiring and purposing, but what they think of is the consequences of their behavior upon that of others and that of others upon themselves.[69]

No person, or any other being in nature (except perhaps the protozoa) can claim to be an isolated individual. Even the choice to "leave society" is influenced by one's social experience and nurturing. Reproduction, for the human animal, requires association and survival requires extended nurturing. Extended nurturing and caring for other beings, however, appears to distinguish human association from the association of electrons and many other animals and gives it its moral element.[70]

With the recognition of our interdependence we begin to take others into account when making decisions about what to do, how to act, and what to believe. Our behavior is affected by anticipation of the response of others; it is affected by our imagined future states. It is our awareness of our connectedness that allows us to direct our behavior to certain goals, and it is this ability to give intentional direction to our actions that, Dewey believes, makes us different from many other beings in our environment. It is our ability to give direction to our future that makes lived experience possible.

To help guide judgments about forms of association, judgments about the ends-in-view that guide our actions, Dewey's work contains at least five criteria. As we have seen, better forms of association, in Dewey's view:

1. Promote free and open participation by all people in a society in order to help develop critical and flexible habits of mind.
2. Lead people to recognize the limits and possibilities of any particular situation and propose realistic choices for action.
3. Avoid making dogmatic claims and are open to change.
4. Do not narrowly focus on the ends to be achieved, but instead focus on developing abilities that allow for multiple ends to be realistically possible.
5. Open up possibilities and promote an awareness of our interconnectedness and diversity.

In *The Public and Its Problems* Dewey presents a vision of a community that meets these five criteria of worthwhile association—a Great Community. Dewey makes an important distinction between a Great Society and his ideal of a Great Community. He says that we live in a Great Society. Born to and dependent on at least one other human being, we are irrevocably connected and associated with one another. Technology has intensified this connectedness by effectively shrinking the world and increasing our dependency on one another. This association, however, is based on the classical liberal view of the individual and lacks the awareness of our interconnectedness and the resultant consideration of each and every other in the making of decisions and the dreaming of the future. A Great Society fails to be a community because there is no conscious integration of people and their activities. Without an understanding of our interdependence and connectedness, it is not possible for individuals to make informed decisions. They lack the knowledge that would make imagined foresight of the possible consequences of any particular action possible. Without such understanding and foresight it is not possible for people to take control and direct their present toward a desired future.[71]

Dewey believes that since much of the world is no longer divided into local, stable communities where family ties and long-time friendships connect people to one another in a direct and perceivable way, the necessary awareness of our connectedness has been lost. One important reason for this change in the world, this loss of our sense of connectedness, is the presence of the doctrine of individualism. Relishing the liberating effect of the doctrine of individualism, the concomitant loss of community has been overlooked by many. Dewey argues that while the philosophy of individualism is an important and emancipatory doctrine, it has another side which we must face and consequences with which we must deal. The liberating effect of the doctrine of individualism is that it freed individuals from the economic domination of the feudal system, the political domination of arbitrary rule, the spiritual domination of the "church," and the creative domination of superstition and custom.

> The new conditions involved a release of human potentialities previously dormant. While their impact was unsettling to the community, it was liberating with respect to single persons, while its oppressive phase was hidden in the impenetrable mists of the future. . . . Meanwhile the liberating effect was markedly conspicuous with respect to the members of the "middle-class," the manufacturing and mercantile class. It would be shortsighted to limit the release of powers to opportunities to procure wealth and enjoy its fruits, although the creation of material wants and ability to satisfy them are not lightly passed over. Initiative, inventiveness, foresight and planning were also stimulated and confirmed.[72]

The oppressive phase of the doctrine of individualism, however, is to be found, in Dewey's view, in the loss of community. The doctrine of individualism was so caught up in freeing the individual from domination that it attempted to free the individual from association altogether. This is not possible and the belief that it is either possible or desirable has the consequence of obscuring our connectedness from us. Without an awareness of our connectedness, people cannot make responsible and intelligent decisions about their actions, they cannot lead integrated lives, and lived experience becomes impossible.

Lived experience requires an understanding of our connectedness; it requires truly associated living. True association, however, is not simply a matter of being within a family, group, or society. It is a matter of how one is in that family, group, or society. Associated living requires that a person realize that her growth is interdependent with the possibilities of growth for others.

Associated living was thus but another name for "moral democracy," a society in which the good of each was the good of all and the good of all the good of each. "Free and open communication, unself-seeking and reciprocal relationships, and the sort of interaction that contributes to mutual advantage, are the essential factors in associated living." Democracy was the embodiment of the possibilities inherent in social life as such because democratic societies, insofar as they were truly democratic, were held together by consensus rather than force and were dedicated to securing the opportunities for self-development for all the members of the society.[73]

Lived experience, then, is to be a possibility only when one is engaged in the process of associated living, or what Dewey calls community. One can live in society with others and not truly be engaged with them or with one's self. In society where there is no recognized interdependence and interaction—where there is no associated living, no community—there can be no lived experience. As lived experience requires our participation with our environment, associated living is a form of association of individuals who participate with their physical and social environments. To live in community is to be engaged with society. This engagement enables us to make sense of and organize society to some purpose and so move experience forward in a cumulating and fulfilling way. It is by being in community that lived experience becomes possible and intelligent imagination and reflection can be applied to the future.

If there is no community there can be no lived experience. Without the possibility of lived experience all our activity seems disjointed and purposeless and people will tend to be apathetic; without lived experience people cannot "make a future such as we desire." Dewey's way out of this quandary is not to be found in the rejection of the doctrine of individualism, but in re-embedding the individual in society. Such an individual will not be dominated by the community nor disassociated from it. With Dewey's notion of the individual the split between the individual and society will be dispelled and the foundation for community laid.

The problem of the relation of individuals to associations—sometimes posed as the relation of the individual to society—is a meaningless one. We might as well make a problem out of the relation of the letters of an alphabet to the alphabet. An alphabet is letters, and "society" is individuals in their connection with one another.[74]

Dewey wants room for the individual, but he also recognizes the legitimacy of certain common interests. It is not as hard to reconcile the individual and the social for Dewey as it is for classical liberals, because Dewey does not see the individual and society as two essentially distinct, opposing, or dueling entities. Neither authority nor community essentially or necessarily places fetters on individuals. They can do so only if the individuals do not take hold of the authority that is ultimately theirs and participate in forming and directing their community.

Given his notion of the relationship of the individual and community, Dewey can answer many of the concerns (especially feminist concerns) about the classical liberal notion of the individual. On the classical liberal model of the individual there is the individual, the maker of contracts, distinct from the community (or association of individuals). With Thomas Hobbes as its progenitor, the individual springs up as a mushroom—a human object with no relationships, attachments, natural commitments. On the classical liberal model such independent individuals, then, formally contract to form a sphere of relatedness—that is, the public sphere.

The main characteristics of this contracting individual are impartiality and rationality. The resulting public sphere is a place where rational, impartial judgment is sought and prized. This is liberation to the degree that prejudice, tradition, and habit are to be replaced by critical thought. Such impartiality is, however, a myth. The individuals involved in the forming of the contract are born and brought up in the private sphere which the classical liberal model characterizes as partial and irrational—ruled by emotion and habit rather than reasoned, critical thought. Since people do not spring up like mushrooms, the private sphere cannot be ignored or made the antipathy of all rational individuals, the receptacle of all evil. Ultimately, there is no isolated individual so no individual–society split, no private–public split.

The individual is an associated social creature prior to any formal contract. The more abstract and impartial public sphere cannot exist separately from the connected and partial private sphere. Most feminists challenge the myth of the isolated individual in much the same way that Dewey does. Charlotte Perkins Gilman, for instance, says:

> Altruism was born of babyhood. The continued existence of the child—of a succession of children; the permanent presence of helplessness and its irresistible demands for care; this forced us into a widening of the sympathies, a deepening of the sensitiveness to others needs; this laid the foundations of human love.[75]

If we forget that our physical origin is inherently social we get a skewed view of the relationship between individuals and society. If we get too carried away with the individual as being free from associations, our sense of connectedness becomes hidden, and lived experience becomes impossible. Instead, life appears as a series of disjointed experiences with little continuity or purpose. Community requires a balance of perspective. One needs a sense of being an individual—an individual capable of experiencing, judging, acting. This individual, however, is socially embedded, socially constituted, and must try to remain attentive to its context.

Dewey calls for the recovery of the "unified individual"—an individual attentive to its context. This is an individual who acts more than it is acted upon; it is involved in, and responsible for, its own creation. It is not thrown around by any "natural forces," but uses such forces with intelligence and purpose. Using education to teach individuals to be critical and constructive, by giving them a role to play in formulating their own direction, one obtains an ethic of social responsibility consistent with the individual. Dewey demands that individuals be educated to take hold of their lives and prepared for rational participation in the creation of their communities.[76] Such preparation requires an education that leads to flexible habits of mind.

> The moral is to develop conscientiousness, ability to judge the significance of what we are doing and to use that judgment in directing what we do, not by means of direct cultivation of something called conscience, or reason, or a faculty of moral knowledge, but by fostering those impulses and habits which experience has shown to make us sensitive, generous, imaginative. . . . Every attempt to forecast the future is subject in the end to the auditing of present concrete impulse and habit. Therefore the important thing is the fostering of those habits and impulses which lead to a broad, just, sympathetic survey of situations.[77]

For Dewey, there is no primacy to either the individual or society. The best that can be hoped for is socially embedded individuals capable of sympathy with others as well as independent and critical thought.

If this all sounds familiar, it should. What has been described here is an individual immersed in the method of democracy. With the recovery of the "unified individual," we have the democratic individual—an individual with critical and flexible habits of mind involved in a social task. Getting past the idea of isolated individuals, and beyond a mere aggregate of individuals into a society, we approach the possibility of community—integrated individuals acting conjointly with intelligence and foresight. On Dewey's view, the possibility of moving from a Great Society to a Great Community depends on our increased capacity for communication.

Since the democratic individuals are to participate in the creation and direction of their communities—government, work, family, religion—they must have means of participation consistent with the end-in-view of extending democracy to "affect all modes of human association."[78] Democracy does not require any particular means of communication (that is, a certain range of suffrage, a certain frequency of elections, a congressional versus a parliamentary order), but it does require that whatever means are chosen, these means should be seen as particular tools that serve particular needs.[79]

> But there is no a priori rule which can be laid down and by which when it is followed a good state will be brought into existence. In no two ages or places is there the same

public. Conditions make the consequences of associated action and the knowledge of them different. In addition the means by which a public can determine the government to serve its interests vary. Only formally can we say what the best state would be. In concrete fact, in actual and concrete organization and structure, there is no form of state which can be said to be the best: not at least till history is ended, and one can survey all its varied forms. The formation of states must be an experimental process.[80]

For example, democracy is not pursued for the sake of achieving free and open elections, but free and open elections are employed as a means for promoting people to participate in their own governing. Elections are tools to promote self-governance and must not come to be seen as an end in themselves. Unless there is constant communication amongst the people of a community, however, it is highly probable that ends-in-view, that is, free and open elections, will come to be seen as ultimate ends. People will forget why they pursued free and open elections as opposed to a monied aristocracy. They will take an end-in-view to be an end and forget that what they pursue now is not really an end but a means for future pursuits. One example of this happening was the drive for women's suffrage. Focusing on gaining the vote, the goals of economic independence, equal education and employment opportunities, and equal standing under the law were put aside. Without the concomitant achievement of these goals, the vote would change little. Focusing on one specific goal can have the effect of pushing into the background other, equally important, goals.

When some end-in-view is pursued as an end, it is likely that some particular point of view will come to dominate the articulation of interests and alternate possibilities will be lost to view. As the end becomes the driving purpose of the community, the interrelatedness of means and ends will be overlooked and the questions of means will seem tangential at best. People whose interests are not being addressed by the pursuit of this end will feel alienated from the community, will become apathetic, and will stop participating. The community will become a mere association with authoritarian control.[81] How can the foundation for community be laid? Can it be laid so that the risk of community disintegrating into mere association is minimized?

A PICTURE OF COMMUNITY

On Dewey's view, democracy, as a method of living, is the necessary method for achieving community. Critical engagement and participation by the citizens of any given society is a choice. It is "a choice, amid a complex of contending forces, of that particular possibility which appears to promise the most good with the least attendant evil."[82] Democracy is not the only or final choice, but a choice presented by present conditions to make true community a viable present and future possibility.

One strong reason Dewey believes democracy makes sense, at least his ideal of democracy, is that it fosters choice and experimentation. It is a method of experimentation applied to social concerns. It gives guidance to experience while remaining open to alternatives and change. It is less a state than it is a method.

> We have every reason to think that whatever changes may take place in existing democratic machinery, they will be of a sort to make the interest of the public a more supreme guide and criterion of governmental activity, and to enable the public to form and manifest its purposes still more authoritatively. In this sense the cure for the ailments of democracy is more democracy. The prime difficulty as we have seen, is that of discovering the means by which a scattered, mobile and manifold public may so recognize itself as to define and express its interests.[83]

A distinguishing characteristic of communities, then, one way of separating them from mere associations, is the evident and effective participation of the public. Why should such participation be seen as a good thing, though? Why should it be believed that "the public" will know what is in "its" best interest? Is the decision to be regarded as just or good simply because it is the result of a democratic procedure? Will it be good for the people just because they were involved in making the choice? Yes and no. While such participation is a necessary condition for community, it is not sufficient to guarantee a healthy, intelligent, or desirable community.

To achieve a Great Community there are some restrictions placed on what counts as healthy interaction and some requirements placed on what counts as constructive participation. As community requires effective communication to sustain participation, a healthy, intelligent, and desirable community must foster the conditions for effective communication. "Interactions, transactions, occur de facto and the results of interdependence follow. But participation in activities and sharing in results are additive concerns. They demand communication as a prerequisite."[84] According to Dewey, the attempt to share experiences, desires, and concerns through some set of shared meanings is a continuous process that, while ongoing, is never finished or foolproof. There will always be room to miscommunicate or fail to communicate, but that does not mean the community must cease to be because of this imperfection. At such a moment the community is not fully integrated, but it still exists if it is positioned to reestablish discourse. It is being associated in such a way as to make the attempt at communication possible and urgent that is important.

It is important to be associated in ways that promote and encourage communication rather than discourage or put an end to such interaction. For an example of a less than satisfactory form of association Dewey uses a robber band. A more contemporary example might be a drug gang. Internally, there can be little cohesiveness because there is little ground for trust. Without trust it is difficult for the group to work together toward a common goal. If, however, there is achieved some semblance of identifiable common interest, the members can direct their actions to serve this interest, but only if they are willing to give up a multitude of other possibilities that could be achieved by acting in or with other groups. While it is the case that one must often choose between mutually exclusive interests, the problem with the drug gang is that membership in the drug gang excludes one from the possibility of membership in a variety of other groups. While an integrated individual recognizes and is able to reconcile multiple memberships (for example, parent, child, work, hobby, religious order, political party), the member of the drug gang is a disintegrated individual who is isolated from her potential by virtue of the drug gang's need for secrecy and isolation from large parts of society. The member of the drug gang needs to hide her affiliation in order to be part of other forms of association. The drug gang, like Dewey's robber band, "cannot interact flexibly with other groups; it can act only through isolating itself."

It must prevent the operation of all interests save those which circumscribe it in its separateness. But a good citizen finds his conduct as a member of a political group enriching and enriched by his participation in family life, industry, scientific and artistic associations. There is a free give-and-take: fullness of integrated personality is therefore possible of achievement since the pulls and responses of different groups reinforce one another and their values accord.[85]

What differentiates community from mere association or society is the mutual recognition of the needs of individuals and the groups in which they participate. A Great Community will be evidenced by the integrated personality of each of its members and the consciously conjoint activity of these individuals toward a common goal. There is an awareness that the potential of individuals is increased when they have a share in a cohesive community and the potential of each group is increased when it is arranged so as to encourage the growth of the individuals through participation in the formation of the common interest (that is, through participating in the choice of a particular end-in-view).

There is a further complication, however. A community is not made up directly of individuals in conjoint activity. It is made up of individuals in a multiple of groups with each group consisting of individuals participating in a common project. It is necessary to integrate the groups' interests so that an individual's involvement in a variety of groups does not lead to irreconcilable conflicts. "Since every individual is a member of many groups, this specification cannot be fulfilled except when different groups interact flexibly and fully in connection with other groups."[86] Not only does community require individuals with flexible habits of mind and the recognition of their interconnectedness—the democratic individual—it requires groups with flexible habits and boundaries and the awareness of their interconnectedness—the democratic society.[87]

> Whenever there is conjoint activity whose consequences are appreciated as good by all singular persons who take part in it, and where the realization of the good is such as to effect an energetic desire and effort to sustain it in being just because it is a good shared by all, there is in so far a community. The clear consciousness of a communal life, in all its implications, constitutes the idea of democracy.[88]

While Dewey's view of democracy is an ideal which has no end-state to be achieved, the process of democracy can be instantiated only when community is a reality.

Because democracy requires community, and community requires conscious conjoint activity, it follows that democracy requires conscious conjoint activity. Such activity is possible only when people combine their various talents and skills to achieve an agreed-upon goal. If all individuals in a community were alike, conjoint activity would not be possible. Community, and so democracy, relies on people being different—having different skills, interests, beliefs. Democracy requires that individuals recognize and respect differences as being what make conjoint action possible, interesting, and fruitful. The ideal of democracy requires that people interact in ways that do not result in either the mere aggregation of different individuals and groups or in the suppression of difference under one dominant individual or group. Instead we must learn to handle difference constructively and make it the basis for community.

Community, then, requires ongoing education. Dewey says that we must learn to be human. Human creatures are born already associated, but not as functioning members of a community. We are not born respecting and appreciating differences. We are not born thinking of the wants and needs of others as being integral to our own wants and needs. Every child must learn to be Dewey's "unified individual," recognizing our interconnectedness and acting in light of this with intelligence and foresight.

> To learn to be human is to develop through the give-and-take of communication an effective sense of being an individually distinctive member of a community; one who understands and appreciates its beliefs, desires and methods, and who con-

tributes to a further conversion of organic powers into human resources and values. But this translation is never finished.[89]

The lifetime of every individual is (or ought to be) spent learning; it is spent experimenting with communicating with others "so that genuinely shared interest in consequences of interdependent activities may inform desire and effort and thereby direct action."[90] Each person must develop and continually sustain the sense of being an individual in a community, and Dewey's education is the necessary condition for developing and sustaining this sense of self.

A Great Community cannot be achieved overnight; in fact it can never be achieved in totality. There will always be people at a variety of stages of consciousness of their interconnectedness and people more and less able to act on this awareness. Given the developmental nature of the human organism it will never be the case that either individual or conjoint action will proceed with perfect understanding of the consequences for the future. There is no procedure for decision making that can ensure the best, or even good decisions will be made. Not only are there people at a variety of stages involved in decisions, but also each individual tends to resist change. The lag time between an individual changing a belief or desire and the same individual acting on this changed conception of her/himself will be reflected in a lag in group action. "Nevertheless, changes take place and are cumulative in character. Observation of them in the light of their recognized consequences arouses reflection, discovery, invention, experimentation. . . . But there is a marked lag in any corresponding change of ideas and desires. Habits of opinion are the toughest of all habits."[91]

Dewey acknowledges that we are creatures of habit as much as or more than we are rational creatures. The only way to combat the habit of being dogmatic, close-minded, or disintegrated is to develop and sustain the habit of free and open inquiry into all matters with the concomitant commitment to act without being closed to revising both the means and ends of one's action.

Pragmatism, a faith in intelligence, carries no overarching or advance guarantees. It provides no specific assurances about the future existence or expansion of democratic life. Indeed, it provides no general warrant for any complacent expectation of progress. It finds nothing in human history, human nature, or the world situation today to support a rosy or comfortable vision of the future. Such mistaken visions merely treat present hopes as future realities. This faith in community, then, supports neither utopian thinking nor even optimism in the abstract.[92]

This freedom of inquiry is not a habit developed for any abstract purpose— utopian in the traditional end-state sense. Deweyan inquiry is to guide concrete action. We must constantly challenge our social habits with critical imagination and experimentation, trying out ideas and examining the results. We must not trust the future to fate (end-state visions) or rely on simple trial and error (anarchist visions). We must critically examine the past, the present, and the possibilities of the future and act with intelligence and foresight. This means thinking things through, acting on our conclusions, and revising our theories. Above all it means accepting responsibility for ourselves and our world.

THE POSSIBILITY OF COMMUNITY

We have but touched lightly and in passing upon the conditions which must be fulfilled if the Great Society is to become a Great Community; a society in which the ever-expanding and intricately ramifying consequences of associated activities shall be known in the full sense of that word, so that an organized, articulate Public comes into being. . . . Democracy will come into its own, for democracy is a name for a life of free and enriching communion. . . . It will have its consummation when free social inquiry is indissolubly wedded to the art of full and moving communication.[93]

If a Great Community requires critical and flexible habits of mind in constant inquiry and experimentation in regard to their individual and social conditions, is it a realistic end-in-view? Does it ask too much of people? Is it able to meet Dewey's own criteria for a desirable end-in-view? As an end-in-view a Great Community does promote free and open participation by all people in a society, developing critical and flexible habits of mind. The whole idea of community is that of integrated individuals, with the realization of their embeddedness, participating in the formation and direction of individual and conjoint action. Such participation will lead to the realization that the future can be chosen, within parameters. Some critics, such as Sidney Hook, believe that Dewey may assign too much of a sense of agency to individuals, forgetting that most often one does not choose, and has little control over, one's circumstances. I believe Dewey acknowledges that circumstances and environment constrain one's possibilities, but he pushes people not to become passive recipients of their future but rather to remain active agents in their respective situations.[94] This responsibility should prompt people to develop and practice their critical skills so as to achieve a desirable future.

As an end-in-view the idea of a Great Community avoids making dogmatic claims and leaves people open to the possibility of change. Community depends on free and open inquiry—on the experimental method. This limits the possibilities of the community, or any individual or group within it, to make claims about having the only right belief about any subject. It also limits the possibilities for the community to get stuck in some habit of organizing and running itself because it is seen as the right way. A Great Community does not promote an end-state—an arrangement which once reached will function once and for all. Rather, community consists in a process of individuals interacting with one another. Any particular stage of such a process may vary greatly from another stage.

As an end-in-view the idea of a Great Community does not promote any particular end. Its main focus is on promoting the development of abilities that allow for multiple ends to be realistically possible. As there is no way to predict the particular needs of the future, the community prepares people in the method of critical intelligence. In this way, not only can the most immediate ends-in-view be evaluated and achieved, but so can any future ends-in-view be evaluated and achieved.[95]

As an end-in-view the idea of a Great Community opens up possibilities and promotes an awareness of our interconnectedness and diversity. The community is both the ground for and the result of our awareness of our interconnectedness. The continued functioning of the community, and its possible flourishing, relies on and promotes our continued consciousness of our embeddedness and the use of this knowledge to direct our present actions and to choose intelligently for the future.

The question remains, however: Does the idea of a Great Community meet Dewey's remaining criteria for a good end-in-view? In particular, does it recognize the limits and possibilities of our particular situatedness in a Great Society and lead to realistic choices for action? Does it ask too much of people? The idea of a Great Community will not be an effective guide to action as long as the notion of the isolated, disintegrated individual has a hold on imagination, policy, and practice. If the idea of a Great Community is to meet this final criterion of a good end-in-view, it must face up to the need to reconstruct the notion of the unified individual and propose a realistic method for achieving this reconstruction.

Dewey proposes that the unified individual can be recovered by reflective investigation and education. Reflective investigation of our situatedness will lead to the realization that neither the individual nor society is primary, but that the activities of individuals and the associations they are in are inseparable. People "are in the concrete what they are, their beliefs and purposes included, because of the social medium in which they live; that they are influenced throughout by contemporary and transmitted culture, whether in conformity or protest."[96] Awareness of our embeddedness frees our critical powers and gives us the necessary ground for being effective in directing our future. Reflective investigation provides the basis for such an awareness. Education, then, must promote and sustain reflective investigation.

One place Dewey presents a method for structuring such investigation and developing the needed democratic citizens is in *Logic: The Theory of*

Inquiry. Here, he argues that a person becomes a knowing subject, an organism capable of directing its future when it engages in controlled inquiry. "Inquiry is the controlled or directed transformation of an indeterminate situation into . . . a unified whole."[97] Such inquiry requires a recognition of the continuity and connectedness of live creatures and their environment, and of each experience to possible future experience. "The process of inquiry reflects and embodies the experiential continuum which is established by both biological and cultural conditions. Every special inquiry is . . . a process of progressive and cumulative re-organization of antecedent conditions."[98] In order to use prior experiences and judgments in directing the future, people must agree to standards and methods for testing and verifying the conclusions they have reached. As in scientific inquiry, social inquiry needs a community in agreement as to methods so conclusions can be verified and future inquiry given intelligent direction and foresight. It is this sense of inquiry that Dewey seeks to embody in his theory of education.

Education must not try to perpetuate the present or achieve a particular closed and static future state. Either goal limits education to a particular end and so then to limited means. This means the future has more limited options than if critical and experimental reflection were the means and end of education. Education should be seen as a process, not as an end in itself, or simply as a tool. It is an enabler. It is to enable people to become the critical thinkers they are capable of being. By immersing people in a task, in the process of resolving conflicts, critical intelligence and imagination will be called into action. Then they can be directed toward an understanding of their embeddedness and encouraged to participate in forming and directing their future. Education must perpetuate social conditions that encourage and prepare people to be involved in decision making. They must not bow to experts, or defer to authority, but participate intelligently in the decisions that affect their lives.

> Until secrecy, prejudice, bias, misrepresentation, and propaganda as well as sheer ignorance are replaced by inquiry and publicity, we have no way of telling how apt for judgment of social policies the existing intelligence of the masses may be. . . . No matter what are the differences in native intelligence (allowing for the moment that intelligence can be native), the actuality of mind is dependent upon the education which social conditions effect.[99]

People must learn how to see their opinions as opinions rather than the only right choice and remain open to discussing and consulting with others to achieve a joint need or desire. In other words, education must foster open and flexible habits of mind. How can human beings, creatures who prefer habitual sameness to radical change, be encouraged to remain open and flexible when faced with momentous decisions about their present and future lives? Is education enough of a safeguard?

Dewey proposes that in addition to this active education we need to return to smaller face-to-face communities. If people are to be deeply aware of their interconnectedness to the point that it forces them to honestly consider views different from their own and prompts them to consult with those with whom they disagree, they need to recover that sense of direct accountability, reciprocity, and continuity with others.

> In its deepest and richest sense a community must always remain a matter of face-to-face intercourse. This is why the family and neighborhood, with all their deficiencies, have always been the chief agencies of nurture, the means by which dispositions are stably formed and ideas acquired which laid hold on the roots of character. . . . Vital and thorough attachments are bred only in the intimacy of an intercourse which is of necessity restricted in range.[100]

Dewey does not draw a picture of any particular community or of a Great Community. Instead he tells us what he thinks can be accomplished with such an end-in-view.

With the idea of a Great Community as an end-in-view Dewey believes that we will be encouraged to develop critical and flexible habits of mind. He believes that we will become immersed in social inquiry, recognize our embeddedness, and become engaged in directing our future. For a Great Community to be a realistic end-in-view, however, for it to be an end-in-view that can prompt us to action rather than despair and apathy, we must realize, and satisfy to some extent, the need for deep and close connections with others. With our interconnectedness in the local community a daily reality rather than an abstract ideal or fantasy, Dewey believes we will be prepared to see our interconnectedness to those we have never seen. As with the anarchist vision, it is only with the bonds at the local level firmly established that we can effectively move to the global or universal notion of embeddedness and responsibility. The notion of a Great Community requires local community.

> The chances of regard for distant peoples being effective as long as there is no close neighborhood experience to bring with it insight and understanding of neighbors do not seem better. A man who has not been seen in the daily relations of life may inspire admiration, emulation, servile subjection, fanatical partisanship, hero worship; but not love and understanding, save as they radiate from the attachments of a near-by union. Democracy must begin at home, and its home is the neighborly community.[101]

How we will return to local face-to-face communities is not spelled out in Dewey. Nor is there any particular prescription for how each community should be organized. Each community will probably be different, with different goals, lifestyles, organization. There are to be found in Dewey, however, both some prescriptions and proscriptions for communities. As with ends-in-view, just because we cannot detail what they will be does not mean there are no guidelines. The guidelines for a desirable community are the same as the guidelines for a good end-in-view, for that is what a community is—an end-in-view.

A good community takes account of its resources and the abilities of its members, and proposes realistic goals and means for reaching those goals. Such a community, recognizing the limits and possibilities of the situation, is then in a position to work on fine-tuning its members' abilities and on developing new abilities. Rather than just focusing on achieving certain ends, such a community will focus on developing abilities that will make a variety of different ends-in-view realistic possibilities. In order to remain open to such a variety of possible ends-in-view, a good community must avoid making dogmatic claims about their purposes and remain open to change. This means they must be willing to reevaluate both their ends and means and be open to changing either one or both. In other words, a good local community can be identified by its flexible habits and boundaries. Certain kinds of community will fail to meet these criteria. Certain kinds of communities will be internally unhealthy and fail to contribute to the possibility of a Great Community; for instance, a local group of white supremacists is an association that serves neither itself well nor the ideal of a Great Community.

To achieve and maintain the necessary flexible attitude, communities must encourage their individual members to develop a sense of their interconnectedness and sustain the flexible habits of mind characteristic of Dewey's unified or democratic individual. A good community promotes free and open participation by all members of that community. White supremacists do not. Such a group ignores and/or denigrates the abilities of whole segments of the population. They seek to eliminate people different from themselves. This desired homogeneity limits the possibilities of the present and the future. Such an arrangement wastes existing talent and fails to encourage further development. It fails to recognize our interdependence, our need to be challenged, and the desirability of growth. This limits the number and character of the ends-in-view the community can realistically pursue. Such a group also encourages fixed and dogmatic habits of mind. By focusing on the supremacy of the white race as an established fact, dogmatism comes to rule over reason. Ends become established, are not open to reevaluation or change, and all manner of means come to be acceptable insofar as they promote the desired future state.

Similarly, it can be argued that patriarchal social arrangements stunt human growth and development. Gilman argues, for instance:

The whole position is simple and clear; and easily traceable to its root. Given a pro-prietary family, where the man holds the woman primarily for his satisfaction and service—then necessarily he shuts her up and keeps her for these purposes. Being so kept, she cannot develop humanly, as he has, through social contact, social service, true social life. . . . Thus checked in social development, we have but a low grade motherhood to offer our children; and the children reared in the primitive conditions thus artificially maintained, enter life with a false perspective, not only toward men and women, but toward life as a whole.[102]

The idea is that subordination to and dependence on another is a perverse re-lationship which adversely affects both the one in power and the one who is disempowered. Patriarchy results in a relationship of dependence which per-verts men by promoting in them a sense of power and a habit of command-ing obedience to their desires. With such power there is no impetus to see that their needs and desires involve the needs and desires of others.

The familial and social arrangements which result from a patriarchal struc-ture promote in women and children obedience and submission rather than self-governing thought and activity. Patriarchy, then, frustrates the develop-ment of democratic citizens. Social arrangements should be such that all peo-ple are encouraged to participate in social tasks so as to develop their critical skills and realize their embeddedness. This participation is the basis for de-veloping democratic citizens. Patriarchy, then, is not a basis for developing democracy.

While Dewey's theory implicitly recognizes and critiques racism and sex-ism (as seen above), he does not adequately address how such systems of op-pression impact the daily lives of the members of the targeted groups. Racism and sexism are not simply encountered as ideas or attitudes. They are en-countered in everyday lived experience. Dewey believes participation helps to develop critical and flexible habits of mind. In a local community, how-ever, encouraging participation by all members of the community may entail encouraging the participation of people who have not yet developed critical and flexible habits of mind—people who do not yet realize their embedded-ness. As was discussed in regard to the anarchist model, people with deep-seated prejudice, chauvinism, hate, or bigotry will be encouraged to put forth their views before they have developed the critical attitudes which will help them to be open to compromise and change. Blinded by emotion, or bound by habit, they will be unable to achieve the necessary critical attitude and people will suffer for this in concrete ways. This will happen on the level of a Great Community too, but then the effects will be more diffuse. On the level of the local community, however, such close-mindedness will have a direct impact on other members of the community and may close down communication or lead to violence. Dewey's call for the formation of face-to-face communities could be problematic because he does not fully acknowledge that many people do not have the power or ability to fully participate in an open, critical, and flexible community.

C. Wright Mills criticizes Dewey's nostalgia for the local community. He sees this as an escape to a simplistic view of reality that covers up the daily reality, for most people, of being a powerless cog in a corporate world. Mills agrees with Dewey that democracy needs to be part of people's everyday lives—exercised at work and home—but he does not believe Dewey has got a realistic method in the call to return to smaller communities.[103] There is something to this critique. It is a critique raised by feminists addressing communitarian theory in general. The worry is that without uncovering and addressing inequality and oppression, the return to face-to-face communities will result in more intolerance and more restriction. Feminist critiques of community raise an important challenge for Dewey's model of democracy. Feminist theory also reinvigorates the discussion of utopia. So now we turn to a discussion of feminism, pragmatism, community, and utopia.

NOTES

1. John Dewey, "Challenge to Liberal Thought," in *John Dewey: The Later Works, Vol. 15: 1942–1948,* ed. Jo Ann Boydston (Carbondale: Southern Illinois University Press, 1989), 273.

2. John Dewey, "Creative Democracy: The Task Before Us," in *John Dewey: The Later Works, Vol. 14: 1939–1941,* ed. Jo Ann Boydston (Carbondale: Southern Illinois University Press, 1988), 228.

3. Justice Holmes, quoted in John Dewey, *Experience and Nature,* in *John Dewey: The Later Works, Vol. 1: 1925,* ed. Jo Ann Boydston (Carbondale: Southern Illinois University Press, 1981), 312.

4. John Dewey, *Art as Experience,* in *John Dewey: The Later Works, Vol. 10: 1934,* ed. Jo Ann Boydston (Carbondale: Southern Illinois University Press, 1987) 177.

5. Thomas M. Alexander, *John Dewey's Theory of Art, Experience, and Nature: The Horizons of Feeling* (New York: SUNY Press, 1987), 260–261.

6. John Dewey, *The Quest for Certainty,* in *John Dewey: The Later Works, Vol. 4: 1929,* ed. Jo Ann Boydston (Carbondale: Southern Illinois University Press, 1984), 218.

7. John Dewey, "Changed Conceptions of Experience and Reason," in *John Dewey: The Middle Works, Vol. 12: 1920,* ed. Jo Ann Boydston (Carbondale: Southern Illinois University Press, 1982), 134.

8. Dewey, *The Quest for Certainty,* 218.

9. Michael Eldridge, *Transforming Experience: John Dewey's Cultural Instrumentalism* (Nashville, Tenn.: Vanderbilt University Press, 1998), 41.

10. There are utopian visions which appear to see science as the problem and eschew all forms of critical investigation. Agrarian visions, such as William Morris's *News From Nowhere* (New York: Penguin Books, 1986), do blame science and technology for prob-

lems such as social alienation and destruction of the environment. Such visions, however, do not deny the possibility of the intelligent use of science and technology. Rather, they serve to point out the danger of allowing science to go unchecked or undirected. Scientific inquiry, without intelligent investigation of its goals and methods, is dangerous and is exactly what Dewey is trying to stop. It is not now a realistic option to do away with science and technology—such visions are fantasy. Utopian vision, grounded in the possibilities of the present and the constraints of the situation, must instead try to give science intelligent direction.

11. John Dewey, *Human Nature and Conduct,* in *John Dewey: The Middle Works, Vol. 14: 1922,* ed. Jo Ann Boydston (Carbondale: Southern Illinois University Press, 1983), 138.

12. Alexander, *John Dewey's Theory of Art,* 276.

13. Alexander, *John Dewey's Theory of Art,* 101.

14. Alexander, *John Dewey's Theory of Art,* 101.

15. Marie Louise Berneri, *Journey Through Utopia* (London: Routledge & Kegan Paul, 1950), 8.

16. John Dewey, *Experience and Nature,* in *John Dewey: The Later Works, Vol. 1: 1925,* ed. Jo Ann Boydston (Carbondale: Southern Illinois University Press, 1981), 86.

17. John Dewey, *Democracy and Education,* in *John Dewey: The Middle Works, Vol. 9: 1916,* ed. Jo Ann Boydston (Carbondale: Southern Illinois University Press, 1980), 110.

18. Dewey, *Democracy and Education,* 137.

19. Alexander, *John Dewey's Theory of Art,* 124.

20. John Dewey, "Nationalizing Education," in *John Dewey: The Middle Works, Vol. 10: 1916–1917,* ed. Jo Ann Boydston (Carbondale: Southern Illinois University Press, 1980), 204.

21. Dewey, *Experience and Nature,* 280.

22. Dewey, *The Quest for Certainty,* 80–81.

23. Dewey, *Art as Experience,* 22.

24. Dewey, "Creative Democracy," 229.

25. Dewey, *Democracy and Education,* 24.

26. Robert B. Westbrook, *John Dewey and American Democracy* (Ithaca, N.Y.: Cornell University Press, 1991), 309.

27. John Dewey, "Culture and Human Nature," in *John Dewey: The Later Works, Vol. 13: 1938–1939,* ed. Jo Ann Boydston (Carbondale: Southern Illinois University Press, 1988), 90.

28. Westbrook, *John Dewey,* 245.

29. Joseph Betz, in his article "John Dewey and Paulo Freire," compares the educational theories of Paulo Freire, a Brazilian philosopher whose work focuses on the education of the oppressed, and John Dewey. He says, "As does Dewey, Freire stressed that the authentically educated new individual comes into being with the new society, but the two authors differ in emphasis. For Freire it is a liberated individual coming into existence with a revolutionary society. For Dewey it is a developed individual coming into existence in a participatory society. But Dewey's explanation is more basic, for what makes Freire's individual liberated is the development of Dewey's powers and what makes Freire's society revolutionary and good is Dewey's participation of all" (*Transactions* 28 [Winter 1992], 117).

30. Dewey, "Human Nature and Conduct," 160.

31. John Dewey, "The Economic Basis of the New Society," in *John Dewey: The Later Works, Vol. 13: 1938–1939*, ed. Jo Ann Boydston (Carbondale: Southern Illinois University Press, 1988), 321.

32. Dewey, " The Economic Basis of the New Society," 321.

33. John Dewey, "Reconstruction in Moral Conceptions," in *John Dewey: The Middle Works, Vol. 12: 1920*, ed. Jo Ann Boydston (Carbondale: Southern Illinois University Press, 1982), 181.

34. Another way to put this: "The one thing constant in education is that the habit of successfully reconstructing serviceable habits which have broken down can and should be learned. Only such a second-order habit will endure because the first-order habits will eventually find themselves invalidated by time" (Betz, "John Dewey and Paulo Freire," 119).

35. Dewey, *Democracy and Education*, 111.

36. Dewey, *Democracy and Education*, 112.

37. Dewey, *Democracy and Education*, 112.

38. Dewey, *Democracy and Education*, 122–123.

39. John Dewey, *Ethics*, in *John Dewey: The Middle Works, Vol. 5: 1908*, ed. Jo Ann Boydston (Carbondale: Southern Illinois University Press, 1978), 389.

40. Westbrook, *John Dewey*, 347.

41. Dewey, *Ethics*, 389.

42. Dewey, *Democracy and Education*, 61.

43. Dewey, *Democracy and Education*, 93.

44. John Dewey, "The Need of an Industrial Education in an Industrial Democracy," in *John Dewey: The Middle Works, Vol. 10: 1916–1917*, ed. Jo Ann Boydston (Carbondale: Southern Illinois University Press, 1980), 139.

45. John Dewey, "Philosophy and Education," in *John Dewey: The Later Works, Vol. 5: 1929–1930*, ed. Jo Ann Boydston (Carbondale: Southern Illinois University Press, 1984), 290.

46. Dewey, "Philosophy and Education," 297.

47. John Dewey, "Dewey Outlines Utopian Schools," in *John Dewey: The Later Works, Vol. 9: 1933–1934*, ed. Jo Ann Boydston (Carbondale: Southern Illinois University Press, 1986), 136–140.

48. Ralph Ross, "Introduction," in *John Dewey: The Middle Works, Vol. 13: 1921–1922*, ed. Jo Ann Boydston (Carbondale: Southern Illinois University Press, 1983), xv.

49. John Dewey, "Report and Recommendation upon Turkish Education," in *John Dewey: The Middle Works, Vol. 15: 1923–1924*, ed. Jo Ann Boydston (Carbondale: Southern Illinois University Press, 1983), 275.

50. Westbrook, *John Dewey*, 109.

51. Charlene Haddock Seigfried, *Pragmatism and Feminism: Reweaving the Social Fabric* (Chicago: University of Chicago Press, 1996), 58.

52. Dewey, *The Quest for Certainty*, 201.

53. Dewey, *The Quest for Certainty*, 29.

54. John Dewey, "Democracy and Human Nature," in *John Dewey: The Later Works, Vol. 13: 1938–1939*, ed. Jo Ann Boydston (Carbondale: Southern Illinois University Press, 1988), 142.

55. Dewey, *The Quest for Certainty*, 199.

56. Seigfried, *Pragmatism and Feminism*, 97.

57. Seigfried, *Pragmatism and Feminism*, 98.

58. John Dewey, "The School and Social Progress," in *John Dewey: The Middle Works, Vol. 1: 1899–1901*, ed. Jo Ann Boydston (Carbondale: Southern Illinois University Press, 1976), 19–20.

59. Dewey, *The Quest for Certainty*, 81.

60. Dewey, *The Quest for Certainty*, 152–153.

61. Dewey, *Democracy and Education*, 131–132.

62. John Dewey, "From Absolutism to Experimentalism," in *John Dewey: The Later Works, Vol. 5: 1929–1930*, ed. Jo Ann Boydston (Carbondale: Southern Illinois University Press, 1984), 160.

63. Dewey, *Human Nature and Conduct*, 139.

64. Dewey, "Reconstruction in Moral Conceptions," 186.

65. Westbrook, *John Dewey*, 164.

66. Murray Murphey, "Introduction," in *John Dewey: The Middle Works, Vol. 14: 1922*, ed. Jo Ann Boydston (Carbondale: Southern Illinois University Press, 1983), xxi.

67. John Dewey, "Democracy and America," in *John Dewey: The Later Works, Vol. 13: 1938–1939*, ed. Jo Ann Boydston (Carbondale: Southern Illinois University Press, 1988), 187.

68. Again, Dewey does not rule out the possibility that violent revolution may appear to be the only effective means of defeating oppression, but he cautions that the violence constrains the possibility of growth and should always be a last resort. Even then, one should act with the awareness that violence as a means will likely produce, for some at least, violence as a way of life—that is, violence as an end. He says, "I know of no greater fallacy than the claim of those who hold to the dogma of the necessity of brute force that this use will be the method of calling genuine democracy into existence—of which they profess themselves the simon-pure adherents. It requires an unusually credulous faith in the Hegelian dialectic of opposites to think that all of a sudden the use of force by a class will be transmuted into a democratic classless society. Force breeds counterforce." ("Liberalism and Social Action," in *John Dewey: The Later Works, Vol. 11: 1935–1937*, ed. Jo Ann Boydston [Carbondale: Southern Illinois University Press, 1986], 60).

69. John Dewey, *The Public and Its Problems*, in *John Dewey: The Later Works, Vol. 2: 1925–1927*, ed. Jo Ann Boydston (Carbondale: Southern Illinois University Press, 1984), 250.

70. There are many highly social nonhuman animals and the moral content of their lives is subject to a lively debate.

71. Dewey, *Public and Its Problems*, 315–316.

72. Dewey, *Public and Its Problems*, 296–297.

73. Westbrook, *John Dewey*, 248–249.

74. Dewey, *Public and Its Problems*, 278.

75. Charlotte Perkins Gilman, *The Home: Its Work and Influence* (Urbana: University of Illinois Press, 1972), 165.

76. Joseph Ratner, *Intelligence in the Modern World: John Dewey's Philosophy* (New York: Modern Library, 1929), 428.

77. Dewey, *Human Nature and Conduct*, 144.

78. Dewey, *Public and Its Problems*, 325.

79. Dewey, *Public and Its Problems*, 326–327.

80. Dewey, *Public and Its Problems*, 256.

81. This is similar to what happens in anarchist communities when individuals fail to realize the necessity of participating in decisions that affect their lives.

82. Dewey, *Public and Its Problems*, 287.

83. Dewey, *Public and Its Problems*, 327.

84. Dewey, *Public and Its Problems*, 330.

85. Dewey, *Public and Its Problems*, 328.

86. Dewey, *Public and Its Problems*, 328.

87. A possible example might be environmentalists who have come together with the end-in-view of saving the spotted owl and its forest environment, and loggers who are joined by the common end-in-view of maintaining their livelihood. If the groups were flexible and farsighted they would realize that the goals of saving the owl and sustainable logging are not necessarily in contradiction with one another. If the interconnectedness of interests were realized, rather than trying to assert that one particular interest has priority, it might become possible to arrive at workable solutions.

88. Dewey, *Public and Its Problems*, 328.

89. Dewey, *Public and Its Problems*, 332.

90. Dewey, *Public and Its Problems*, 332.

91. Dewey, *Public and Its Problems*, 336.

92. John Stuhr, *Genealogical Pragmatism: Philosophy, Experience, and Community* (New York: SUNY Press, 1997), 246.

93. Dewey, *Public and Its Problems*, 350.

94. Cornel West, *The American Evasion of Philosophy* (Madison: University of Wisconsin Press, 1989), 115.

95. C. Wright Mills warns that capitalist America may not be in a position to produce people prepared in the method of critical intelligence. "A society that is . . . a network of smart rackets does not produce men with an inner moral sense; a society that is merely expedient does not produce men of conscience." Nevertheless, Mills ultimately agrees with Dewey that an effort must be made to set free people's critical intelligence and imagination so that they can become active and responsible agents in the forming of the future (West, *The American Evasion of Philosophy*, 135–138).

96. Dewey, *Public and Its Problems*, 357.

97. John Dewey, *Logic: The Theory of Inquiry*, in *John Dewey: The Later Works, Vol. 12: 1938*, ed. Jo Ann Boydston (Carbondale: Southern Illinois University Press, 1986), 108.

98. Dewey, *Logic*, 245.

99. Dewey, *Public and Its Problems*, 366.

100. Dewey, *Public and Its Problems*, 367.

101. Dewey, *Public and Its Problems*, 368.

102. Charlotte Perkins Gilman, *The Man-Made World* (New York: Charlton Co., 1911), 39–40.

103. West, *American Evasion*, 125–126.

Chapter Five

Feminism, Pragmatism, Community, and Utopia

Pragmatist theory itself provides strong resources for feminist thinking since many of its positions address current feminist interests and debates. Among these are a pluralism and perspectivism that go beyond theory to advocate the actual inclusiveness of appropriately diverse viewpoints, including those of class, color, ethnicity, and gender, as a precondition for resolving problematic situations, whether these involve political, economic, epistemological, or ethical issues.[1]

Pragmatism and feminism both require the rejection of dualisms and hierarchical thinking.[2] Specifically, thinking and doing should not be seen as separate, neither should mind and body be distinguished, nor theory and practice divided. The rejection of these dualisms is a rejection of the superiority of a fixed reality over the notion of changing realities. It is the embracing of plurality and process.

Dewey advocates that philosophers cease trying to formulate general theories which seek to settle for all time the nature of truth, knowledge, and value. Instead we should find out "how authentic beliefs about existence as they currently exist can operate fruitfully and efficaciously in connection with the practical problems that are urgent in actual life."[3]

These commonalities are why I call the process model of utopia a pragmatist and feminist model of utopia.

This pragmatist focus on concrete practical problems has obvious connections to feminist research and activism concerning such issues as housework, childcare, and body image. These are not seen as philosophical issues from the traditional perspective of philosophy. However, as women's perspectives are introduced, the perspective of philosophy is expanded and so to the issues

129

it addresses. It also demonstrates the ways in which knowledge itself is perspectival. The notion of "objective" knowledge is overcome, but pure subjectivity is not embraced.

> Dewey's philosophy is a major achievement precisely because it combines explanations of the perspectival character of our grasp of reality, which is active and transformative, with analyses of the ways in which we can legitimately distinguish merely subjective from warrantably objective claims about reality.[4]

People's lived experiences come to matter. Experience and feelings form the basis of both knowledge and values. And knowledge and values shape one's experiences and feelings. Once one realizes this transactive nature of experience and feelings it becomes important not to universalize one's own particular perspective. Many feminists argue that the history of western philosophy is an example of taking a particular perspective—privileged male—as if it were universal. It becomes the standard by which all "others," and their experiences and feelings, are judged. Not surprisingly, those "others" usually fail to meet the standard. We need to count these "other" experiences and feelings. No one's experiences are to be taken as totally objective, or as completely subjective. This is yet another dualism to dismiss. Experience has "objective" components in the physical and social structures that exist at the time. Such experiences, however, are had by people. "Selves are specifiable, definable events within experience and not occurrences outside, underneath, or beside experience, as they are traditionally held to be in the pernicious dualisms of spirit and matter, mind and body."[5] We must learn to respect and incorporate a plurality of perspectives and see that "defenses of the objective character of experience can be made without denying that gender, as well as race, class, sexual orientation, and many other distinctions contribute to its objectivity, and therefore it is not only appropriate but imperative to question whose experience is being used as a paradigm for explication."[6]

The pragmatist and feminist model presented here pushes us to embrace plurality as a way to more workable knowledge, to take concrete lived experience seriously, and to embrace the changing and plural nature of realities. Visions which seek final and fixed ends do not fit in such theories, for they go against our very experience. Visions which require, or tend to promote, homogeneity do not fit such theories, for they result in limited ways of knowing that are less flexible than our changing world requires. The process model of utopia is a pragmatist and feminist model which embraces plurality and process and so prepares us to make a "future such as we desire."

A FEMINIST CRITIQUE OF DEWEY'S CALL FOR COMMUNITY

Dewey's model of this "future such as we desire" is not any particular model of the state. But as discussed, he does suggest that we need to develop from a Great Society to a Great Community. A Great Community requires local communities. These communities are to engage in the method of intelligence, develop flexible habits and boundaries, and understand and embrace their interconnectedness with others. It has already been argued that patriarchal communities do not meet Dewey's requirements because they encourage dependence and frustrate the development of democratic citizens. There are some other concerns, however, that emerge from a feminist analysis of Dewey's model.

People who have suffered oppression are often suspicious of the idea of returning to small communities. Feminist analysis of communitarian theory points to the fact that women often have more narrowly prescribed domestic roles in such community life. The work women do to sustain such community and family life is often ignored by such theories. Also, local face-to-face communities can be less than welcoming of difference, a worry raised earlier in the analysis of the anarchist model.

At the local community level, rather than realizing our interconnectedness and moving from this realization to an attitude of respect and sympathy for others, it is possible that one will see the possibilities of dominating others as more attractive than the possibilities of working with them. As with the anarchist model, it is possible that difference will come to be seen as something to be eliminated or controlled, rather than as an asset for the future. Being of the same community is not enough to ensure tolerance and respect among people. Unless the members of the community are already Dewey's democratic individuals, the local community may be as disintegrated a place as a Great Society. If this is so, the ideal of a Great Community may not be worth risking the intolerance, and its effects, found in the local community.

It seems that Dewey's ideal of a Great Community may run into some of the same difficulties encountered by the anarchist visions. Unless people are already transformed into Dewey's unified individual, Dewey's notion of community may be very restrictive and intolerant. How can institutionalized prejudice and discrimination be dismantled and flexible habits put in their place? Returning to local communities, then, cannot be the whole of the method for transforming individuals into unified individuals. With Dewey's ongoing education as a complement to face-to-face relations, there seems to be more of a chance of making some progress toward community and away from mere association or society, but there is also an ever-present risk of progressing toward a rule of domination. Good community requires unified individuals and becoming such an individual is a lifelong process and very hard work. As it will be difficult to fully transform any individual from their habits of prejudice to habits of critical investigation and imagination, it will be impossible to have all members of any community so transformed at any one time. The return to local community has inherent risks and seems likely to be a positive ideal only among those who have experienced little or no discrimination or oppression.[7] This is where a feminist analysis can strengthen Dewey's pragmatism.

Iris Marion Young, a feminist philosopher who shares many ideas and commitments with Dewey, does not find local community, or the idea of a Great Community, to be a good end-in-view. She, like Dewey, seeks a form of social life in which people can interact in a positive way to solve common problems, not in spite of their differences but because of their differences. However, she does not find local face-to-face communities, or ideas of a global community, to be workable. She believes that small face-to-face communities may entail too much social pressure to conform to a single standard, and the idea of a global community may require too much abstraction and the loss of individual and unique strengths. Instead, she proposes city life as a possible model for a society in which people, complete in their variety, can participate together in making decisions and directing their future. She argues that the anonymity of the city, rather than the close ties of a "village," will free people to explore their uniqueness and accept the differences of others. With the distance of strangers living in a common space, people will not feel as threatened by what is unfamiliar because it does not affect their daily lives. Secure in their own ways, they will be strong enough to have an open mind about others.

Young believes that the ideal of face-to-face community has value, but she is not as optimistic as Dewey and believes it is a dangerous ideal if it is taken as the only ideal.[8] The ideal of face-to-face community encourages a recognition of our embeddedness and the corresponding need to balance multiple commitments in making choices. It encourages a recognition of intimate relationships and the corresponding responsibilities of such relationships. It encourages close interaction where one must acknowledge the effects of any given choice upon the people of the community, rather than providing a "safe" bureaucratic distance. Such communities, however, can also encourage social and personal pressure to conform to certain community norms.[9] They can encourage one to suppress difference for the sake of others, failing to realize how the expression of difference could enrich the community.[10] Difference can seem more threatening when it is expressed in a small, close-knit community because, as with the end-state model of utopia, in such a community change and difference are often seen as a threat to the order and stability of the community, and so to the lives of each person in the community. Being open about difference within a local community, then, is often seen as an irresponsible, inconsiderate, and threatening social act and so is opposed.

Difference may seem less personally and socially threatening, however, if people are connected but have more individual space. Young proposes the model of city life to stand in the place of small face-to-face communities.

> By "city life" I mean a form of social relations which I define as the being together of strangers. In the city persons and groups interact within spaces and institutions they all experience themselves as belonging to, but without those interactions dissolving into unity or commonness. City life is composed of clusters of people with affinities—families, social group networks, voluntary associations, neighborhood networks, a vast array of small "communities." City dwellers frequently venture beyond such familiar enclaves, however, to the more open public of politics, commerce, and festival, where strangers meet and interact.[11]

People involved in this array of small communities can gain from them the positive aspects of face-to-face community and retain a certain amount of individual space and distance from others. They can be involved with other people without as much pressure to be like them. People can come together to solve common problems (such as busing, sewage, waste disposal, education, drug trafficking, gun control) without having to agree on other issues, and go their own ways when and if the common focus fades away. One can come to be in community with people of different political associations, different sexual orientations, different races, different religions, different educational backgrounds—all of whom share a common interest or concern. Coming together with a shared concern one can learn about these differences but not see them as threatening or directly challenging to any particular way of life as a whole.

With such experiences one is more likely, though not inevitably, to become open to learning about different perspectives as these perspectives can offer a variety of opinions and a greater breadth of knowledge and ideas about how to deal with the common problem or promote the common project. Being immersed in a task, one is more likely to see the educational aspects of plurality and not focus so much on any one perspective. Given the fluidity of the groups and their transitory nature, it will be harder for any particular individual or group with deep-seated prejudices to dominate multiple aspects of another's life, even if they are able to become dominant in a certain community. Since people are involved in a variety of groups, the impact of individuals who have not yet recognized their embeddedness participating in decision making will be more diffuse than if we simply return to stable local face-to-face communities where there could be an attempt to define a public interest—an impartial or unified position that excludes certain voices.

Furthermore, to call for a return to small face-to-face communities is not re-alistic if one means by this that cities be dismantled and small towns set up in-stead. Such a goal does not seem to qualify as a good end-in-view as it does not take into account the actual situatedness of people in the urban present, and, as we have seen, ignores the risks of small communities limiting horizons, pushing for homogeneity, and frustrating the method of democracy. A more consistent Deweyan account might not ask for stable face-to-face communities to be the basis of a Great Community, but take up the idea of people involved in a variety of fluid task-oriented groups, but not focused on achieving a stable community. Young's communities of interest are dynamic, coming in and going out of exis-tence as needs and interests change. While it is the case that affinity groups are small face-to-face communities, none is expected to be too long lasting or sta-ble, and each person is expected to be involved in several such groups simulta-neously. This variety and fluidity of connectedness should, ideally, help each person see and build connections with those people they may not directly choose to be associated with. Young may be too optimistic here, for many interest groups become institutionalized and grow into stable and inflexible bureaucra-cies of their own. There is also the risk that the city model will not be able to nur-ture the kind of close relationships and interactions which help nurture our awareness of each other's needs and the willingness to compromise and cooper-ate, even when it hurts. Nonetheless, Young's model of city life fits the process model of utopia as it encourages participation in a variety of communities, a recognition of our interconnectedness and embeddedness, and a commitment to developing open and flexible habits of mind.

It is important to note that on the process model of utopia the main focus is on developing people capable of critical thought. The process model is not so concerned with an end-state, but with developing the means of continued, critical engagement between live creatures and their environment. Young's idea of task-oriented groups is a very Deweyan concept and it helps to expand the options available for fostering his notion of a Great Community. With such flexible communities we can learn to appreciate differences by coming together with others with a certain shared end-in-view. This coming together is as important as achieving any particular goal as this task-oriented commu-nity will help people realize their embeddedness, encourage their participa-tion in directing their future, and make it possible for them to act with intel-ligence and foresight. For Dewey, acting with intelligence and foresight requires a community involved in conscious conjoint activity, and conscious conjoint activity entails the recognition and appreciation of differences as be-ing what makes fruitful activity possible.

The process model of utopia embraces democracy as a method which ap-preciates and encourages differences within a variety of shared but shifting contexts. Involved in a variety of tasks people become aware of a variety of perspectives, expand their horizons, and see community as a dynamic, interactive process. The process model of utopia does not seek stable, unchanging communities, but dynamic and fluid associations that encourage people to become Dewey's unified individual. The process model of utopia does not seek a specific arrangement of society, but a critical, flexible, and open-minded citizenry. We can find this process model in action in many contemporary feminist utopian novels.

FEMINIST UTOPIAS

As has been discussed, the possibility of a process model of utopia has certain implications. The process model of utopia developed out of Dewey's work, and feminist theory is a model that calls people to participate with critical intelligence in the formation of future possibilities. It is a model that requires people to understand themselves as socially embedded creatures who must be actively engaged in and reflectively aware of their lived experience if they are to move forward in a satisfying and fulfilling way. The process model recognizes the ongoing, rather than the static, nature of social experience and tries to develop methods for sustaining in people an open and flexible attitude that can enable them to see diversity and change as an opportunity and challenge, rather than as an obstacle or threat.

The keys to this process model are lived experience and critical intelligence. As discussed before, lived experience is characterized by an intense participatory relationship between the environment and the live creature. This engagement with the world gives experience structure and enables one to live the experience and integrate it into another, more complete experience, which in turn will become the ground for yet another experience, and so on. Lived experience is dynamic and has a cumulating effect. When one understands the dynamic nature of human experience, discerns its rhythm, it becomes possible to organize experience to move it forward in a satisfying and fulfilling way. It is important to keep in mind that, even with lived experience, it will happen that one runs into obstacles. Every solution creates new problems; progress is neither inevitable nor continuous. Lived experience embraces the possibilities of this movement.

If one comes to understand the dynamic nature of experience, if one connects with what Dewey calls the rhythm or relational nature of live creatures and their environment, then one is in a position to apply critical intelligence to understand one's past and present and to guide one's future. With an understanding of one's embeddedness, namely, that one's potential for growth is interdependent with the possibilities for others, then one is what Dewey calls a unified individual. It is also important to realize one is embedded in a particular history, a present culture, and certain sets of habits. The unified individual is able to act with foresight. Proposals for the future, however, that are developed without an understanding of our connectedness are more likely to fall short. Without an understanding of our interdependence and connectedness it is not possible for individuals to make informed decisions; it is not possible to exercise critical intelligence. Without such understanding critical foresight is not possible. Feminist utopian fiction provides such critical foresight.

From the early 1980s to the mid-1990s there was a surge of interest in women's utopias. This interest came primarily from literature professors who were rediscovering women's utopias of the late nineteenth century and those who were beginning to explore the exciting revival of feminist utopias written in the 1970s and 1980s—books such as Frances Bartkowski's *Feminist Utopias*; Angelika Bammer's *Partial Visions: Feminism and Utopianism*; N. B. Albinski's *Women's Utopias*; N. Rosinsky's *Feminist Futures*; Marlene Barr's *Future Females: A Critical Anthology;* Marlene Barr and Nicholas Smith's *Women and Utopia: Critical Interpretations*; Libby Falk Jones and Sarah Webster Goodwin's *Feminism, Utopia, and Narrative*; and Ruby Rohrlich and Elaine Hoffman Baruch's *Women in Search of Utopia: Mavericks and Mythmakers*.[12] There was no corresponding surge in analysis from the perspective of political theory and/or philosophy, though. Lucy Sargisson's *Contemporary Feminist Utopianism,* which explores utopian theory and literature from a postmodern perspective, is the only one that comes to mind. That is why I believe developing this pragmatist and feminist (process) model of utopia is important.

Sargisson provides a nice history of utopian theory and develops a postmodern–poststructuralist feminist account of the need for what she calls a transgressive utopianism. The pragmatist and feminist model of utopia which I have developed here is both similar to and different from Sargisson's transgressive utopianism. Informed by feminist theory and Derridian and Cixousian poststructuralism, Sargisson concludes "that the new utopianism represents the manifestation of a conscious and necessary desire to resist the closure that is evoked by approaches to utopia as perfect, and that this has far-reaching implications."[13] On this model "*process* becomes the focus of political theoretical research, rather than result or consequence."[14] Sargisson's themes of rejecting the blueprint notion of utopia (or the end-state model) and embracing the open-ended notion of experience is very much in line with the pragmatist and feminist model I have proposed. She argues that contemporary feminist utopias avoid the blueprint model because they are influenced by contemporary feminist theory which questions the notion of an essential human nature. Specifically, the idea of an essential male nature and an essential female nature are disputed. As discussed before, the end-state model of utopia requires a notion of human nature around which the society is built. This notion of human nature has often been the result of universalizing the perceived male nature and calling it human. This has at least two problems: (1) universalizing the particular and (2) assuming an absolutist view that does not allow for change. Sargisson turns to postmodern and poststructuralist theory because she believes it addresses many of the same concerns addressed by feminist theory. She uses the work of Jacques Derrida to suggest that:

> Universalism is a masculine construct in a libidinal-economic sense, and that the (universalist, blueprinting and perfectionist) utopianism created by some approaches is disempowering to all but those who constructed it. . . . In this reading, masculinity is not essentially gender-specific; it is not a sociological phenomenon, but it does characterize the dominant values and norms which can be found to advantage men over women.[15]

In her Derridian reading Sargisson focuses on issues of constructing concepts. I very much agree when she says, "Deconstruction, from this perspective, strips the construct of utopia of its pretensions towards neutrality and universalism. Thus deprived, the blueprinting approach to utopia as perfection can be seen to be uncompromisingly exclusive."[16] However, this approach can run the danger of becoming a word game. She says:

> Deconstruction as a process is profoundly creative. At its most obvious level this creation comes in the form of neologisms. . . . A less apparent, but equally important, creative act of deconstructive thought is the (utopian) space that it creates in which reconceptualization can occur.[17]

It allows us to create new meanings. All of this is very important and consistent with pragmatism. Pragmatism, however, requires a continual checking with actual concrete problems of people. It also requires that we try out new meanings in action and see how they work. This is an important correction if political theory in general, and utopia in particular, is not to become an abstract intellectual game with little bearing on our everyday lives. While Sargisson and I have our differences, we both focus on the feminist utopian literature that emerged in the 1970s and 1980s. It is this literature that tends to embrace change and open-endedness.

What makes these utopian novels feminist utopian novels? Sally Miller Gearhart offers a working definition of a feminist utopian novel.

> A feminist utopian novel is one which a. contrasts the present with an envisioned idealized society (separated from the present by time or space), b. offers a comprehensive

critique of present values/conditions, c. sees men or male institutions as a major cause
of present social ills, and d. presents women not only as at least the equal of men but
also as the sole arbiters of their reproductive functions.[18]

The first two criteria seem to hold of any utopian novel. It is the critique of
male institutions (and sometimes men themselves) and a focus on developing
female equality and autonomy that makes a novel feminist. Carol Pearson
says:

> Feminist utopian fiction implicitly or explicitly criticizes the patriarchy while it em-
> phasizes society's habit of restricting and alienating women. . . . It assumes that the
> patriarchy is unnatural and fails to create environments conducive to the maximiza-
> tion of female—or male—potential.[19]

It is important to stress that pragmatist and feminist utopian novels seek to
make a better future for everyone, not just women. These novels demonstrate
an understanding that the interests of any one person or group are intricately
connected to the interests of other individuals and groups.

The women's utopias of the late nineteenth century offered a critical view
of the position of women and the meaning of being female. Even if all are not
feminist, embracing the classical female role, they do still raise issues of gender as important social and political concerns. The feminist utopian and
dystopian fiction of the 1970s and 1980s takes up these concerns and offers
more radical revisions. Jean Pfaelzer says:

> I believe that our task now is to explore the political implications of the transition
> from a teleological view of the future to a deconstructionist view of the future. To
> what degree is the retreat from a totalized or absolute representation of the future a
> democratizing and antipatriarchal act, encouraging the reader to participate in the
> creation of alternative possible worlds . . . and to what degree does it represent our
> "incapacity to imagine utopia"? This is a troubling question.[20]

Even here there is the recognition of a move to a different kind of vision, but
a hesitation to call it utopian because it does not offer a totalizing and absolutistic vision. As she comes to embrace this new vision Pfaelzer goes on to
say:

> In the 1970s and 1980s, the new utopias are part of political practices and social vi-
> sions which have repudiated most totalizing solutions. Utopian dynamics reside in a
> context of local, disparate, and autonomous politics: hostility to worldwide corporate
> structures, critiques of centralized and homogenized media, demands for control of
> the workplace, and resistance to the commodification of special activity. Recent
> utopians call for individual sovereignty, local community, sexual pluralism, and the
> creative devastation of class, region, gender and race.[21]

It is clear that Pfaelzer's description of these new utopias is very much in line with the process model of utopia developed in the last chapter. These new utopias are pragmatist and feminist utopias.

I have chosen to focus on feminist utopian novels that address issues of male violence (among other things). "Violence, coupled with a desire to master others, is antithetical to a feminist utopian vision."[22] I think it is clear that the novels discussed so far—Sheri S. Tepper's *The Gate to Women's Country* and Marge Piercy's *Woman on the Edge of Time*—do meet the requirements of Gearhart's definition of a feminist utopian novel.[23] They both see men and male institutions as a major cause of social ills and present women as equal to men and in control of their reproductive functions. The means by which these issues are addressed in these future societies, however, are at odds with a pragmatist understanding of the continuum of means and ends and the pragmatist understanding of ends as ends-in-view. While both Tepper and Piercy are critical of the visions they present, they do not give us an alternative way of envisioning the future. Visions that are pragmatist, as well as feminist, do.

The two novels to be discussed in this chapter also meet the definition of a feminist utopia, but they add something important. They are pragmatist as well as feminist novels. They embrace a notion of process and change, see the importance of diversity, and seek to avoid the division of means from ends. They see that how they get to the future is part of what they achieve.[24] Ursula K. Le Guin says:

> Our curse is alienation, the separation of Yang and Yin. Instead of a search for balance and integration, there is a struggle for dominance. Divisions are insisted upon, interdependence is denied. The dualism of value that destroys us, the dualism of superior/inferior, ruler/ruled, owner/owned, user/used, might give way to what seems to me, from here, a much healthier, sounder more promising modality of integration and integrity.[25]

The search for balance and integration is obviously in line with the process (pragmatist and feminist) model of utopia presented in chapter 4. I believe that many pragmatist commitments have come to be part of most feminist theory, though the connection is largely unacknowledged. I think a model which acknowledges these commonalities can strengthen both feminist and utopian theory and enliven pragmatist social/political theory.

In her book *Partial Visions,* Bammer argues that the notion of utopia as perfection is a dead concept. It tends to ignore issues of race, class, and gender and allows for no change. She says, "As soon as we abandon the conventional concept of utopia, we find that the utopian is not dead at all, but very much alive in people's longing for a more just and human world, their belief that such change is possible, and their willingness to act on the basis of the belief."[26] She sees a change occurring in the feminist utopias of the 1970s. They begin to embrace a vision in process.

> The difficulty faced by such a movement is sustaining the very principle on which it is predicated, namely the idea of the future as possibility rather than a present goal. The difficulty, in other words, is to sustain the concept of utopia as process. In the face of external and internal challenges to legitimate both its ends and its means, it is all too easy for even the most progressive movement to foreclose process and construct and image of utopia as historical telos.[27]

Even the title of her book brings to mind the pragmatist and feminist notion that vision, all knowledge, is partial. This means that we are not in a position to make absolutistic claims, but rather to form hypotheses which are subject to change. We must be willing to change and adapt to new information and needs as they arise. In "Change and Art in Women's Worlds," Lee Cullen Khanna writes:

> For women, however, the "best social order" is dynamic. The inevitable changes of life are not denied or down graded in the rush to produce and accumulate. Rather, each stage of life is respected, attended by communal concerns and ritual, even celebrated. In addition, the recognition that change is necessary allows for tolerance in human development and a more relaxed sense of human interaction, certainly a more fluid political structure. The good society is thus viable only so long as it is constantly re-evaluated, revised, responsive to individual and communal growth. . . . In fact, women's utopias differ markedly from the male utopian tradition in the importance attached to both change and creativity.[28]

I would suggest that when Khanna distinguishes the male utopian tradition from women's utopians she is really pointing to the problems of the end-state model of utopia. While I would agree that this has largely been a privileged, white, male tradition, we need to be careful about assuming that being of a different race, class, or gender would be enough to prevent one from seeking the more fixed and final kinds of visions. *The Gate to Women's Country* shows us that women's visions can fail to appreciate the importance of change and creativity. However, it does seem to be the case that women's utopias do tend to avoid the idea of a fixed and final solution and when such a vision is employed, there is usually more than a hint of critique implicit in the novel (including in *The Gate to Women's Country*). In discussing Doris Lessing's *Canopos of Argos* series, Khanna further says that we learn "what every reader of feminist utopias must come to understand. There can be no better society without allowance for growth, variety, and change."[29] This focus on, and acceptance of, growth, variety, and change is central to both pragmatism and feminism. This is something that the two novels to be discussed in this chapter—Le Guin's *Always Coming Home* and Gearhart's *The Wanderground*—represent. They are pragmatist and feminist utopias.

These novels are representative of the process model of utopia. Both books stress the social embeddedness of individuals and the connectedness of every live creature and its environment. Where the Kesh of *Always Coming Home* imbue everything with a sense of spirituality and purpose, the Hill Women of *The Wanderground* literally communicate with and work together with the world and the creatures in it. Both books stress learning to live with the world and all its inhabitants.

Both of these books embody Dewey's idea of lived experience. They both stress the need to develop an understanding of the relational nature of things in order to save the future from individual men who lack such understanding. The Hill Women have a deep psychic bond with the earth and all live creatures in it (a process called enfoldment) which reveals the rhythm of lived experience and moves their experience forward in a fulfilling way. So too, the Kesh have discovered their relatedness with all things and the transactional nature of this relationship. To act with an awareness of the purpose and connectedness of all is called mindfulness. Both novels present a fluid structure that embraces growth, variety, and change. Both require that a person internalize a sense of others as part of her own experience and understanding. There are social arrangements, rituals, and practices that encourage and reinforce such an understanding and habit of flexibility in each community; and there is a real sense in which people (and this can include the reader) understand themselves as active participants in the formation of their future.

I will explore these two books in terms of how they may be seen as an instantiation of the process model of utopia. Both books are so rich and complex, with many layers of meaning and purpose, that inevitably the descriptions will be simplified and much will be left out. These books create interesting and rich societies. I am focusing, however, on the developmental and changing character of the societies. Both of these books model the process model of utopia not just in content, but in form as well. They do not present a grand unifying narrative, but rather interconnected partial stories. As for content, their ends-in-view change as they encounter different people and situations. They recognize the impact of means on ends, the relational nature of experience, the connectedness of method and purpose. They do not present final perfect end-states, but possible futures-in-process.

THE KESH

The Kesh are a possible people of the future. In the book *Always Coming Home,* Le Guin employs what she calls an archaeology of the future to see what may come to be, given what is now, in a valley of the northern Pacific coast of what was the United States. One of the first things that distinguishes this book from traditional utopian novels is its format. The book does not present a still life of a perfect society, but actively encounters the developing practices of a people in transition. It is not a novel so much as a collection of stories and artifacts. There are stories (written and oral), poems, plays, songs, dances, recipes, explanations of social practices and arrangements, some maps, and a language is explained (complete with a dictionary). There are, in the back of the book, descriptions of marriages, eating, medicine, instruments, playing, and architecture. A tape, "Music and Poetry of the Kesh," accompanies the book.

An entire future culture and people come to life when one engages this book. The reader is asked to participate in the making and unmaking of the world; the reader is asked to imagine this future possibility and to change what is now in light of what has been seen. As with the Kesh themselves, it is expected that learning is a sharing, not a receiving, and all must learn together to shape the future in a better way.

Translator's Note:
    p. 290. . . . he learned arboriculture with his mother's brother . . . and with orchard trees of all kinds.
    We would be more likely to say that he learned *from* his uncle *about* orchard trees; but this would not be a fair translation of the repeated suffix *oud,* with, together with. To learn *with* an uncle and trees implies learning is not a transfer of something by someone to someone, but is a relationship. Moreover, the relationship is considered to be reciprocal. Such a point of view seems at hopeless odds with the distinction of subject and object considered essential to science.[30]

The book challenges the notion of presenting a finished picture of a perfect society for others to simply take over and learn from and, instead, presents ideas and possibilities that people can consider, learn, and experiment with together.

Another feature that distinguishes this book from most more traditional utopian novels is its acknowledgment of how the present will impact and constrain the future. During the time of the Kesh there is still evidence of the industrial age—roads, a train, electricity, pollution, satellites, and a central computer (the City of Mind) connected to each town by Exchanges. Since knowledge is respected, it is stored in the computer. The information on how to make tanks, planes, bombs is all kept, but the priorities for using knowledge have changed. The limited resources and great pollution have forced this change, but it does not result in the wholesale abandonment of technology. The industrial age has been replaced by "the very loose, light, soft network of the human cultures, which in their small scale, great number, and endless diversity, manufactured and traded more or less actively, but never centralised their industry."[31] Despite this change, however, technology still exists and is used, but now in a more limited and mindful way.

> To construct, say, a battery to power a flashlight was not an easy matter, though at need it was done; the technology of the Valley was completely adequate to the needs of the people. To construct a tank or a bomber was so difficult and so unnecessary that it really cannot be spoken of in terms of the Valley economy. After all, the cost of making, maintaining, fueling, and operating such machines at the very height of the Industrial Age was incalculable, impoverishing the planet's substance forever and requiring the great majority of humankind to live in servitude and poverty.[32]

The computer keeps information, but the people make different use of it than their forebears because they *see* the costs. The computer network that is The City of Mind is not only consulted for information, it also serves as a network for communication between communities. So widespread is the use of the computer that the computer language TOK is used as a universal language in travel and trade.

A final distinguishing feature of this book as a utopian fiction is its lack of concern with a final end or perfect state. The Kesh are not a perfect untroubled people, nor is the world a perfect untroubled world. There is pollution left from the industrial age, radiation exposure has led to a high infant mortality rate, severe deformities are common, and debilitating sicknesses affect many in middle age. This is true of all animals, not just humans. The earth and the live creatures who inhabit it are working together to adjust and survive—to learn to live together gently.

The Kesh are a cooperative people who see the spirit of life in everything. Rocks, streams, trees, animals—all are worthy of respect. Animals are raised for food, but they have a good life and are slaughtered carefully to avoid causing fear or pain. All killing requires a woman to be present to speak the words of death to the animal, to reinforce the connectedness and mutual respect between all live creatures. While it is not explicitly stated why a woman must be present at the killing, there does appear to be an ongoing debate within the community about men participating in sacred acts.

> With Tarweed she was polite, but it was plain that her manners masked contempt. She thought a man's place was in the woods and fields and workshops, not among sacred and intellectual things. In the Lodge I had heard her say the old gibe, "A man fucks with his brain and thinks with his penis." Tarweed knew well enough what she thought, but intellectual men are used to having their capacities doubted and their achievements snubbed; he did not seem to mind her arrogance as much as I sometimes did, even to the point of trying to defend him against her once, saying, "Even if he is a man he thinks like a woman!"[33]

It appears that what was once an occupation only for women is becoming an occupation shared by both.

When hunting (mainly an occupation of children) one must sing to the prey and speak to the death. "Even when a corn-borer was squashed, a mosquito swatted, a branch broken, a flower picked, the formula was muttered. . . . The speaking of it maintained and contained the idea of need and fulfillment, demand and response, of relationship and interdependence."[34] The Kesh community, as it sees itself now, includes the whole Valley—the air and water as well as every plant, rock, and animal. Dying is seen as a rejoining of the whole, for animals and people. There is a cycle of reincarnation that keeps the energy flowing forward. The ceremonies around death express "the emotional and social interdependence of the community, their profound sense of living and dying with one another."[35] The sense of interdependence and relatedness that is central to their way of life is the basis for their ability to live with intelligence and foresight.

The most sacred ceremony, the World Dance, represents this interconnectedness for the Kesh.

The World Dance celebrated human participation in the making and unmaking, the renewal and continuity, of the world.

While the people of the Valley danced the Sky Dance for all people and beings of the earth, the Sky People were dancing their part of the ceremony, the Earth Dance. The dead and the unborn danced on the wind and in the sea, birds in the air, the wild animals in secret places in the wilderness. . . . The linked spirals of these two cosmic dances formed the sacred image, the Heyiya-if.[36]

As indicated by this dance, the world is divided into two—Sky and Earth. There is neither hierarchy nor primacy between the two groups or within either group. Each is a necessary part of the whole which is harmony. There are five Houses of Earth and four Houses of Sky. Houses are like clans or family groups. Sexual relations with another member of one's House are considered inappropriate. Each house is matrilineal and exogamous (homosexual marriages are recognized too).

The Houses of Earth are inhabited by the Earth, moon, rocks, fresh water, living individual animals and human beings, plants used by human beings, ground-living birds, domestic animals, and game. Each House of Earth— Obsidian, Blue Clay, Serpentine, Yellow Adobe, Red Adobe—is responsible for certain social tasks, performs certain festivals or rituals, makes up the membership of certain societies, and participates in certain crafts or arts. These Houses are the basic divisions of society. The Houses of Sky—Rain, Cloud, Wind, Still Air—are inhabited by most birds, fish, wild animals not hunted for food, reptiles, insects, the dead, the unborn, beings in stories or dreams, the oceans, stars, the sun, and everything considered together as a species, tribe, nation, or people.[37]

The World Dance brings all the Houses together and reinforces an understanding of the whole. To be wise, or to act mindfully, is to act with this understanding. As with Dewey, one must recognize the interdependence of live creatures and their environment (social and physical) and take others into account when making decisions about what to do, how to act, and what to believe. "To be singleminded is to be unmindful. Mindfulness is keeping many different things in mind and observing their relations and proportions."[38] Not all people in the time of the Kesh act mindfully, however, as will be seen later when discussing the Condor people.

When the Kesh encounter other people while traveling or trading, they can seem judgmental as they point out and discuss different customs and values. They acknowledge most differences as part of a whole, however, rather than competing ways of being. This does not mean that they make no judgments. They judge both their own society and others they encounter, and as with other utopian novels some people and practices are seen as problematic. Of a trading partner the Usudegd (to the Kesh, the cotton people), they say "they are not an unreasonable people, except in making little paths everywhere and being ashamed to admit they have had troubles."[39] The Condors they judge as sick. "The people of the Condor, those men who have come here from that people, are sick. Their heads are turned backwards."[40] And the people of the past are also considered backwards headed people. The desolation of the earth required human action and so could not have been an accident. They did wrong mindfully in that they were aware of the connectedness of all things and willfully chose to ignore the impact of their actions on others and on the future.

> Accidents happened to people, but what people did they were responsible for. So these things human beings had done to the world must have been deliberate and conscious acts of evil, serving the purposes of wrong understanding, fear, and greed. The people who had done these things had done wrong mindfully. They had had their heads on wrong.[41]

Note that though these people acted mindfully the result is considered negative. To act mindfully is to act with an awareness of the connectedness of all things. The Kesh believe the people of the past had such an understanding but, perversely, acted against it. There is no guarantee of wise choice, or progress on the process model. Negative judgments are made if the society or person does not recognize their interconnectedness to other things or if they choose to overlook the connectedness. This is seen as bad, not so much because it goes against some truth about the world (their view of the world is considered metaphorical, not literal), but because it leads to a stressful, combative, and limited way of being in the world. If people fail to see themselves as part of a continuum they live only for the present, hoarding, owning, using up, destroying. Like the Condor people, they will be poor in spirit and alienate those around them. The Kesh believe that things work out better if people have an eye to building and maintaining the future, if they can see the connectedness of all things and times. If people do not look to the future, if they are not mindful, or if they choose to ignore what they know of their interconnectedness, it will go badly for them and those with whom they have contact.

The Condor people are the best example of unmindfulness encountered in the stories of the book. They are a patriarchal society of warriors. They worship the One all powerful god or spirit under which all can be ordered and unified. They develop a corresponding hierarchy, placing themselves at the top, just below the One, and seek to conquer and control everything else in an attempt to achieve the proper order and unification. The Kesh consider them sick and infectious. Contact with Condor soldiers led to the creation among the Kesh of a Warrior Lodge for men and boys and the Lamb Lodge (butchering) for the women. These lodges were eventually eliminated (at the conclusion of a four-day meeting and much debate) as the sickness was recognized. The Condor people themselves, because of their need to conquer, control, and destroy their land and other people, alienated those around them, stagnated, and died out.

The Condors not only failed to conquer others, but they failed to sustain themselves because they lacked what Dewey calls critical intelligence. The Condors had isolated and alienated themselves from the earth and the creatures in it. "The Condor people seem to have been unusually self-isolated; their form of communication with other peoples was through aggression, domination, exploitation, and enforced acculturation."[42] This lack of understanding, their unmindfulness, put them at a disadvantage. Since they looked only to themselves, they learned nothing about or from those they sought to conquer and so acted without understanding or foresight. "To conquer is to be careless. Carefulness is holding oneself and one's act in appropriate relation and proportion to the many other beings and intentions."[43] This sickness of single-mindedness is something the Kesh, and all peoples, must continually guard against. They see it is a risk of being human that one forgets that human people are part of a larger fellowship. (This is the sickness that affected those who were members of the Warrior and Lamb Lodges.) In this sense of isolation there is a fear which pushes one to try to control what is seen as separate.

I have come to think that the sickness of Man is like the mutating viruses and the toxins; there will always be some form of it about, or brought in from elsewhere by people moving and traveling, and there will always be the risk of infection. What those sick with it said is true: It is a sickness of our being human, a fearful one. It would be unwise in us to forget the Warriors . . . lest it need all be done and said again.[44]

Respect and the recognition of reciprocity between all beings of the earth is the only way to guard against such unmindfulness. As with Dewey, the Kesh believe that one must recognize the relational nature of live creatures with each other and their environment if lived experience is to be possible. It is only with lived experience that it becomes possible to act with understanding and foresight; it is only with lived experience that it becomes possible to apply critical intelligence to the present and guide the future in a satisfying and fulfilling way. It is only with the recognition of our interdependence and interaction that intelligent engagement with the world becomes possible and the formation of community becomes a live option.

The recognition of the continuity and connectedness of life is central to the Kesh in much the same way that the recognition of the rhythm which makes lived experience possible is for Dewey. If our sense of connectedness is lost, lived experience becomes impossible. It is necessary, then, that the individual understand herself as a socially embedded yet active agent. As the Kesh put it:

Personal energy was of course a personal matter; the individual made the choices, and the choosing, wise or foolish, mindful or careless, was the person. But no choice could be made independent of the superpersonal and impersonal energies, the cosmic/social/self-relatedness of all existences. Another word very important in Kesh thinking, *tuuvyai*, mindfulness, might be described as the intelligent awareness of this interdependence of energies and beings, a sense of one's place and part in the whole.[45]

The shaping of the world—the unending dance of the world—depends on this recognition of embeddedness and use of critical intelligence in regard to the whole. Even if the world is broken and visions of better futures are incomplete, the mind and heart can act together to make the world and our experience in it better, to make it whole again. "Even if the bowl is broken (and the bowl is broken), from the clay and the making and the firing and the pattern, even if the pattern is incomplete (and the pattern is incomplete), let the mind draw its energy. Let the heart complete the pattern."[46]

THE HILL WOMEN

Similarly to Le Guin's creation of the Kesh, Sally Miller Gearhart describes the lives of the Hill Women in her book *The Wanderground*. Again, it is not one sustained story, but a variety of stories of different parts of different women's lives. There is more of a central concern than in *Always Coming*

Home, however, that eventually brings all the lives together. This central concern is the problems of the city and male violence. A distinguishing feature of this book is the nature of the changes that take place to arrive at this future. The earth itself revolted against the violence, industry, and pollution which have ripped her apart. One day all the machines and motors quit working, guns did not fire, animals refused to carry men, and men became impotent outside the cities. At the same time women, especially lesbians, were fleeing the violence against women and homosexuals that was becoming more prevalent and more extreme.

Some of the women who made it out into the country had telepathic powers, which all the women of the Wanderground eventually learned. It was a situation in which they had to learn to change or die. Now they communicate mind to mind, in what is called an enfoldment, with other women, animals, plants, water, air, and the earth itself. They can move objects and even transport their own bodies through mental effort. They have also learned to procreate without men, through a process of egg-merging, and only girls are born.

These women are a cooperative people. Each child has a flesh mother and seven sisters who help to raise and teach the child.[47] They share cooking duties, serve on rotating councils, and share guard duties in addition to whatever task or craft they practice. The women share serving on rotating watches during which they guard the Wanderground from men. They also serve on rotations in the city, disguised as men, to monitor the continuing violence there. Theirs is not a perfect world, it is a world of conflict. They consider themselves to be at war with men and must be alert and watchful.

These women seem to have an essentialist view of male nature as combative and destructive. Men have almost destroyed the earth and have shackled, enslaved, and maimed women. The women work on changing themselves and guard themselves as the men self-destruct.

> "Aha! You slay the slayer, then!"
> No! changing not, he dies.
> "Then you do not slay him?"
> The rhythm moved just a hair's breadth:
> We do not slay him
> But aid him in his dying
> Show him how to bear himself
> Into his own stilldeath.[48]

Unless the men change, though, it is possible that all will die. In an effort to hold things steady while they learn to change themselves, and practice new ways, the women keep up the rotations in the cities. There are some men who help them in the cities and befriend the women on rotations. These are the Gentles. These are men who agree with the women of the Wanderground that at this time, with people as they are now, men and women can only do violence to one another and so should stay separate. "Even beneath his cultivated hard exterior she could feel his understanding of the essential fundamental knowledge: women and men cannot yet, may not ever, love one another without violence; they are no longer of the same species."[49] The Gentles are also working on changing themselves, however, and practicing new ways of being in hope that the human species may become one again sometime in the future. Both the Hill Women and the Gentles hope that things can change, that people can live in harmony with one another, the planet, and the other creatures.

The model for the change is the lifestyle and social arrangements being developed and practiced by the Hill Women. As with Dewey, a main component of the needed changes is improved communication. In this case what is needed is more than improved communication between individual humans but improved communication between all live creatures and the earth. Each woman first learns to trust her own body and mind and then begins to stretch out to the creatures of the world with her mind. Each girl has one special friend, her "learntogether," with whom she experiments and pushes her abilities. It is also necessary to learn to shield oneself. If one takes on another's experiences directly, as Seja did with Margaret's rape, it can be overwhelming and dangerous. "Seja had yielded entirely to the memory, yielded with no protection. She was clearly in full retrosense, tensed in rigid paralysis there on the floor . . . Inside her head Margaret's ugly drama was still raging; apparently even the remember rooms had not prepared Seja for this more visceral experience of rape."[50] Seja becomes so enraged she tries to kill the woman she is with. It is important to learn how to use this telepathy carefully and wisely because without shielding one is in the experience and can be destroyed by it.

The necessity for survival required the development of these telepathic abilities. It also required the development of people on the model of Dewey's integrated individual immersed in critical intelligence. As with Dewey, the women of the Wanderground realize it is important not to get stuck in confining habits, but to develop critical and flexible habits of mind. The older women remember the difficulties of breaking their old, confining habits.

"Demanding," she grumbled. "Don't ask for help out of my nest. Take my turn at the soap cauldron. Demanding. Demanding, demanding, demanding. Demand some respect. Haven't been where I've been; got a lot to teach them." She shook her head. What was happening? She had lapsed again. So hard to escape the patterns, even when you've been away from them over seventy years.[51]

But they have broken the pattern of living they had been taught and are learning to live cooperatively with each other, the earth, and other creatures. They
have learned to communicate and make lived experience possible. "'Meaningful communication is the meeting of two vessels, equally vulnerable,
equally receptive, and equally desirous of hearing. In the listening is all real
speaking.'"[52] They have learned to listen. They work at listening. They listen
to and accept what each other has to say. They see each person's limits—called
carjer—such as impatience, desire for dominance, dislike of children or animals, or temper. It is not the case that everyone gets along well, but they have
developed ways of working it out and being tolerant of each other's limits.

> Ono remembered Egathese's carjer, one of those personal bands of prejudice where
> hard things had to be worked out or at least understood. One of Egathese's carjers
> was her antipathy to dogs. Ono slipped into a mantle of tolerance, though underneath
> she wondered if Egathese were not all carjery, so many people and things did she dis-
> like, so grumpy was she always. "And I guess all that is my own carjery," Ono
> thought to herself.[53]

Each person works on softening herself and others help her to do so.

> *Your trouble,*
> *My trouble.*
> *Our ease.*[54]

No matter what one's personal limits of understanding are, however, all the
women are always part of discussion and decisions.

The community of the Hill Women is one of many communities in the
Wanderground. When there are decisions to be made all the communities
meet in what is called a "gatherstretch"—a connection of minds. There are
twelve women (everyone serving on rotation) representing the various communities, called the Long Dozen, who serve as a council and decide when to
call everyone together in such a mind stretch. "They brought to each other for
sharing or decision all the woman-matters, from threats of external danger to
work rotations or the discovery of a covey of quail at a meadow's edge."[55] In
such a meeting, problems are presented for discussion and everyone who
wants to may speak. When the discussion is ended a vote is taken to see if
there is a clear wish, that is, unanimous agreement. If not, those who disagree
discuss whether they can yield. They are not asked to yield, just to express
their willingness to do so. If one or more are not willing, they can separate. It
is this freedom that is the basis of their unity and strength. "'I am called to re-
mind us that at any moment we can cease to be one body. No woman has to
follow the will of any other. Always we must know that we can separate, even
splinter or disperse one-by-one, for a little while or forever. We rest our unity

on the possibility.'"[56] If there is a willingness to yield, the involved parties continue to argue until agreement is reached, they decide to come back to it another time, or people do as they please.

The "gatherstretch" discussed in the book is the largest ever held—it reminds everyone of the possibility of all coming together to fight violence.

What if it were too big? What if the combined energy were too great? What vast consequence could occur if hundreds of women inhaled together and then released their spirit into the biosphere beyond themselves? She shook. That prospect, she knew, could be a reality someday. All the women were preparing for that—. . . all of them were preparing for the time when it would be possible to gather their power, to direct it, and to confront whatever murderous violence threatened the earth. Many hoped it would not be necessary, that the violence would continue to be contained in the cities, but all held in common the knowledge that even if unnecessary, such an energy-gathering must be made possible.[57]

It is one potentiality they have been preparing themselves for—one end-in-view. This particular time they have been called together because the Gentles want to meet with them outside the city. To be asked to meet with men brings out the most basic anger, hatred, and fear in many of the women. It forces them to examine the very core of their being and their purpose. The Gentles are men and so some women, given their essentialist view of male nature as combative and destructive, believe they should have nothing to do with them. Men are violent and power-hungry. Men rape and "he who rapes must die."[58] Yet, the Gentles blur this absolute essentialist view; they are different. There has been built a basis for trust between the women serving rotations in the cities and the Gentles. They work together for a different future. This position is again countered with a sense of mistrust and independence. There is also apprehension that the women's energy will once again be drained by the needs of these men and misdirected. There is a strong feeling that men are just different by nature. They seek power and control. Whatever they can do they think they must do, regardless of the consequences for others. Even the Gentles have had trouble really sharing power. Some of the Hill Women believe that men do not, and cannot, have a relational understanding of the world and the creatures in it, only an understanding of a desire for dominance.

"That's the mistake the men made, sisterlove, and made over and over again. Just because it was possible they thought it had to be done. They came near to destroying the earth—and may yet—with that notion. Most of us like to think that even long ago women could have built what's been called 'western civilization'; we knew how to do all of it but rejected most such ideas as unnecessary or destructive."[59]

After much debate, several women decide to meet with the Gentles on their own. They agree to make it clear to the men that they are acting on their own and nothing they do or say will bind anyone else. They meet and the Gentles inform them that they have observed an interesting phenomenon. When there are, for any reason, fewer than the normal number of Hill Women in the cities, violence increases, some motors will start, and an occasional gun will fire. When the number of women increases it stops again. The women listen and are convinced that this is important and will be carried back to the others and discussed in another "gatherstretch." It appears their presence and their changed way of being is making a difference.

Equally of interest, though, in this face-to-face meeting of men and women outside the city, is the acknowledgment that they need each other but are not dependent. They have come to respect each other's need for independence, but may no longer have to fear or distrust each other. The Hill Women are no longer seen as superior by the Gentles but as possible partners. The Gentles have even begun to develop telepathic powers themselves. These abilities are different in both means and end, unique to the men. What most of the women can do by themselves takes four men in unison to do, such as communicate with an animal or move an object. The nature of the communication is also different. What the women do when they meet mind to mind is called enfoldment. The men do not enfold, but build a bridge.

The women's first reaction to this revelation is one of surprise and anger.

"How will you use that power? To pry into the lives of others? To conquer them?"
. . . "When have men ever used their power for anything else?" . . . "The whole raped world is a testimony to that."[60]

The men argue that they have developed and changed, discovering their own nonviolent psychic powers. While the women are still nervous, they realize they must learn to respect these men and their abilities even if they continue to distrust the traits which they have identified with maleness. Their situation has changed and, having begun to develop critical and flexible habits of mind, at least some of the women see the need to adapt to and use the change. They see the need to get beyond their essentialist view of male nature and see individuals for who they are. They had held the belief that "'it is too simple . . . to condemn them all or to praise all of us. But for the sake of the earth and all she holds, that simplicity must be our creed.'"[61] With the changes in these men they can now move beyond this creed. Now they can get beyond this simplicity and move in the gray area where absolutes do not apply—the situation has changed and so must the relations of the Hill Women and the Gentles. There is hope that these men have overcome the need for violence and power, and they must try to work together to save the mother—this is their task.

To work as if the earth, the mother, can be saved.
To work as if our healing care were not too late.
Work to stay the slayer's hand,
Helping him to change
Or helping him to die.
Work as if the earth, the mother, can be saved.[62]

The overwhelming urgency of the task and the presence and development of the Gentles allow for no essentialist views, no absolutes, no final ends, but require the women to modify and expand their vision for peaceful coexistence.

THE VALLEY AND THE WANDERGROUND—GOOD ENDS-IN-VIEW?

On the process model there are no fixed or final ends, but guiding aims or ends-in-view. Given the process view of our social existence, different societal arrangements or forms of association will count as ends-in-view, not final or static states. As has been discussed, to judge ends-in-view, or particular forms of association, there are at least five considerations. Does the particular form of association:

1. Promote free and open participation by all people in the society in order to help develop critical and flexible habits of mind.
2. Lead people to recognize the limits and possibilities of any particular situation and propose realistic choices for action.
3. Encourage people to avoid making dogmatic claims and to remain open to change.
4. Encourage people not to focus on achieving some end, but on developing abilities that allow for multiple ends to be realistically possible.
5. Open up possibilities and promote an awareness of our interconnectedness and diversity.

How do the societies of the Kesh and the Hill Women measure up in regard to these five criteria, developed out of Dewey's work, for judging a good end-in-view?

First, do the societies of the Kesh and the Hill Women promote free and open participation by all the people in the societies in order to develop critical and flexible habits of mind? The basis for both communities is the notion of the integrated individual, which includes the realization of her embeddedness and participation in the formation and direction of individual and conjoint actions. The Kesh see education and learning as a collaborative effort with others—people, animals, and nature. The Kesh are continually immersed in the relatedness of things. Each is responsible for certain aspects of community life and comes to learn, through the performance of her craft or art, that all is interconnected. Stories tell of people who do not do their share and so are poor because they have little to give to others. Stories tell of people who deny their connectedness to others and not only bring pain to others, but find that their own purposes are frustrated by their isolation. Living is a collaborative effort for the Hill Women, too, each having a special friend, her "learntogether," with whom she explores her ability to connect with all live creatures. The Hill Women see the relatedness of all things and see any one person's problems as the problems of all to be worked out together.

> *Your trouble,*
> *My trouble.*
> *Our ease.*[63]

Given this deep sense of embeddedness in each society, each individual sees participation in decision making as important and necessary. Each is affected by others and in turn affects others, so decisions must reflect the positions of all who are involved. The Kesh meet in their lodges regularly and all come together when faced with problems such as the Condor soldiers. The Hill Women serve on councils and all come together in a "gatherstretch" when faced by important decisions that deeply affect them all, such as the meeting with the Gentles. In both societies such meetings can be long, all sides having time and opportunity to voice their view and to be heard. Reconciliation and unanimity are the goal, although it is not always attained, and this goal requires a great deal of effort by all involved and a willingness to yield one's position and be flexible. Through such participation the people of these communities begin to form the critical and flexible habits of mind needed to act with understanding and foresight and to guide their future intelligently.

This brings us to the second criterion for judging forms of association. Are people led to recognize the limits and possibilities of their particular situation and to propose realistic choices for action? This proved to be a possible sticking point for Dewey's notion of a Great Community and may prove a difficult standard for the Kesh and Hill Women as well. As with Dewey, Le Guin and Gearhart may be overly optimistic about human possibilities for change and overlook some constraining features of our current situatedness and habits of living. All three believe that it is possible for people to gain a sense of themselves as integrated individuals, realizing their connectedness to all things. Dewey believed that advances in technology were shrinking the world and would force us to realize our connectedness. He also gives us a sketch of an educational method to help in achieving this sense of integration and to enable us to act with intelligence and foresight.

Le Guin and Gearhart also believe that advances in technology will force us to realize our interconnectedness or to die out. They then sketch what societies may look like if we choose to change and survive. The Kesh do not use their "expensive" technology except for pressing needs; the Hill Women continue their efforts to live cooperatively and change the violent energy of the cities. But we have realized for quite some time that our technologies are depleting the planet's resources and that violence is very costly. However, change is sometimes imperceptibly slow. While the visions of the Kesh and the Hill Women are certainly based on a realization of current situatedness, the solutions they purport to represent may exceed the possibilities for change for creatures of habit such as ourselves.

The third criterion raises the question of whether the Kesh and the Hill Women succeed in remaining open to change and in avoiding making dogmatic claims. Both communities depend on free and open inquiry, on trying different ways to live with the earth, on a willingness to change and adapt. Neither society presents a picture of an end-state—an arrangement which once reached will function once and for all. Rather, they present pictures of societies in which individuals are interacting with each other and their environment in an ongoing process. Ends-in-view change as people and situations develop and change. The Kesh begin to rethink their ways of living when they encounter the Condors. The Hill Women begin to rethink their positions and goals when they see that the Gentles have changed. As the conditions of the planet change, the possibilities and priorities for each people are rethought and adjusted to the new needs and desires of the people.

If a community does not focus on set ends, but is arranged around changing ends-in-view, it becomes necessary for the community to focus on developing the abilities of individuals that allow the community to achieve its multiplicity of ends-in-view and to adapt to changes in focus and circumstance. Hence, we come to the fourth criterion. Since there is no way to predict the particular needs of the future, each community needs to prepare people in the method of critical intelligence so that they can evaluate, guide, and adapt to changing ends-in-view.

While the need to develop a deep understanding of the relational nature of the world is seen to be the strongest basis for preparing people to act with critical intelligence, there is not much done in either book beyond pointing to this need and describing some community practices that encourage such an understanding. The Kesh have developed mindfulness—the intelligent awareness of interdependence. Mindfulness is a deep understanding of the world that helps them guide their future intelligently and to adapt to changing needs.

The Hill Women have developed their telepathic abilities to help them achieve a deeper understanding of the world, which in turn prepares them to adapt to changing needs. Their telepathy is an ability which is useful in achieving a variety of immediate ends-in-view and as a continual means to further and deeper understanding. As with most utopian novels, however, these two books are somewhat sketchy as to how the people come to have such understanding and provide only brief glimpses of such understanding being applied to problematic situations. Here, Dewey's notion of the integrated individual, developed and sustained through active inquiry, could go some way to filling in the needed methods of transition.

The final criterion for judging forms of association is the ability for the societal arrangement to open up possibilities and promote an awareness of our interconnectedness and diversity. Realizing one's social embeddedness should push her to be a reflective thinker who is able to engage difference in others as an opportunity for growth. On Dewey's view, plurality is a necessary condition for growth. As developmental creatures, we use the variety of experience to expand ourselves. The perspectives that we as individuals embody need to encounter and learn to communicate with other perspectives for growth to be possible.

Although the Kesh do not encounter other peoples all that frequently, they do seem open to those they do encounter. They seek to understand others and as a result prove to be good negotiators of trade agreements and good arbitrators in settling disputes. In general, they remain open to a variety of perspectives and so are able to bring them together and to learn from them. Sometimes, as with the Condors, what they learn is that these people are not open and it would be best not to deal with them now. The Kesh are also open to differences within their communities. Each town has its own idiosyncrasies and character. Some people prefer to attend certain rituals in one town or another because of different styles and interpretations; some just get along better in one place, among certain people, than in another. People are also encouraged to pursue their unique callings. Visionaries are as important to the community as electricians, tanners, and farmers. There does seem to be a limit to this openness, however. While homosexual marriages are recognized, and apparently not uncommon, it seems few people marry someone outside the Kesh people. In fact, non-Kesh people are referred to as no-House people. They are outside the community. There are several examples of friendly relations with non-Kesh people, however, and no clear reason is ever given for the infrequency of intermarriage.[64]

The Hill Women are open to and seek to learn from the diversity of nature (the various plants and animals) and from each other. Most of the women are dark skinned, though it would seem little notice is taken of skin color. There is no age prejudice. Young and old are seen as integral members of the community and as potential teachers. Each woman is seen as having an interesting perspective that is valuable, even within each one's individual limits — each one's carjer. In regard to men, however, there is little openness. Some women are absolutists on this score and want nothing to do with those they see essentially as rapists. For others this simplicity and absolutist attitude is troubling. This whole debate is changed, however, when the Gentles reveal their own changing natures. At this point it becomes possible to begin the process of opening up to at least some men and to begin to learn from each other.

It would appear that both the societies of the Kesh and of the Hill Women meet most of the criteria of the process model for a satisfying form of association. They represent possibilities for the future without proposing fixed and final ends, and without manipulating people into homogeneity. They promote growth, variety, and change in the process of dealing with real social concerns and problems. They show flexible individuals engaging the world with critical intelligence. They embrace the dynamic nature of the world and come to understand the rhythms of their experience in it. These societies show us unified individuals acting with foresight to address problems and form the future. These pragmatist and feminist visions encourage the reader to do the same.

NOTES

1. Charlene Haddock Seigfried, *Pragmatism and Feminism: Reweaving the Social Fabric* (Chicago: University of Chicago Press, 1996), 187–188. This book provides an excellent and comprehensive discussion of the connections between pragmatism and feminism (not to mention that it is the only one currently available). She discusses the historical links between pragmatism and pioneering women teachers and reformers. She discusses the feminist and anti-feminist aspects of the personal lives of canonical figures of pragmatism with particular focus on William James and John Dewey. She discusses the feminist and anti-feminist aspects of the philosophical theories of canonical figures of pragmatism, again with a particular focus on James and Dewey. Her discussion is very rich and deserves our attention. For my purposes here, however, I will focus on her discussion of pragmatism in general and John Dewey in particular.

2. Feminist theory, in all its variety, challenges dualisms and hierarchies. Radical feminists may present the most devastating challenge, seeking to eliminate such conceptual schemes. However, even liberal feminists challenge dualisms and hierarchical thinking as they challenge the placement of women in such schemes. I would like to again acknowledge, though, that I am not providing a full-blown analysis of the variety and complexity within feminist theory but examining and employing some fairly widely accepted feminist conceptualizations and challenges.

3. Seigfried, *Pragmatism and Feminism,* 148.

4. Seigfried, *Pragmatism and Feminism,* 154.

5. Seigfried, *Pragmatism and Feminism,* 158.

6. Seigfried, *Pragmatism and Feminism,* 158.

7. W.E.B. Du Bois argues that pragmatism in general fails to take the experience of those who are oppressed into account and this blocks its potential to realize the ideals of participatory democracy. The perspectives of those who are shut out must be acknowledged and their needs addressed. As long as any group is kept from participation, the radical potential of pragmatism will remain unfulfilled.

8. A specific example of what Young fears from such communitarianism can be found in Jean Bethke Elshtain's *Public Man, Private Woman* (Princeton, N.J.: Princeton University Press, 1981). Elshtain seeks a stable organization of community. The result is a rather traditional division of male/female spheres, work, and opportunities. Her focus on traditional family eclipses the reality of differences and limits the possibilities for the future. For an interesting discussion of this work, see Sally J. Scholz, "A Critique of Jean Bethke Elshtain's Reconstruction of the Public and the Private," *Contemporary Philosophy* 13 (July/August 1991): 19–23.

9. According to Young, these norms are usually the result of the "impartial" stance that masks the privileged, white, male perspective.

> The stances of detachment and dispassion that supposedly produce impartiality are attained only by abstracting from the particularities of situation, feeling, affiliation, and point of view. These particularities still operate, however, in the actual context of action. Thus the ideal of impartiality generates a dichotomy between universal and particular, public and private, reason and passion. It is, moreover, an impossible ideal, because the particularities of context and affiliation cannot and should not be removed from moral reasoning. Finally, the ideal of impartiality serves ideological functions. It masks the ways in which the particular perspectives of dominant groups claim universality, and helps justify hierarchical decision-making structures (97).

10. In Young's view, a "blind" society is not the ideal. As we cannot truly be impartial, trying not to see or acknowledge difference—racial, sexual, religious—only serves to block understanding, reaffirms the status quo, and forces some to deny their distinctiveness. We cannot make responsible choices for the present or the future if we are pretending differences are not important enough to accept and discuss and we cannot expect participation in social decision making from those people whose experiences and points of view are being overlooked. Groups who are affected by any combination of Young's five faces of oppression (exploitation, marginalization, powerlessness, cultural imperialism, and violence) need support to get their voices heard. Young proposes the following:

> Such group representation implies institutional mechanisms and public resources supporting (1) self-organization of group members so that they achieve collective empowerment and a reflective understanding of their collective experience and interests in the context of society; (2) group analysis and group generation of policy proposals in institutionalized contexts where decisionmakers are obliged to show that their deliberations have taken group perspectives into consideration; and (3) group veto power regarding specific policies that affect a group directly, such as reproductive rights policy for women, or land use policy for an Indian reservation (184).

11. Iris Marion Young, *Justice and the Politics of Difference* (Princeton, N.J.: Princeton University Press, 1990), 237.

12. There were also a few books on women and utopian experiments. Carol Kolmerton's *Women in Utopia: The Ideology of Gender in the American Owenite Communities* (Bloomington: Indiana University Press, 1990) comes to mind. There are also books on the women's utopias of the late nineteenth and early twentieth centuries: Darby Lewes' *Dream Revisionaries: Gender and Genre in Women's Utopian Fiction, 1870–1920* (Tuscaloosa: University of Alabama Press, 1995), and Carol Kessler's *Daring to Dream: Utopian Stories by United States Women, 1836–1919* (Boston: Pandora, 1984).

13. Lucy Sargisson, *Contemporary Feminist Utopianism* (London: Routledge, 1996), 226.

14. Sargisson, *Feminist Utopianism*, 227.

15. Sargisson, *Feminist Utopianism*, 87.

16. Sargisson, *Feminist Utopianism*, 91.

17. Sargisson, *Feminist Utopianism*, 105.

18. Sally Miller Gearhart, "Future Visions: Today's Politics: Feminist Utopias in Review," in *Women in Search of Utopia*, ed. Ruby Rohrlich and Elaine Baruch (New York: Schocken Books, 1984), 296.

19. Carol Pearson, "Coming Home: Four Feminist Utopias and Patriarchal Experience," in *Future Females*, ed. Marlene Barr (Bowling Green, Ohio: Bowling Green State University Popular Press, 1981), 63.

20. Jean Pfaelzer, "Response: What Happened to History?" in *Feminism, Utopia, and Narrative*, ed. Libby Jones and Sarah Goodwin (Knoxville: University of Tennessee Press, 1990), 193.

21. Pfaelzer, "Response," 195.

22. Pfaelzer, "Response," 64.

23. *The Ruins of Isis* and *The Dispossessed* also meet this definition. Though they have been discussed in less detail, they are important books.

24. I would argue that *The Gate to Women's Country* and *Woman on the Edge of Time* also demonstrate some of these commitments. Tepper's novel is ambiguous and acknowledges the flaws of the society in a back-handed way, suggesting other commitments. Piercy also takes an ambiguous stand on the violence in her novel. They do not unequivocally support the societies they create. They may well be read as pointing to the need for something else.

25. Ursula K. Le Guin, quoted in Pearson, "Coming Home," 68.

26. Angelika Bammer, *Partial Visions: Feminism and Utopianism* (New York: Routledge, 1991), 3.

27. Bammer, *Partial Visions*, 48.

28. Lee Cullen Khanna, "Change and Art in Women's Worlds," in *Women in Search of Utopia*, ed. Ruby Rohrlich and Elaine Baruch (New York: Schocken Books, 1984), 271.

29. Khanna, "Change and Art," 277.

30. Ursula K. Le Guin, *Always Coming Home* (New York: Bantam Books, 1987), 291–292.

31. Le Guin, *Always Coming Home*, 404.

32. Le Guin, *Always Coming Home*, 404–405.

33. Le Guin, *Always Coming Home*, 311.

34. Le Guin, *Always Coming Home*, 98.

35. Le Guin, *Always Coming Home*, 93.

36. Le Guin, *Always Coming Home*, 484.

37. Le Guin, *Always Coming Home*, 48–49.
38. Le Guin, *Always Coming Home*, 331.
39. Le Guin, *Always Coming Home*, 153.
40. Le Guin, *Always Coming Home*, 406.
41. Le Guin, *Always Coming Home*, 167.
42. Le Guin, *Always Coming Home*, 404.
43. Le Guin, *Always Coming Home*, 331.
44. Le Guin, *Always Coming Home*, 411.
45. Le Guin, *Always Coming Home*, 526.
46. Le Guin, *Always Coming Home*, 56.

47. Gearhart does not explain why there should be seven women, in addition to the flesh mother, or how they are chosen. It is mentioned that one can decline to be a seven sister.

48. Sally Miller Gearhart, *The Wanderground: Stories of the Hill Women* (Boston: Alyson Publications, 1979), 194.

49. Gearhart, *Wanderground*, 115.
50. Gearhart, *Wanderground*, 23.
51. Gearhart, *Wanderground*, 77.
52. Gearhart, *Wanderground*, 115.
53. Gearhart, *Wanderground*, 34–35.
54. Gearhart, *Wanderground*, 42.
55. Gearhart, *Wanderground*, 122.
56. Gearhart, *Wanderground*, 129.
57. Gearhart, *Wanderground*, 123.
58. Gearhart, *Wanderground*, 25.
59. Gearhart, *Wanderground*, 145.
60. Gearhart, *Wanderground*, 179.
61. Gearhart, *Wanderground*, 2.
62. Gearhart, *Wanderground*, 195.
63. Gearhart, *Wanderground*, 42.

64. One woman, Willow, marries a Condor soldier and has a daughter—Stone Telling, who becomes Woman Coming Home. When she was Stone Telling she always felt herself to be half a person, not fully accepted by the community and with no real place in it. She leaves with her father and lives with the Condor people for a while. After she returns home she is more secure in herself and apparently reenters Kesh life with little problem. A Condor woman who returns with her also assimilates into Kesh society and marries a Kesh man, and this seems to cause little notice. Perhaps the problem with Willow's marriage was the nature of the Condor men, not the fact that he was not Kesh, but it is not clear from the story which explanation is correct.

Chapter Six

The Future of Utopia

All three models of utopia discussed here can serve to critique past and present societal arrangements, principles, and objectives. All three can serve to push people to take a critical look at how they live their lives. All three can serve to encourage people to take action to transform their individual and societal situatedness. Each model, however, has its own problems and limits. We no longer live in a world that can find end-state and anarchist visions helpful in the task of directing change toward a fulfilling future. Given the need to cope with a global community, these visions are now inadequate and even dangerous. Intricately linked through business relations, environmental concerns, advances in technology, vulnerability to disease (such as AIDS), and fear of nuclear devastation, we need visions that take this connectedness into account and prepare people to cope with the multiplicity and complexity of possibilities the future may hold.

This does not mean the end of utopia, however. If we give up the task of utopia we surrender our future. We still need to formulate visions of the future to guide our goals and actions. It is the process model that offers the most help and opens up the most possibilities. It is important to retain utopian thought and dreams in order to create and nurture reasonable hope; utopia is an important task that we must undertake. The process model of utopia does not offer castles in the air, it does not rely on technology to solve all our problems, it does not allow people to sit passively, hoping for their dreams to materialize. The process model seeks to actively engage people in the task of making the future, accepting problems and conflicts as challenges to be met with critical reflection and intelligent action.

I propose the process model of utopia as an alternative to the end-state and anarchist models. I believe the end-state and anarchist models of utopia encourage habits of mind that can result in dogmatism, passivity, and violence. I believe we need to shift to the process model if we hope to shift our habits of mind. In this complex world we need the habit of flexible, critical engagement with the uncertain and the changing. I think visions based on the process model more realistically reflect and help transform our current situatedness.

Another possibility, however, is to see this process model of utopia as a metatheory which can guide our reading and formation of end-state and anarchist visions.[1] This can be a very productive approach as well. It would allow us to use end-state visions to transform our present, but prevent us from expecting them to provide final answers or perfect systems. It would allow us to seek the kind of equality and freedom proposed by anarchist visions, but prevent us from employing violent or restrictive means of transformation which are incompatible with our goals. Using the process model as a metatheory would be a way to find and use the best any vision has to offer without falling into the trap of thinking it has to provide all the answers or fix all our problems. I see great potential for this use of the process model and would not discourage others from employing it in this way. It may be a necessary stage in the transition of our thinking. I, however, have something else in mind.

As I have said, the process model is about different habits of mind. I resist the metatheory interpretation because the focus on process, rather than a plan, is a guide to ends-in-view that can guide our actions today. It provides a kind of vision that is, in many ways, antithetical to the end-state and anarchist visions. We must give up end-state visions that tend to be preoccupied with ends and indifferent to means, view individuals and society as a totality, make dogmatic assumptions, are preoccupied with management, and neglect human variety. Because end-state visions try to achieve a final lasting harmony through rational control of people and nature, they tend to be static, totalitarian nightmares. Such visions have little room for difference, see change as a sign of disintegration, and rely on an authoritarian system to keep people in the proper order.

In Sheri S. Tepper's *The Gate to Women's Country* we see a vision preoccupied with the end-state of a world without violence. An authoritarian elite makes the judgment that it is the warrior nature of most men that is the problem and undertakes to control the actions and choices of people in order to eliminate such individuals; they manage and direct human life as a mere tool to gain their desired end. Both overt violence, that is, killing off garrisons and attacking individuals who are seen as threatening, and more subtle genetic violence are used as means to achieve the end of a world without violence. The end-state vision lacks any understanding of the continuum of means and ends, is comfortable making dogmatic assumptions about human nature, and believes that rational control over the world and the live creatures in it can be gained and will fix problems once and for all. The result is a totalitarian, homogeneous society heading toward stasis. Such forced homogeneity and harmony are rather empty and do little to promote growth.

If we use the process model as a metatheory to read this particular vision, we could see Stavia's discomfort with the Council's (the Damned Few) actions as encouraging us to critique this authoritarian approach. When she weeps at the end, knowing she is sending her son to die, we would realize that this is a dystopia (or a very ambiguous utopia)—a vision we do not want to pursue. I think this is a very possible and useful reading of *The Gate to Women's Country*. I do not think Tepper herself endorses Women's Country as an ideal. She pushes us to object, along with Stavia, and to see the complexity and ambiguity of the choices people are making. However, since no alternative is provided, this vision does not take us very far. It does succeed in unsettling most readers. I use this book in my "Women and Philosophy" class and invariably students are angry when they figure out what is going on. Then, as we discuss it, there is usually a shift in tone and some begin to suggest that, given the situation, this is what the women had to do. Stavia's weeping is not seen as a critique, but as acceptance of a hard but necessary reality. Since there is no hint that Stavia plans to change things now that she understands what is going on, I think this is the more likely message that readers will take away. Even using the process model as a metatheory to frame interpretation I worry that this vision reinforces the notion that we need to try to control and manage our world, and the people in it, through some authority.

Anarchist visions are better in that they do take into account the connectedness of the world and the live creatures in it; they do see multiple possibilities for the future rather than a final, static, homogeneous end-state. However, such visions do not provide a method through which to prepare people to participate in the ongoing experiment. This lack of preparation may pose a threat to diversity. People may seek conformity to avoid disorder. Further, without people prepared to direct and control themselves it can easily happen that they will fall back into allowing someone else to define a desired end-state and direct them toward it.

In *Woman on the Edge of Time* we see a vision preoccupied with increasing the probability of their anarchist federation coming into existence. The people of Mattapoisett not only fight a war in their time, they encourage people of our time to strike out against the violence, manipulation, and control that are part of daily life (doctors, pimps, government). Their response to violence is more violence. While the people tacitly acknowledge that Mattapoisett is only one of several possible futures, and is in itself an ever-changing social arrangement, they are willing to kill (and ask others to kill) for its achievement and its continued existence. In addition to the war, there is internal violence against those who are violent, those who do not get along well with others, and those who do not do their share of the work. If someone fails to gain and act on a sense of mutual reciprocity, they are ostracized, fixed (healed), or killed. Some propose to begin genetically shaping people to fit. The idea that there is a shape that fits implies, once again, a focus on an end-state and a desire to manage and direct human life as a mere tool to gain the desired end. Without more of a focus on developing people immersed in critical intelligence, and so able to adapt to future changes without becoming dogmatic and manipulative, there is still little potential for growth and little chance that the people will move experience forward in a satisfying and fulfilling way.

If we use the process model as a metatheory to read this particular vision we could see Connie's concerns about killing the doctors as encouraging us to critique the violent means being employed to reach this future end. When she kills the doctors we would realize that this is a dystopia (or a very ambiguous utopia) that we cannot afford to achieve. The means employed betray the desired goals. As with Tepper, it is not clear that Piercy endorses Connie's actions and she too pushes us to see the complexity and ambiguity of the choices people are making. However, since (as with *Women's Country*) no alternative is provided or explored, this vision does not take us very far. This book also tends to unsettle students. In my "Making the Future" class, students sympathize with Connie, but at first they are not sure that her actions are warranted. Since the future of Mattapoisett is not *guaranteed* by her killing the doctors, only made more possible, they are not sure she is justified. What usually starts to come through these conversations, though, is the idea that if her actions were *very likely* to bring about the desired future, then she was justified. As with Stavia, Connie and my students seem to accept what they perceive as the hard reality that sometimes violent methods are necessary and justified if the end is important enough and likely to be achieved. I think this is the most likely message readers will take away. Even with using the process model as a metatheory to frame interpretation, I worry that this vision reinforces the notion that "'we must fight to come to exist, to remain in existence, to be the future that happens.'"[2] We need an alternative. We need the process model of utopia.

Paying attention to feminist theory, the process model acknowledges the need to develop a method for sustaining open and flexible citizens who respect differences if they are to avoid having small, closed, homogeneous communities. The process model does not seek to achieve a specific plan of action, but to form the ability in each of us to develop various plans to try out. A participatory democracy, inhabited by people with critical and flexible habits of mind, is the necessary ground for a process model of utopia, though it is not a final end itself. It is hoped such citizens can be created, and their participation sustained, through education. Education can be used to create socially responsible citizens embedded in the method of intelligence and experimentation. A task-oriented education that involves students in live inquiry is the means for developing individuals committed to the method of intelligence—observation, reflection, judgment, and vision. While human creatures are born already associated, they are not born as functioning members of a community; they are not born as socially responsible individuals immersed in the method of intelligence. They must grow into being socially responsible individuals. It takes effort to combat the habit of being close-minded and to strive to develop and sustain the habit of free and open inquiry. This means thinking things through, acting on transitory conclusions, and revising our theories. It means learning to live with uncertainty.

In *Always Coming Home* and *The Wanderground* we see visions of people living with uncertainty. In these books people are dealing with the aftermath and possible resurgence of violence. Rather than trying to eliminate the people who are considered violent, though, there is instead a focus on transforming the way people look at themselves in relation to the world and other creatures in it. Neither society seeks to achieve a specific arrangement, but to form the ability in each person to develop, try out, and evaluate a variety of plans. These people have to unlearn old habits of seeking rational control to gain a perfect world and learn new habits that help them to be continually adaptive—participating in free and open inquiry. In each society there are social arrangements, rituals, and practices that encourage and reinforce an understanding of the relational nature of things and help people to see themselves as active participants in the formation of their futures.

Both societies see education and learning as a collaborative effort—it is an activity done with others. In fact, these people see living as a collaborative effort. Everyone has individual responsibilities, but each understands her connectedness to others and her social responsibilities. Given this sense of embeddedness, each individual sees participation in social decision making as important and necessary. These people form the critical and flexible habits of mind needed to act with understanding and foresight and to guide their future intelligently. They achieve lived experience. By using the process model of utopia, not as a metatheory but as an actual guide in forming the visions, we begin to see how it would be possible to live with more open, critical, and flexible habits of mind. Students who chose to work on feminist utopias for their presentation in my "Women and Philosophy" class found these books challenging but invigorating. At first they complained that these books spent too much time on the personal transformation of the women and were not sufficiently focused on social transformation. As they struggled with how to do their class presentation, though, they came to see that it was the change in the habits of mind of these future people that constituted the hope of the visions.

People can become capable of directing their future when they engage in controlled inquiry. Such inquiry requires a recognition of the continuity and connectedness of live creatures and their environment and of each experience to possible future experiences. People who come together to solve common problems, or to investigate common interests, can learn about one another's differences but not see them as threatening or directly challenging to any particular way of life as a whole. People engaged in controlled inquiry are more likely, though not inevitably, to become open to learning about different perspectives as these perspectives can offer a variety of opinions and a greater breadth of knowledge and ideas about how to deal with common problems and promote common projects.

Being immersed in a task, one is more likely to see the educational aspects of plurality, be encouraged to participate in directing one's life, and to develop flexible habits of mind. The process model of utopia takes into account the connectedness of the world and the live creatures in it; it postulates multiple possibilities for the future rather than a final, static, homogeneous endstate, and seeks to sustain a critical, flexible, and open-minded citizenry. Process visions represent possibilities for the future without proposing fixed and final ends, and without manipulating people into homogeneity. Visions on this model can help us understand, cope with, and transform our current situatedness. Visions on this model can move experience forward in a satisfying and fulfilling way, but only if people are willing to work at remaining critical, flexible, and open-minded.

Herein lies the biggest obstacle for the process model. On the end-state model it is proposed to arrange things so that people behave or think in a certain way according to a certain vision. The changes are not so much the choice of the people or in the people's control; it is done for them by the authoritarian elite who has defined the end. There is little or no effort called for, or responsibility taken by, the majority of the people on end-state visions. Anarchist visions require people to participate in the directing of their lives, but they, too, can fall back on end-state visions if the people are not prepared to think critically for themselves in an open-minded and flexible manner. Even if the process model can prepare people to be the critical citizens it needs (a huge task in itself), how can it ensure that they actually will participate and take on their responsibilities? The process model asks a great deal of people in terms of time and effort. Apathetic or lazy citizens will not take up the critical stance easily. Where the end-state vision does not ask enough of people, or give enough responsibility to them, the process model may ask and give too much. If we are to gain a sense of ourselves as integrated individuals, realizing our connectedness to all things, we must change many habitual ways of conceiving of ourselves and others. It means changing how we relate to the earth and the other creatures in it. While the process model may require more of people than we are prepared to give now, visions on this model can provide us with insight into the means available to change our attitudes and action and show us the possibilities of the future if we are willing to try to change and become Dewey's integrated individual.

I believe there is reason to hope for the success of the process model. It is never a complete success because at any given time there will be people who refuse to take an active part in forming the future. However, a large-scale attitudinal shift is possible. People are not apathetic or lazy by nature (we are future-oriented creatures), but become so by being alienated from the processes that direct our lives. The participation called for by the process model will take a leap of faith by some, but will produce concrete consequences. Not everyone will get what they want all the time, but they should see a system that takes their engagement seriously and a society in which their actions do make a difference.[3] If apathy is lifted and lived experience is seen to be possible, people will realize their dissatisfaction with received experience; and so many will continue the effort of engagement that makes lived experience possible.

On the process model it becomes important for us to critically examine the goals we choose to pursue since what we choose to pursue now defines what we will be able to pursue in the future. On this model we must accept responsibility for creating the future and develop a critical method of directing it, and not wait for it to simply unfold. We need to see life, and our visions of what could be possible, as an experimental process—an experimental coping with conflict and difficulties. Rather than seek perfection, the process model of utopia seeks to create and sustain people willing to take on responsibility and participate in directing their present toward a better, more desirable future. We need to continue to try; we must have hope and remain active agents in forming the future. We must take on the task of utopia.

Utopian thought, by providing visions to which we might aspire, helps us to understand ourselves both as we are and as we might be. Such visions can help us decide what to do now to improve how we live; they can provide a description of an end-in-view which can serve to guide what goes on in our present actions. "Art is a mode of prediction not found in charts and statistics, and it insinuates possibilities of human relations not to be found in rule and precept, admonition and administration."[4] Utopian visions are visions of hope that can challenge us to explore a range of possible human conditions. If one can get beyond trying to achieve final perfect end-states and accept that there are instead multiple possible futures-in-process, one has taken the first step in understanding the responsibility each of us has to the future in deciding how to live our lives now.

NOTES

1. I am indebted to Lisa Heldke for providing this suggestion.

2. Marge Piercy, *Woman on the Edge of Time* (New York: Fawcett Crest, 1976), 197–198.

3. One can hope that here, in the United States, the elections of 2000 have awakened people to the importance of their responsible participation in the political process.

4. John Dewey, *Art as Experience,* in *John Dewey: The Later Works, Vol. 10: 1934,* ed. Jo Ann Boydston (Carbondale: Southern Illinois University Press, 1987), 352.

Bibliography

Albinski, N. B. *Women's Utopias*. New York: Routledge, 1988.

Alexander, Thomas M. *John Dewey's Theory of Art, Experience, and Nature: The Horizons of Feeling*. New York: SUNY Press, 1987.

Bakunin, Mikhail. "Protestation of the Alliance." In *Quotations from the Anarchists*, ed. Paul Berman (p. 8). New York: Praeger, 1972.

———. *Statism and Anarchy*, trans. Marshall S. Shatz. Cambridge: Cambridge University Press, 1990.

Baldelli, Giovanni. *Social Anarchism*. Chicago: Aldine Atherton, 1971.

Bammer, Angelika. *Partial Visions: Feminism and Utopianism*. New York: Routledge, 1991.

Barr, Marlene. *Future Females: A Critical Anthology*. Bowling Green, Ohio: Bowling Green State University Popular Press, 1981.

Barr, Marlene, and Nicholas Smith, eds. *Women and Utopia: Critical Interpretations*. New York: University Press of America, 1983.

Bartkowski, Frances. *Feminist Utopias*. Lincoln: University of Nebraska Press, 1989.

Bellamy, Edward. *Looking Backward*. New York: Penguin Books, 1988.

Benhabib, Seyla. *Situating the Self: Gender, Community, and Postmodernism in Contemporary Ethics*. New York: Routledge, 1992.

Berkman, Alexander. *What Is Communist Anarchism?* New York: Dover, 1972.

Berman, Paul, ed. *Quotations from the Anarchists*. New York: Praeger, 1972.

Berneri, Marie Louise. *Journey Through Utopia*. London: Routledge & Kegan Paul, 1950.

Bernstein, Richard J. "Community in the Pragmatist Tradition." In *The Revival of Pragmatism*, ed. Morris Dickstein (pp. 141–56). Durham, N.C.: Duke University Press, 1998.

Betz, Joseph. "John Dewey and Paulo Freire." *Transactions* 28 (Winter 1992): 107–126.

Bloch, Ernst. *The Principle of Hope*, trans. Neville Plaice, Stephen Plaice, and Paul Knight. Cambridge, Mass.: MIT Press, 1986.

Boyd, William. *The Education Theory of Jean Jacques Rousseau*. New York: Russell & Russell, 1963.

Bradley, Marion Zimmer. *The Ruins of Isis*. New York: Pocket Books, 1978.

169

Campbell, James. *The Community Reconstructs: The Meaning of Pragmatic Social Thought.* Urbana: University of Illinois Press, 1992.

Cassirer, Ernst. *An Introduction to a Philosophy of Human Culture.* New Haven, Conn.: Yale University Press, 1944.

Crockatt, Richard. "John Dewey and Modern Revolutions." *REAL—Yearbook of Research in English and American Literature,* vol. 7 (1990): 191–220.

Dahrendorf, Ralf. "Out of Utopia: Toward a Reorientation of Sociological Analysis." In *Utopia,* ed. George Kateb (pp. 103–126). New York: Atherton Press, 1971.

Davies, Sir Alfred T., ed. *Robert Owen (1771–1858) Pioneer, Social Reformer and Philanthropist—A Memoir.* Manchester, England: Cooperative Wholesale Society, 1948.

Davis, J. C. *Utopia and the Ideal Society.* Cambridge: Cambridge University Press, 1981.

Dewey, John. *Art as Experience.* In *John Dewey: The Later Works, Vol. 10: 1934,* ed. Jo Ann Boydston. Carbondale: Southern Illinois University Press, 1987.

———. "Challenge to Liberal Thought." In *John Dewey: The Later Works, Vol. 15: 1942–1948,* ed. Jo Ann Boydston (pp. 261–275). Carbondale: Southern Illinois University Press, 1989.

———. "Creative Democracy: The Task Before Us." In *John Dewey: The Later Works, Vol. 14: 1939–1941,* ed. Jo Ann Boydston (pp. 224–230). Carbondale: Southern Illinois University Press, 1988.

———. "Freedom and Culture." In *John Dewey: The Later Works, Vol. 13: 1938–1939,* ed. Jo Ann Boydston (pp. 63–188). Carbondale: Southern Illinois University Press, 1988.

———. *Democracy and Education.* In *John Dewey: The Middle Works, Vol. 9: 1916,* ed. Jo Ann Boydston. Carbondale: Southern Illinois University Press, 1980.

———. "Dewey Outlines Utopian Schools." In *John Dewey: The Later Works, Vol. 9: 1933–1934,* ed. Jo Ann Boydston (pp. 136–140). Carbondale: Southern Illinois University Press, 1986.

———. "The Economic Basis of the New Society." In *John Dewey: The Later Works, Vol. 13: 1938–1939,* ed. Jo Ann Boydston (pp. 309–322). Carbondale: Southern Illinois University Press, 1988.

———. *Ethics.* In *John Dewey: The Middle Works, Vol. 5: 1908,* ed. Jo Ann Boydston. Carbondale: Southern Illinois University Press, 1978.

———. *Experience and Nature.* In *John Dewey: The Later Works, Vol. 1: 1925,* ed. Jo Ann Boydston. Carbondale: Southern Illinois University Press, 1981.

———. "From Absolutism to Experimentalism." In *John Dewey: The Later Works, Vol. 5: 1929–1930,* ed. Jo Ann Boydston (pp. 147–60). Carbondale: Southern Illinois University Press, 1984.

———. *Human Nature and Conduct.* In *John Dewey: The Middle Works, Vol. 14: 1922,* ed. Jo Ann Boydston. Carbondale: Southern Illinois University Press, 1983.

———. "Liberalism and Social Action." In *John Dewey: The Later Works, Vol. 11: 1935–1937,* ed. Jo Ann Boydston (pp. 1–65). Carbondale: Southern Illinois University Press, 1986.

———. *Logic: The Theory of Inquiry.* In *John Dewey: The Later Works, Vol. 12: 1938,* ed. Jo Ann Boydston. Carbondale: Southern Illinois University Press, 1986.

———. "The Logic of Judgments of Practice." In *John Dewey: The Middle Works, Vol. 8: 1915,* ed. Jo Ann Boydston (pp. 14–83). Carbondale: Southern Illinois University Press, 1979.

———. "Nationalizing Education." In *John Dewey: The Middle Works, Vol. 10: 1916–1917,* ed. Jo Ann Boydston (pp. 202–210). Carbondale: Southern Illinois University Press, 1980.

———. "The Need of an Industrial Education in an Industrial Democracy." In *John Dewey: The Middle Works, Vol. 10: 1916–1917,* ed. Jo Ann Boydston (pp. 137–143). Carbondale: Southern Illinois University Press, 1980.

———. "Philosophy and Education." In *John Dewey: The Later Works, Vol. 5: 1929–1930,* ed. Jo Ann Boydston (pp. 289–298). Carbondale: Southern Illinois University Press, 1984.

———. *The Public and Its Problems.* In *John Dewey: The Later Works, Vol. 2: 1925–1927,* ed. Jo Ann Boydston (pp. 235–372). Carbondale: Southern Illinois University Press, 1984.

———. *The Quest for Certainty.* In *John Dewey: The Later Works, Vol. 4: 1929,* ed. Jo Ann Boydston. Carbondale: Southern Illinois University Press, 1984.

———. *Reconstruction in Philosophy.* In *John Dewey: The Middle Works, Vol. 12: 1920,* ed. Jo Ann Boydston (77–201). Carbondale: Southern Illinois University Press, 1982.

———. "Report and Recommendation upon Turkish Education." In *John Dewey: The Middle Works, Vol. 15: 1923–1924,* ed. Jo Ann Boydston (pp. 279–297). Carbondale: Southern Illinois University Press, 1983.

———. "The School and Society." In *John Dewey: The Middle Works, Vol. 1: 1899–1901,* ed. Jo Ann Boydston (pp. 5–109). Carbondale: Southern Illinois University Press, 1976.

Eldridge, Michael. *Transforming Experience: John Dewey's Cultural Instrumentalism.* Nashville, Tenn.: Vanderbilt University Press, 1998.

Elshtain, Jean Bethke. *Public Man, Private Woman.* Princeton, N.J.: Princeton University Press, 1981.

Eltzbacher, Paul. *Anarchism: Exponents of the Anarchist Philosophy.* New York: Libertarian Book Club, 1960.

Fanon, Frantz. *The Wretched of the Earth.* New York: Grove Weidenfeld, 1963.

Fourier, Charles. *The Social Destiny of Man.* New York: Gordon Press, 1972.

Fox, Richard G. *Gandhian Utopia.* Boston: Beacon Press, 1989.

Gearhart, Sally Miller. "Future Visions: Today's Politics: Feminist Utopias in Review." In *Women in Search of Utopia,* ed. Ruby Rohrlich and Elaine Baruch (pp. 296–309). New York: Schocken Books, 1984.

———. *The Wanderground: Stories of the Hill Women.* Boston: Alyson Publications, 1979.

Gilman, Charlotte Perkins. *Herland.* Introduction by Ann J. Lane. New York: Pantheon Books, 1979.

———. *The Home: Its Work and Influence.* Urbana: University of Illinois Press, 1972.

———. *The Man–Made World.* New York: Charlton Co., 1911.

Godwin, William. *Enquiry Concerning Political Justice,* ed. Raymond A. Preston. 2 vols. New York: Alfred A. Knopf, 1926.

Goldman, Emma. *Anarchism and Other Essays.* New York: Kennikat Press, 1910.

———. "Anarchism: What It Really Stands For." In *Anarchism,* ed. Robert Hoffman (pp. 34–49). New York: Atherton Press, 1970.

———. *My Further Disillusionment in Russia.* New York: Doubleday, Page & Co., 1924.

———. "The Place of the Individual in Society." In *Quotations from the Anarchists,* ed. Paul Berman (p. 39). New York: Praeger, 1972.

Golffing, Francis, and Barbara Golffing. "An Essay on Utopian Possibility." In *Utopia,* ed. George Kateb (pp. 29–39). New York: Atherton Press, 1971.

Goodwin, Barbara. *Social Science and Utopia: Nineteenth Century Models of Social Harmony.* Atlantic Highlands, N.J.: Humanities Press, 1978.

Goodwin, Barbara, and Taylor, Keith, eds. *The Politics of Utopia: A Study in Theory and Practice*. New York: St. Martin's Press, 1982.

Grimshaw, Jean. *Philosophy and Feminist Thinking*. Minneapolis: University of Minnesota Press, 1986.

Guerin, Daniel. *Anarchism: From Theory to Practice*, trans. Mary Klopper. New York: Monthly Review Press, 1970.

Hansot, Elisabeth. *Perfection and Progress: Two Modes of Utopian Thought*. Cambridge, Mass.: MIT Press, 1974.

Hickman, Larry A. *Reading John Dewey: Interpretations for a Postmodern Generation*. Bloomington: Indiana University Press, 1998.

Hocking, William Ernest. "The Philosophical Anarchist." In *Anarchism*, ed. Robert Hoffman (pp. 115–124). New York: Atherton Press, 1970.

Hoffman, Robert, ed. *Anarchism*. New York: Atherton Press, 1970.

Huxley, Aldous. *Brave New World*. New York: Harper & Row, 1946.

Jacoby, Russell. *The End of Utopia: Politics and Culture in an Age of Apathy*. New York: Basic Books, 1999.

Jaggar, Alison. *Feminist Politics and Human Nature*. Totowa, N.J.: Rowman & Littlefield, 1988.

James, William. *Pragmatism*. Indianapolis: Hackett, 1981.

——. "What Makes a Life Significant." In *The Writings of William James*, ed. John J. McDermott (pp. 645–60). Chicago: University of Chicago Press.

Johnson, Greg. "The Situated Self and Utopian Thinking." *Hypatia* (forthcoming, Summer 2002).

Jones, Libby Falk, and Sarah Webster Goodwin. *Feminism, Utopia, and Narrative*. Knoxville: University of Tennessee Press, 1990.

Kateb, George. *Utopia and Its Enemies*. London: Collier-Macmillan, 1975.

——, ed. *Utopia*. New York: Atherton Press, 1971.

Kessler, Carol F. "Bibliography of Utopian Fiction by United States Women, 1836–1988." *Utopian Studies* 1 (1990): 1–58.

——. *Daring to Dream: Utopian Stories by United States Women, 1836–1919*. Boston: Pandora, 1984.

Khanna, Lee Cullen. "Change and Art in Women's Worlds." In *Women in Search of Utopia*, ed. Ruby Rohrlich and Elaine Baruch (pp. 269–279). New York: Schocken Books, 1984.

Kohak, Erazim. "Central Europe's Post-Captive Minds." *Harper's* (June 1992): 15–19.

Kolmerton, Carol A. *Women in Utopia: The Ideology of Gender in the American Owenite Communities*. Bloomington: Indiana University Press, 1990.

Kropotkin, P. A. *The Great French Revolution 1789–1793*. New York: Vanguard Press, 1909.

——. *Revolutionary Studies*. London: Office of the Commonweal, 1892.

Kumar, Krishan. *Utopia and Anti-Utopia in Modern Times*. New York: Basil Blackwell, 1987.

——. *Utopianism*. Minneapolis: University of Minnesota Press, 1991.

Le Guin, Ursula K. *Always Coming Home*. New York: Bantam Books, 1987.

——. *The Dispossessed: An Ambiguous Utopia*. New York: Harper Paperback, 1974.

Levitas, Ruth. *The Concept of Utopia*. Syracuse, N.Y.: Syracuse University Press, 1990.

Lewes, Darby. *Dream Revisionaries: Gender and Genre in Women's Utopian Fiction 1870–1920.* Tuscaloosa: University of Alabama Press, 1995.

Malatesta, Errico. "Umanita Nova." In *Quotations from the Anarchists,* ed. Paul Berman (p. 9). New York: Praeger, 1972.

Manuel, Frank E., and Fritzie P. Manuel. *Utopian Thought in the Western World.* Cambridge: Belknap Press, 1979.

Marcuse, Herbert. *An Essay on Liberation.* Boston: Beacon Press, 1969.

Misenheimer, Helen Evans. *Rousseau on the Education of Women.* Washington, D.C.: University Press of America, 1981.

Morris, William. *News From Nowhere and Selected Writings and Designs.* New York: Penguin Books, 1986.

Mumford, Lewis. *The Story of Utopia.* New York: Boni & Liverright, 1922.

Murphey, Murray. "Introduction," in *John Dewey: The Middle Works, Vol. 14: 1922,* ed. Jo Ann Boydston (pp. ix–xviii). Carbondale: Southern Illinois University Press, 1983.

Okin, Susan Moller. "Rousseau's Natural Woman." *Journal of Politics* 41 (May 1979): 393–416.

Parker, S. E. *Individualist Anarchism: An Outline.* London: S. E. Parker, 1965.

Parsons, Lucy. "Interview with the New York *World.*" In *Quotations from the Anarchists,* ed. Paul Berman (p. 49). New York: Praeger, 1972.

Patai, Daphne. "Beyond Defensiveness: Feminist Research Strategies." In *Women and Utopia,* ed. Marlene Barr and Nicholas Smith (pp. 148–169). New York: University Press of America, 1983.

Pateman, Carole. *The Disorder of Women.* Stanford, Calif.: Stanford University Press, 1989.

———. *The Sexual Contract.* Stanford, Calif.: Stanford University Press, 1988.

Pateman, Carole, and Elizabeth Gross, eds. *Feminist Challenges.* Boston: Northeastern University Press, 1986.

Pearson, Carol. "Coming Home: Four Feminist Utopias and Patriarchal Experience." In *Future Females,* ed. Marlene Barr (pp. 63–70). Bowling Green, Ohio: Bowling Green State University Popular Press, 1981.

Pfaelzer, Jean. "Response: What Happened to History?" In *Feminism, Utopia, and Narrative,* ed. Libby Jones and Sarah Goodwin (pp. 191–200). Knoxville: University of Tennessee Press, 1990.

Piercy, Marge. *Woman on the Edge of Time.* New York: Fawcett Crest, 1976.

Plato. *The Republic and Other Works,* trans. B. Jowett. New York: Anchor Press, 1973.

Popper, Karl. *The Open Society and Its Enemies.* Princeton, N.J.: Princeton University Press, 1950.

Ratner, Joseph. *Intelligence in the Modern World: John Dewey's Philosophy.* New York: Modern Library, 1929.

Rawls, John. *The Law of Peoples.* Cambridge, Mass.: Harvard University Press, 1999.

Read, Herbert. *Anarchy and Order.* London: Faber & Faber, 1954.

Rohrlich, Ruby, and Elaine Hoffman Baruch. *Women in Search of Utopia: Mavericks and Mythmakers.* New York: Schocken Books, 1984.

Rorty, Richard. "For a More Banal Politics." *Harper's* (May 1992): 16–21.

———. *Philosophy and the Mirror of Nature.* Princeton, N.J.: Princeton University Press, 1979.

Rosinsky, N. *Feminist Futures.* Ann Arbor, Mich.: UMI Research Press, 1988.

Ross, Ralph. "Introduction." In *John Dewey: The Middle Works, Vol. 13: 1921–1922,* ed. Jo Ann Boydston (pp. ix–xxix). Carbondale: Southern Illinois University Press, 1983.

Rousseau, Jean Jacques. *Emile.* London: Everyman's Library, 1972.

———. *On the Social Contract,* trans. Judith Masters. New York: St. Martin's Press, 1978.

Sargent, Lyman Tower. *British and American Utopian Literature 1516–1985: An Annotated, Chronological Bibliography.* New York: Garland, 1988.

———. "Social Decision Making in Anarchism and Minimalism." *The Personalist* 59 (October 1978): 358–369.

———. "William Morris and the Anarchist Tradition." In *Socialism and the Literary Artistry of William Morris,* ed. Florence S. Boos and Carole G. Silver (pp. 61–73). Columbia: University of Missouri Press, 1990.

Sargisson, Lucy. *Contemporary Feminist Utopianism.* London: Routledge, 1996.

Schehr, Robert C. *Dynamic Utopia: Establishing Intentional Communities as a New Social Movement.* Westport, Conn.: Bergin and Garvey, 1997.

Scholz, Sally J. "A Critique of Jean Bethke Elshtain's Reconstruction of the Public and the Private," *Contemporary Philosophy* 13 (July/August 1991): 19–23.

Seigfried, Charlene Haddock. "John Dewey's Pragmatist Feminism." In *Reading Dewey,* ed. Larry A. Hickman (pp. 187–216). Bloomington: Indiana University Press, 1998.

———. *Pragmatism and Feminism: Reweaving the Social Fabric.* Chicago: University of Chicago Press, 1996.

Shklar, Judith. *After Utopia: The Decline of Political Faith.* Princeton, N.J.: Princeton University Press, 1957.

Silbergleid, Robin. "Women, Utopia, and Narrative: Toward a Postmodern Feminist Citizenship." *Hypatia* 12: 4 (1997): 156–172.

Skinner, B. F. "Freedom and the Control of Men." In *Utopia,* ed. George Kateb (pp. 57–75). New York: Atherton Press, 1971.

Stuhr, John J. "Dewey's Social and Political Philosophy." In *Reading Dewey,* ed. Larry A. Hickman (pp. 82–99). Bloomington: Indiana University Press, 1998.

———. *Genealogical Pragmatism: Philosophy, Experience, and Community.* New York: SUNY Press, 1997.

Taylor, Michael. *Community, Anarchy, and Liberty.* Cambridge: Cambridge University Press, 1982.

Tepper, Sheri S. *The Gate to Women's Country.* New York: Bantam Books, 1988.

Tiger, Lionel. *Optimism: The Biology of Hope.* New York: Simon & Schuster, 1979.

Tong, Rosemarie Putnam. *Feminist Thought: A More Comprehensive Introduction.* Boulder, Colo.: Westview Press, 1998.

Weiss, Penny. *Gendered Community: Rousseau, Sex, and Politics.* New York: New York University Press, 1993.

Wellmer, Albrecht. "Models of Freedom." *Philosophical Forum* (1990): 227–252.

West, Cornel. *The American Evasion of Philosophy.* Madison: University of Wisconsin Press, 1989.

Westbrook, Robert B. *John Dewey and American Democracy.* Ithaca, N.Y.: Cornell University Press, 1991.

Wieck, David Thoreau. " Essentials of Anarchism." In *Anarchism,* ed. Robert Hoffman (pp. 86–97). New York: Atherton Press, 1970.

Young, Iris Marion. *Justice and the Politics of Difference.* Princeton, N.J.: Princeton University Press, 1990.

Index

Alexander, Thomas M., 85, 88–89, 90–91
Always Coming Home (Le Guin), 12, 141–47, 153–57, 165–66
anarchist model: description of, 11–12, 49–53; Dewey's rejection of, 94–95; examples of 11–12, 62–63, 67–74; problems of 11–12, 50, 53–58, 65–68, 74–80; strengths of, 11–12, 49, 74–75. *See also* utopia
animals, 82n50, 127n70, 144, 148, 150, 154

Bakunin, Mikhail, 52, 54, 60
Bammer, Angelika, 136, 139–40
Bellamy, Edward, 1, 27
Bernstein, Richard, 5
Bradley, Marion Zimmer, 22–23
Brave New World (Huxley), 18, 24

Cassirer, Ernst, 51
change: acceptance of, 5–6, 9, 20, 47n42, 49–50, 84, 91–92, 96, 117, 140–41, 155, 165; fear of, 7, 17–19, 35–36, 94, 96
community. *See* Great Community
critical intelligence: description of, 8, 12, 43, 83–84, 95, 155; need for, 3, 5, 79, 88–89, 106

Davis, J. C., 22
democracy: as association, 100, 110, 116; as community, 116, 118, 121–22; and education, 100–102; as experimental inquiry, 83–84, 93–94, 112–14; as method, 12, 83, 93–95, 112, 114; moral meaning, 93, 106, 110; as a way of living, 12, 83, 93, 112–13, 123
Dewey, John: *Art as Experience*, 10, 85, 92, 167; on democracy (*see* democracy); *Democracy and Education*, 90, 94, 98, 100; on education (*see* education); *Ethics*, 99; *Experience and Nature*, 84, 89, 91; *Human Nature and Conduct*, 6, 88, 106, 112; on lived experience (*see* experience); *Logic: Theory of Inquiry*, 119–120; *The Public and Its Problems*. 6, 107–10, 112–18, 120–22; *Quest for Certainty*, 35, 86–87, 92, 103–5; on utopia, 5–6, 101–2. *See also* process model; utopia
difference. *See* diversity; pluralism
disintegration of visions, 8, 34, 79–80, 82n64
The Dispossessed (Le Guin), 62–63, 67–68, 69, 159n23

diversity: end of, 21, 28–29; fear of,
    35–36, 45, 67–8, 79–80; need for,
    35–36, 66, 73, 76, 84, 91, 100, 116,
    134; as a problem, 42; response to,
    29, 66–8, 77–9, 82n57, 129, 132–5,
    156–7, 164. *See also* pluralism
dualisms, 4, 84, 129
DuBois, W. E. B., 158n7

education: on anarchist model, 63–65,
    74, 81n34; on end-state model,
    27–34; on process model, 82n57,
    97–98, 100–05, 112, 116–17,
    119–120, 125n29, 126n34, 142, 149,
    153–54, 165
Eldridge, Michael, 87
Emile (Rousseau), 29–34, 36, 44, 68
ends-in-view: definition of, 89, 91,
    96–97, 122; as goal, 86, 90 (*see also*
    means and ends); judging, 88,
    97–100, 108, 122–23, 153; as
    opposed to fixed ends, 96, 113, 119,
    122–23, 134, 153
end-state model: description of, 2–3,
    10–11, 17–21; Dewey's rejection of,
    6, 95–97; examples of, 10–11, 20,
    22–23, 36–40, 48n48; problems with,
    10–11, 18, 21–26, 34–36, 40–46. *See
    also* utopia
experience: lived, 12, 84–86, 88–90,
    92–93, 99, 109–13, 130, 135, 141;
    received, 85, 88, 167
experimentation. *See* scientific method

Fanon, Franz, 54
feminism: and critique of community,
    123–24, 131–35, 158n8; definition
    of, 4, 14n12, 137–38, 157n2; and
    pragmatism, 3, 5, 14n14, 84, 129–30,
    157n1; and utopias; 4–5, 135–41;
    and utopian experiments, 159n12
flexibility: evidence of, 93, 122, 157,
    166; lack of , 88, 115; need for, 49,
    84, 88, 93, 98, 100, 120–22, 128n87
foresight, 8, 43, 85, 88, 109, 116, 134

Fourier, Charles, 28
freedom: from arbitrary will, 29–34;
    from government, 50–52, 56–62, 70,
    75; to direct one's life, 50–53, 65,
    102, 104; as ongoing task, 8, 53,
    56–58, 65–66

Gearhart, Sally Miller: definition of
    feminist utopia, 137–38; *The
    Wanderground*, 12, 141, 147–57,
    165–66
Gilman, Charlotte Perkins: *Herland*, 27;
    *The Home: Its Work and Its
    Influence*, 111; The Man-Made
    World, 122–23
Godwin, William, 45, 50, 58, 64
Goldman, Emma, 49, 52–53, 55, 66
Great Community, 94, 108, 112,
    114–24, 131–35; feminist critique of,
    123–24, 131–35, 158n8
Great Society, 94, 108, 112, 118, 131
growth: as guiding aim, 86, 96–97, 100,
    105–6, 136; judgment of, 97,
    99–100, 122

Hertzler, Joyce, 7
Hobbes, Thomas, 56, 60, 111
hope, 1, 3, 5–6, 8, 21, 35, 51, 167;
    Bloch, Ernst, 35, 46
human nature: on anarchist model,
    51–52, 56–58, 60; on end-state
    model, 26–29, 43–44, 46n24; on
    process model, 86, 88, 101, 103–5
Huxley, Aldous: *Brave New World*, 18,
    24; *Island*, 27

imagination, 84–89, 91–94, 98,
    100–101, 105–6, 110
individual: on anarchist model, 51–52,
    56–58, 60; as associated, 107–10; as
    developmental, 86, 88, 104, 107,
    111, 116–17; as disassociated, 115,
    122–23; on end-state model, 26–29,
    43–44, 46n24; liberal, 60, 109–11;
    loss of, 20–25, 29, 32–33, 41–42, 57,

66; unified, 106, 112–13, 116, 119,
122, 131–32, 136, 156–57, 165–67
interconnectedness: failure to realize,
85, 99, 108–10, 145–46; need to
recognize, 29, 33, 58–61, 65, 70,
85–86, 99, 108–13, 116, 121–22,
128n87, 135, 141, 144–47, 150,
154–55
inquiry, 83, 101, 105, 117, 119–21, 155,
166. *See also* method of intelligence;
scientific method
Island (Huxley), 27

Jacoby, Russell, 2–3, 13n1
James, William, 2, 24–25

Kateb, George, 17, 21, 23, 25, 28–29
Khanna, Lee Cullen, 140
Kropotkin, P. A., 53–55, 65
Kumar, Krishan, 20

Le Guin, Ursula K.: *Always Coming
Home*, 12, 141–47, 153–57, 165–66;
The Dispossessed, 62–63, 67–68, 69,
159n23; on integration and integrity,
139
Levitas, Ruth, 7–9
lived experience. *See* experience, lived
Looking Backward (Bellamy), 1, 27

Malatesta, Enrico, 54
Marcuse, Herbert, 55
means and ends: as continuum, 12,
55–56, 86, 88–89, 95, 98–99, 102,
106–7, 127n68, 141, 162; separation
of, 17, 21, 36, 42–43, 53–55, 89
method of intelligence, 87, 91–3, 97,
105, 107, 116. *See also* inquiry;
scientific method
mind, 85, 90, 92, 98, 100, 120–21. *See
also* mindful; unmindful
mindful, 145–46, 155–56. *See also*
mind; unmindful

Nineteen Eighty-Four (Orwell), 1, 18

On the Social Contract (Rousseau),
29–30
Orwell, George, 1, 18
Owen, Robert, 27, 81n37

Pearson, Carole, 138
Peirce, Charles Saunders, 14n18
perfection: as final, 2–3, 7–8, 10, 17–20,
34–36; as process, 3, 6, 45, 92, 96,
167–68
Pfaelzer, Jean, 138–39
Piercy, Marge: *Woman on the Edge of
Time*, 11–12, 69–79, 139, 159n24,
163–64
Plato, 19–20, 48n48, 96
pluralism, 2–3, 99–100, 129–30, 156.
See also diversity
Popper, Karl, 19–21, 36
pragmatism: characteristics of, 3–5, 89,
129–130; and feminism (*see*
feminism); and utopia (*see* utopia)
process model: description of, 2–3, 8–9,
12–13, 89–92, 97–100, 107–21,
134–36, 161; examples of, 12–13,
141–53; as metatheory, 162–64;
problems with, 118, 124, 131–35;
strengths of, 12–13, 88–89, 97,
113–18. *See also* utopia

Rawls, John, 13n1
reconstruction, 55–56, 87, 95, 102–3,
119
responsibility: for future, 3, 6, 9, 52–53,
83, 86, 91, 106, 118–20, 161, 165,
167–68; for self, 9, 52–53, 118; for
others, 9, 108, 118
revolution, 11, 53–56, 59, 68, 94–95,
127n68; alternatives to (*see*
reconstruction)
Rorty, Richard, 15n32
Rousseau, Jean-Jacques: *Emile*, 29–34,
36, 44, 68; *On the Social Contract*,
29–30; on Sophie, 30–31,
47n32
The Ruins of Isis (Bradley), 22–23

Sargisson, Lucy, 136–37
Schehr, Robert, 13n1, 14n18
scientific method, 20, 86–88, 93–94, 98, 118, 120, 124–25n10. *See also* inquiry; method of intelligence
Seigfried, Charlene Haddock, 103–5, 129–30, 157n1
Skinner, B. F., 27–28
Stuhr, John, 5, 117

task: of critical intelligence, 84, 88, 97, 123; of democracy, 100, 112, 123; of education, 64, 97, 100, 120, 152, 166; of making the future, 6, 41, 46, 100, 152–53, 161, 166–68; of utopia, 3, 9, 46, 138, 161, 166–67
Taylor, Michael, 59–63
Tepper, Sherri: *The Gate to Women's Country*, 10–11, 36–46, 48n48, 139–40, 159n24, 162–63

unmindful, 145–47. *See also* mind; mindful
utopia: anarchist, 11–12, 49–80; dangers of, 1, 7–8, 37, 161 (*see also* disintegration of visions); death of,

1–3, 8, 15n32, 161; definitions of, 3–4, 7–9, 14n8, 21; end-state, 2–3, 7, 10–11, 17–46; engineering/ management, 17–20, 27–29, 36–37, 40–41, 44–46; feminism and (*see* feminism); postmodernism and, 13n6, 136–37; pragmatism and, 5–6, 14n15, 83; process, 2–3, 8–9, 12–13, 83–124, 135, 138–40, 141–57, 161–62, 164–68; renewed interest in, 1–2, 13n1; as static (*see* end-state); threat to individuality, 18, 20–25, 32–33, 41–42, 57, 78–79, 132–33; use of, 1, 8–9, 81n29, 85–86, 97, 161, 167–68; violence and, 18, 40, 44, 54, 70, 75–76, 95, 162–63

The Wanderground (Gearhart), 12, 141, 147–57, 165–66
Wellmer, Albrecht, 8
Westbrook Robert B., 94–95, 99, 102, 106, 110
Woman on the Edge of Time. See Piercy, Marge

Young, Iris Marion, 132–34, 158n9, 158n10

About the Author

Erin McKenna teaches philosophy at Pacific Lutheran University in Tacoma, Washington. Her regular teaching schedule includes courses such as "Women and Philosophy," "Pragmatism and American Philosophy," "Introduction to Moral Theory," and a freshman writing seminar "Making the Future." McKenna's previously published essays include work on social and political theory, feminist theory, pedagogy, the moral standing of animals, and vegetarianism. Her current research focuses on pragmatism and the moral standing of animals, specifically primates.